Metaphor and Corpus Linguistics

Metaphor and Corpus Linguistics: Building and Investigating an English as a Medium of Instruction Corpus offers a model for building a corpus of oral EMI seminars. It demonstrates how incorporating metaphor to the process of corpus building affords a more comprehensive description of the role of metaphor in discourse.

EMI is the specific context outlined in this volume, and as such it will be of particular interest to researchers in this area, though the design and model can be easily generalised and applied to other corpora focusing on metaphor. Alejo-González argues for the need to build such a corpus given the scarcity of corpora being tagged for metaphor as well as the shortage of those dealing with the EMI phenomenon.

This book will be of practical use and interest to those researchers of corpus linguistics or related areas looking to explore metaphor through their corpus studies.

Rafael Alejo-González is Associate Professor of English at the University of Extremadura, Spain.

Routledge Applied Corpus Linguistics

Series Editor: Michael McCarthy
Michael McCarthy is Emeritus Professor of Applied Linguistics at the University of Nottingham, UK, Adjunct Professor of Applied Linguistics at the University of Limerick, Ireland and Visiting Professor in Applied Linguistics at Newcastle University, UK. He is co-editor of the Routledge Handbook of Corpus Linguistics, editor of the Routledge Domains of Discourse series and co-editor of the Routledge Corpus Linguistics Guides series.

Series Editor: Anne O'Keeffe
Anne O'Keeffe is Senior Lecturer in Applied Linguistics and Director of the Inter-Varietal Applied Corpus Studies (IVACS) Research Centre at Mary Immaculate College, University of Limerick, Ireland. She is co-editor of the Routledge Handbook of Corpus Linguistics and co-editor of the Routledge Corpus Linguistics Guides series.

Series Co-Founder: Ronald Carter
Ronald Carter (1947–2018) was Research Professor of Modern English Language in the School of English at the University of Nottingham, UK. He was also the co-editor of the Routledge Corpus Linguistics Guides series, Routledge Introductions to Applied Linguistics series and Routledge English Language Introductions series.

Editorial Panel: IVACS (Inter-Varietal Applied Corpus Studies Group), based at Mary Immaculate College, University of Limerick, is an international research network linking corpus linguistic researchers interested in exploring and comparing language in different contexts of use.

The Routledge Applied Corpus Linguistics Series is a series of monograph studies exhibiting cutting-edge research in the field of corpus linguistics and its applications to real-world language problems. Corpus linguistics is one of the most dynamic and rapidly developing areas in the field of language studies, and it is difficult to see a future for empirical language research where results are not replicable by reference to corpus data. This series showcases the latest research in the field of applied language studies where corpus findings are at the forefront, introducing new and unique methodologies and applications which open up new avenues for research.

RECENT TITLES IN THIS SERIES

Corpus Applications in Language Teaching and Research
The Case of Data-Driven Learning of German
Nina Vyatkina

Language and Creativity at Work
A Corpus-Assisted Model of Creative Workplace Discourse
Michael Handford and Almut Koester

Metaphor and Corpus Linguistics
Building and Investigating an English as a Medium of Instruction Corpus
Rafael Alejo-González

Discourse Markers in Doctoral Supervision Sessions
A Multimodal Perspective
Samira Bakeer

Inter-Varietal Applied Corpus Studies

More information about this series can be found at www.routledge.com/series/RACL

Metaphor and Corpus Linguistics

Building and Investigating an English as a Medium of Instruction Corpus

Rafael Alejo-González

Routledge
Taylor & Francis Group

LONDON AND NEW YORK

First published 2024
by Routledge
4 Park Square, Milton Park, Abingdon, Oxon OX14 4RN

and by Routledge
605 Third Avenue, New York, NY 10158

Routledge is an imprint of the Taylor & Francis Group, an informa business

© 2024 Rafael Alejo-González

British Library Cataloguing-in-Publication Data
A catalogue record for this book is available from the British Library

Library of Congress Cataloging-in-Publication Data
Names: Alejo-González, Rafael, author.
Title: Metaphor and corpus linguistics: building and investigating an English as a medium of instruction corpus / Rafael Alejo-González.
Description: Abingdon, Oxon; New York, NY: Routledge, 2024. |
Series: Routledge applied corpus linguistics | Includes bibliographical references and index. |
Identifiers: LCCN 2023047687 (print) | LCCN 2023047688 (ebook) |
Subjects: LCSH: Corpora (Linguistics) | Metaphor–Data processing. |
English-medium instruction–Data processing.
Classification: LCC P128.C68 A435 2024 (print) | LCC P128.C68 (ebook) |
DDC 420.1/88–dc23/eng/20231106
LC record available at https://lccn.loc.gov/2023047687
LC ebook record available at https://lccn.loc.gov/2023047688

ISBN: 978-1-032-51057-6 (hbk)
ISBN: 978-1-032-51059-0 (pbk)
ISBN: 978-1-003-40090-5 (ebk)

DOI: 10.4324/9781003400905

Typeset in Sabon
by Deanta Global Publishing Services, Chennai, India

To M. Carmen, Nacho and María

Contents

Acknowledgements

Many of the findings presented in this book originate from the MetCLIL Project, which received funding from the Spanish Ministry of Economy, Industry, and Competitiveness (reference: FFI2017-86320-R). I am profoundly grateful to the entire research team for their contributions and in particular to my colleagues Ana Piquer Píriz and Irene Castellano Risco, from the Department of English Philology at the Faculty of Education and Psychology of the University of Extremadura, for their support and collaboration. I extend my heartfelt thanks to Fiona MacArthur for her inspirational insights and for paving the way for a research journey that has greatly enriched my work.

1 Metaphor and corpus linguistics

Introduction

In the era of big data, it is only natural that corpus linguistics has taken on an ever-increasing dimension and importance in the study of how language works. In the same way that big data in the social sciences are helping to understand a host of contemporary phenomena, linguistic data, mostly in the form of linguistic corpora, are making a substantial contribution to the development of a wide range of linguistic disciplines. The number and quality of publications is constantly growing, and a mere indication would be the host of handbooks (e.g. Friginal & Hardy, 2020; O'Keeffe & McCarthy, 2022; Paquot & Gries, 2020; Stefanowitsch, 2020; Tracy-Ventura & Paquot, 2020) or of practical resource books related to the application of 'corpus linguistics' to different areas (Friginal, 2018; Friginal et al., 2017; Lange & Leuckert, 2020; Pérez-Paredes, 2021 or Szudarski, 2018) that have appeared in the last five years alone.

Within this increased focus on corpus linguistics, there are, however, two areas, connected respectively to what the research refers to as language-internal and -external parameters of texts, that may not have received the same amount of attention. Thus, in connection to factors related to the internal functioning of the language, where consideration to aspects such as grammar or vocabulary is usual, it seems important to add an element such as metaphor, whose relative lack of attention may be due to the fact that meanings are obviously less easily amenable to the use of a corpus-based methodology. For its part, in the second area, that of linguistic-external factors, which has taken on board a diversity of contextual situations where language is used, the relatively recent emergence of English as a Medium of Instruction (EMI) has not been given sufficient consideration. Closely related to English as a Lingua Franca projects (e.g., the Vienna-Oxford International Corpus of English [VOICE] and the English as Lingua Franca in Academic Contexts [ELFA] corpus), EMI as such has not given rise to a specific corpus, especially one where a variety of European institutions of higher education are represented.

The present book aims to fill this gap by providing a detailed description of the process of creation and the results obtained from a corpus, the Metaphor Production in Content and Language Integrated Learning (CLIL)[1]

DOI: 10.4324/9781003400905-1

seminars corpus (under the acronym MetCLIL), specifically designed to study metaphor in English as a Medium of Instruction (EMI) seminars dealing with business and marketing. By describing the main methodological problems posed and the solutions adopted, as well as the way the corpus could be exploited, I address the questions and issues that may arise in these two areas of linguistic inquiry, metaphor and EMI, that have not received much attention in corpus linguistics.

Introduction to a cognitive-linguistic approach to metaphor

When dealing with metaphor, it is important to take into consideration that the study of metaphor has evolved significantly over the years, from the initial attention paid by literary studies to the more recent approach carried out by Cognitive Linguistics. Initially, literary studies focused on metaphor as a tool for literary expression and interpretation, emphasising its aesthetic and rhetorical functions. However, with the emergence of Cognitive Linguistics in the 1980s, metaphor was re-conceptualised as a cognitive phenomenon, with a focus on its role as a meaning-making device. This shift was largely due to the influence of George Lakoff and Mark Johnson's seminal work, *Metaphors We Live By* (1980), which argued that metaphor is a fundamental cognitive process that shapes our understanding of the world. This new approach has led to a greater appreciation of the role of metaphor in language and cognition and has opened up new avenues of research into the cognitive and linguistic aspects of metaphor. Cognitive Linguistics has thus become the dominant approach to studying metaphor, focusing on how metaphors are used to structure our understanding of the world and how they shape our language and thought.

The importance of Cognitive Linguistics can only be understood against the backdrop of formal and generative approaches to language that were predominant in most of the twentieth century and whose most prominent representative was Noam Chomsky. Cognitive Linguistics proposes a different approach to language in which linguistic meaning is not independent of the system of combinatorial rules governing language, but rather is a reflection of human cognition. In contrast to many formal approaches, Cognitive Linguistics claims that linguistic structures are based on the mental processes of its users. In other words, for this new approach to Linguistics, language structure and cognition are related.

A good example of the difference between Cognitive Linguistics and formal approaches is how constructional variants, i.e., linguistic constructions referring to the same event, are explained. Take, for example, the often-cited contrast between active and passive sentences (see examples a and b). According to the early Chomsky (1957), even if these two constructions have a different surface structure, i.e., the actual words used are not the same, their underlying or deep structure is certainly the same. This would mean that their meaning is the same, whereas their syntactic structure differs. Meaning and syntax are ultimately kept separate in this view.

a. The boy threw the ball
b. The ball was thrown by the boy

For Cognitive Linguistics, the separation between semantics and syntax should be called into question. From a cognitive-linguistic perspective, different ways of rendering meaning are not simply formal variations but correspond to different conceptualisations or to differences in cognitive construal. Thus, a and b above correspond to different ways of construing the same scene and paying attention to different aspects, the agent (i.e. the boy), or the patient (i.e. the ball) of the action. The sentences are not simply two versions of the same underlying meaning – they certainly refer to one event – but their meaning is certainly constructed in different ways (cf. Lee, 2001). Linguistic expression is tightly knit to conceptual structures in the mind. Language has a psychological reality that is no different from any other thought process.

Construal and conceptualisation, which are the notions that explain phenomena such as the one explained above, are also relevant processes in the cognitive-linguistic explanation of metaphor. First, metaphor is no longer viewed as a substitute for a literal phrase, which could be used to express the same meaning. Metaphors bring a meaning that is usually not very easily paraphraseable (cf. Croft & Cruse, 2004). Second, metaphor is mostly conceived within this theory as a conceptual mapping. In other words, a metaphor is a mental structure that allows us to understand a usually more abstract concept, i.e., the target domain, in terms of another, the source domain.

Related to the idea that language is a product of human cognition is the notion that language is shaped by usage. Indeed, mental processes underlie language use, but both thought and linguistic structures emerge in connection to specific contexts of use. Thus, the environment can help to identify the underlying cognitive processes that are involved in language use, such as, for example, how people interpret and use language to communicate in specific contexts. Thus, a phrase like "Take it easy" is often used to tell someone to relax or not to worry in stressful contexts, which is associated with the need to express comfort and reassurance. Both the interpretation of the phrase and its linguistic expression are acquired by language speakers from their experience of contexts where speakers need to convey those communicative needs.

Although early cognitive linguists were concerned with understanding how language is used in different contexts and for different purposes, their work was subjected to some criticisms related to the fact that the examples used in their research were invented, rather than taken from real language use. This was considered to be contradictory with some of the tenets of Cognitive Linguistics and there was a felt need to incorporate the analysis of real language. This is where corpus linguistics joined the Cognitive Linguistics enterprise. By analysing large collections of language data, researchers could gain insight into how language is used in real-world contexts and would thus be able to access the raw data from which the knowledge of language emerges in the users' minds. In this way, corpus linguistics becomes a valuable tool for cognitive linguists to better understand the mental processes that underlie language use.

Metaphor in thought vs metaphor in language

Under the auspices of Cognitive Linguistics, the study of metaphor has seen an incredible expansion, which has taken the form of a movement called Conceptual Metaphor Theory (CMT). Besides the already cited work by Lakoff and Johnson (1980), to which we could also add another pioneer contribution, that of Ortony's edited collection *Metaphor and Thought* (1979), a group of researchers (cf. e.g., Gibbs, 1994, 2008; Grady, 1998; Kövecses, 2000, 2005, 2010; Lakoff &Turner, 1989) began to develop the idea that metaphor is a fundamental mechanism of thought that helps us make sense of the world around us and to give it meaning as already explained in the previous section.

The view of metaphor proposed by CMT researchers is quite different from the one that had prevailed up to that moment. Researchers generally approached metaphor as a linguistic device used for stylistic or aesthetic purposes, because it serves to make language more interesting and engaging for the listener or reader. Deignan (2005) summarises this approach by labelling it as the 'decorative' view of metaphor and argues that for researchers preceding the CMT approach, metaphor would normally be used to create a sense of novelty or surprise, which would make the message more memorable or persuasive. This approach was derived from the understanding of metaphor as a type of linguistic substitution replacing a literal word or phrase. In other words, metaphors would not be necessary in so far as it would be possible to find a literal phrase to be used in its place (see Ricoeur, 1977 for an overview). This substitution is possible because metaphor is the result of a comparison or analogy between two different things. In a metaphor like "all the world's a stage", from *As you like it*, the word "world" is replaced by "stage" because Shakespeare wants to assimilate some of the features of theatre and drama into the way we live in the world.

CMT's new understanding of metaphor also leaves aside its analysis as a 'deviant' linguistic manifestation and posits that metaphors are pervasive. They are found not simply in literary works, but also in everyday communication even if we do not notice them. The reason for this is simple: many metaphors are conventionalised. They are the usual way in which we refer to something.

Here are some examples of these conventionalised metaphors often cited in the CMT literature (see for example Kövecses, 2010):

- The metaphor LIFE IS A JOURNEY evident in expressions *I've hit a rough patch in my journey, He's at a crossroads in his life*. According to this metaphor, life is viewed as a purposeful, directed experience that involves progress, obstacles and change.
- The metaphor ARGUMENT IS WAR reflected in expressions such as *She attacked every point I made* or *He defended his position fiercely*, which frames arguments as combative encounters, rather than opportunities for discussion and collaboration.

- The metaphor TIME IS MONEY found in expressions such as *I'm running out of time, I wasted time on that project, I'm investing my time in this*, which indicates that time is a valuable resource, to be spent carefully, saved or lost.
- The metaphor IDEAS ARE FOOD are reflected in expressions like *I'm chewing on that idea, I've had my fill of that, That idea is half-baked*. This metaphor implies that ideas can nourish or satiate, be satisfying or unsatisfying.

In his book *Metaphor Wars: Conceptual Metaphors in Human Life* (2017), Ray Gibbs poses the question of how many conceptual metaphors like the ones exemplified above there are (cf. p. 34 ff.). Obviously, no final answer can be provided, as there is always the possibility of new metaphors being created, but the number is certainly large. A first attempt was made with the "Master Metaphor List" (Lakoff et al., 1991). A more recent project, "MetaNet", has also compiled a large list of metaphors for English which is available from the University of Berkeley (Dodge et al., 2013). The project, which is multilingual, including other languages such as Spanish or Persian, among others, was mainly intended to attend public discourse and to develop methods for automatic metaphor search that we will see later in the book. This new list of conceptual metaphors offers connections with the FrameNet database, which is another multilingual online resource, in this case collecting frames, i.e., the structures organising speakers' understanding of a given concept or event.

However, the concept of frame is less essential to understand the notion of conceptual metaphor than the idea of 'domain', which is capital in its definition. Deignan (2005) explains it in this way: "a conceptual metaphor is a connection between two semantic areas, or *domains*" (emphasis in the original, p. 14). In the metaphor IDEAS ARE OBJECTS, the two domains involved are IDEAS and OBJECTS. Thus, the sentence *Who's been putting ideas into your head* makes reference to a conceptual metaphor where an abstract concept like an idea and a concrete physical item are connected by the intention to represent the abstract nature of ideas as something tangible and transferrable. For CMT, in this metaphor, as in all conceptual metaphors, there are two domains, the 'target domain', in this case IDEAS, and the 'source domain', OBJECTS. The formulation is conventionally presented in the literature as TARGET DOMAIN IS/ARE SOURCE DOMAIN, where the domain appearing first is always the 'target' and the one after the verb 'to be' is the 'source'. This is important since, as we will see later, some scholars doing corpus analysis of metaphor (e.g., Stefanowitsch, 2006) start their corpus analysis of metaphor by selecting a 'source' domain (e.g., WEATHER) and then elaborating a list of lexical items from that domain or semantic field (*climate, storm, bubble*, etc.), which can be used to search a corpus and then decide whether they are used metaphorically in the context (Lederer, 2016). It is important to note that a single 'source' domain can be used with several 'target' domains. Thus, a very common source domain is JOURNEY, or MOTION if we want to refer to it more generally. JOURNEY metaphors have been used to talk about TIME, COMMUNICATION, LIFE, or CAREER.

To fully understand a conceptual metaphor, the connection between the two domains tells us only part of the story as we sometimes need to see how the meaning of the source domain is projected onto the target domain. Therefore, a full comprehension of a metaphor also takes into consideration the mappings, i.e., "systematic set of correspondences between [the] two domains of experience" (Kövecses, 2017a, p. 14). Take the example of a conceptual metaphor related to emotion used by Kövecses, i.e.., ANGER IS FIRE, which can be instantiated in some linguistic expressions like a) That *kindled* my ire, b) Those were *inflammatory* remarks and c) *Smoke* was *coming out* of his ears (cf. 2017a, p.14). In this conceptual metaphor, the connection between the domain of ANGER and the domain of FIRE is understood if we identify some of the specific mappings or correspondences involved: (a) the cause of fire > the cause of anger; (b) causing the fire > causing the anger; and (c) the thing on fire > the angry person.The explanation provided by Kövecses is quite clear:

> This set of mappings is systematic in the sense that it captures a coherent view of fire that is mapped onto anger: There is a thing that is not burning. An event happens (cause of fire) that causes the fire to come into existence. Now the thing is burning. The fire can burn at various degrees of intensity.
>
> Similarly for anger: There is a person who is not angry. An event happens that causes the person to become angry. The person is now in the state of anger. The intensity of the anger is variable.
>
> (Kövecses, 2017a, p. 14)

Another important feature of conceptual metaphors, which was already referred to when we talked about IDEAS ARE OBJECTS, is that the mappings between domains usually go from concrete to abstract domains. This means that the source domain is typically more concrete than the target domain, which is usually more abstract. You can see this in some of the metaphors we have seen: LIFE (abstract) IS A JOURNEY (concrete), TIME (abstract) IS MONEY (concrete), IDEAS (abstract) ARE FOOD (concrete), ANGER (abstract) IS FIRE (concrete). The explanation seems simple. The world of concrete things is usually more accessible and better understood than abstract concepts that often evade easy comprehension by humans. In fact, many conceptual metaphors can be, and have been, used to explore ideas and generate hypotheses. Thus, for example, the metaphor THE MIND IS A COMPUTER has been used by cognitive science to generate new hypotheses about the structure and function of the mind. A linguistic metaphor like *language processing* is probably a widely accepted realisation of THE MIND IS A COMPUTER in the sense that it builds on the idea that the mind works in a computational way. In general, this would explain why metaphors are certainly frequent in academic language and in science, where the subject matter is typically abstract and difficult to understand, and where the use of metaphor allows for more concrete and accessible explanations of complex concepts. The use of metaphor in these contexts is said to be heuristic, i.e., it serves as a tool for exploration and discovery.

This heuristic use of metaphor is certainly important for the creation and exploitation of what are known as novel metaphors. These metaphors are seen in a different way than rhetoricians and stylists did before the emergence of CMT. Before the development of this theory, novelty was simply considered at the linguistic level, i.e., when considering the specific linguistic metaphor created by literary authors (e.g.: Jorge Luis Borges referring to a complex novel as a "labyrinth of symbols"). In CMT, the term novel metaphor, or as some call them 'live' metaphor, is ambivalent since it can refer to both the linguistic expression and the conceptual metaphor. Thus, in the specific example by Borges, the expression "labyrinth of symbols" used to refer to a book is certainly novel, but the conceptual metaphor on which it is based is more conventional (i.e., LITERACY IS MOTION ALONG A PATH), as it is used in many sentences like *The text got straight to the point* or *She ran through the pages of the book*. Given that CMT is mostly interested in the presence of metaphors in the language we ordinarily use, their attention has mostly been placed on the conceptual metaphors that give rise to conventionalised language. CMT researchers refuse to call them 'dead' metaphors, as they were traditionally called, because for them (cf. Lakoff & Johnson, 1980; Lakoff & Turner, 1989) these conceptual metaphors are active, i.e., their linguistic instantiations can be expanded even if the mapping remains the same.

One of the reasons for the extensive use of conceptual metaphors is related to the fact that many are immediately available to speakers in so far as they are grounded in human bodily sensorimotor experience. CMT subscribes to the cognitive-linguistic approach to human thinking as not only symbolic and abstract but also as rooted in the way humans interact with their environment. In other words, many metaphors can only be understood by reference to the physical experience they refer to. Take, for example, the sentence *Prices have gone up*, where the particle 'up' instantiates the conceptual metaphor MORE IS UP. In this sentence and in the conceptual metaphor, the source and target domains are not connected by similarity but by their usual correlation in human experience. We usually associate an increase in quantity (MORE) with an upward direction or movement (UP) because in our experience both these things co-occur. Thus, for example, if we pile up books one on top of the other, an increase in the number of books corresponds with a rise in their level and the same thing happens if we pour water into a jug; the more water there is the higher the level of the water. Many of these metaphors tend to go unnoticed. They are so entrenched in the way we usually think that not many people realise that in fact there is an association between different domains. In CMT, these metaphors are called Primary Metaphors and their theorisation began with a researcher like Grady (1997). In the second part of the book, we will see some of the Primary Metaphors, which are usually formulated at a very general level, used to talk about the domain of communication. Some of these metaphors are:

- LINGUISTIC EXPRESSIONS ARE CONTAINERS, which in the domain of communication refers to the way in which the message of human interactions, written or spoken, is seen as contained within linguistic expressions: *He always packs many ideas into his speeches.*
- BECOMING ACCESSIBLE IS EMERGING, which refers to the fact that the meaning contained in linguistic expressions becomes accessible and therefore comprehensible: *This sentence makes clear the idea being conveyed.*
- TRANSMISSION OF ENERGY IS TRANSFER (OF OBJECTS), which describes how when speaking, ideas can be perceived as the transfer of objects: *She delivered a brilliant speech that left the audience in awe.*

To end this section, it is important to bring your attention to something you have probably noticed from the examples used so far. As is usual in the CMT literature, conceptual metaphors are written in small caps (LOVE IS A JOURNEY) to indicate that they are referring to a metaphorical mapping in thought, whereas the specific words or phrases instantiating them (*I realized that I was in a dead-end relationship*) are not. This typographic tradition already points to the need to separate between the conceptual metaphor and the linguistic expression given the primacy given to the former by CMT. As already explained, CMT is very clear about this:

> The language is secondary. The mapping is primary, in that it sanctions the use of source domain language and inference patterns for target domain concepts.
>
> (Lakoff, 2006[1993], p. 192)

However, certain authors have begun to point out the limitations of CMT's preferential attention to thought and not to language. Karen Sullivan is one of them:

> It is specifically the noun *argument* in *the lawyer built an argument* that ensures that the verb *built* is interpreted metaphorically. The sentence *the lawyer built a house,* in which both direct object and verb are related to buildings, is most easily interpreted as referring to the literal building of a literal house; so it is only the choice of *argument* as opposed to *house* that makes *the lawyer built an argument* metaphoric. The metaphoric sentence needs a combination of a metaphoric verb (*built*) and non-metaphoric nouns such as *argument* to be understood metaphorically. That is, the grammatical constructions in the sentence help convey the metaphor. The sentence's grammar dictates that the choice of the verb (*devised* vs. *built* vs. *concocted*) determines whether the sentence evokes theories are buildings, ideas are food, or neither of these metaphors.
>
> (Sullivan, 2016, p. 143)

Linguistic approaches to metaphor: basic context for a Corpus-Linguistic methodology

As we have seen in the previous section, CMT has developed a whole new theory of metaphor. However, stemming from CMT, another strand of metaphor research begins to pay more attention to the linguistic manifestation of conceptual metaphors (e.g., Deignan et al., 2013). This new strand mainly focuses on the analysis of figurative language in different types of discourse and emphasises the need to go back to a more linguistic approach to metaphor. In their view, the concern with cognition by CMT may have led to a decontextualised study of language, which would obviously be a misrepresentation of how language works. In her review article entitled "From Linguistic to Conceptual Metaphors", Alice Deignan (2017) summarises some the criticisms levelled at a strict CMT approach, which she and other colleagues such as Cameron (2003), Semino (2008) or Stefanowitsch (2006) have repeatedly pointed out. For Deignan, the main problem resides in that the examples of metaphors that the CMT literature uses are "generated intuitively" (p. 103) or to put it in the words of some of the most prominent figures of mainstream CMT: "The early work on conceptual metaphors ... is commonly regarded as eclectic, introspective, intuitive, unsystematic and so on" (Kövecses et al., 2019, p. 150).

It is this second, more linguistic, approach to metaphor that has sprung the interest in corpus linguistics (CL) as a methodology of great utility in describing how metaphor behaves in actual discourse. CL is thus seen as one of the ways to end the practice of using invented examples of metaphors usually followed by CMT scholars (cf. Deignan, 2005; Deignan et al., 2013) and, more generally, it could be said that this discipline has enabled researchers to fully develop this more linguistic approach to metaphor. The different developments in the linguistic approach to metaphor research have made use of CL.

First, CL has played an important role in establishing metaphor as an emergent phenomenon in discourse (Cameron & Deignan, 2006). This means that the way metaphor works in language is not a function of its stable representation in cognition but rather the result of the complex network of metaphors that are used in a given situation. According to Dorst, the linguistic approach to metaphor has enabled researchers to perceive how language users "introduce, develop, negotiate, challenge, reject and adapt metaphors within the context of the discourse event in order to achieve their rhetorical goals and meet the needs of their addressees" (2017, p. 178). In other words, from the analysis of metaphor as a dynamic system, where both elements of stability and elements of change can be found, it is possible to identify certain patterns of metaphor use that are typically used in a particular discourse context. These patterns, mostly identifiable by using a CL methodology, include: repetition of metaphors, typically used to give coherence to the text (cf. Semino, 2008); recurrence, i.e. the reference to the same source domain within the same speech event; clustering, which refers to greater metaphor density that can be found in certain stretches of discourse; extension, which could be defined as recurrent clusters; combination and mixing, which is the way people use different metaphors in their discourse (cf. also Gibbs, 2017).

An additional perspective in the study of metaphor where the use of corpora is particularly important is the one provided by the notion of genre, a perspective that according to Caballero (2017) has not yet been fully exploited by metaphor researchers. As argued by Deignan et al. (2013), the framework provided by the concept of genre, with the key notions of discourse community, purpose and staging, can help researchers in the explanation of the way certain metaphors are used. In this way, for example, it is easier to understand why texts with similar subject matter differ in metaphor use. Thus, the metaphors used in scientific research articles, with a specialist audience in mind, are different from those used in a popular journal like the *New Scientist* (cf. Deignan et al., 2013, chap. 4), a phenomenon which is closely connected to the concept of 'recontextualization' (cf. Linell & Sarangi, 1998 cit. in Caballero, 2017, p. 198; Deignan et al., 2013 cf. also Skorczynska & Deignan, 2006). It could be argued that the metaphors used in lectures or in office hour consultations should, one way or another, be 'recontextualized' in discussion seminars. The relationship between the metaphors used by the most important spoken academic genres is clearly an aspect to explore in detail.

Connected to the discourse approach, and more particularly to genre, are many aspects of research focusing on English for Specific Purposes, which also benefit from the use of CL. Within this area, we find the research dealing with the complex metaphor systems underlying the construction of specialist discourse. This is the case of disciplines such as economics (Alejo-González, 2010, 2011; Skorczynska & Deignan, 2006), politics (Mio, 1996), business (Arleo, 2000; Morgan, 1996), architecture (Caballero, 2003, 2006), winegrowing (Caballero, 2007), cancer treatment (Semino, 2011), engineering (Roldán-Riejos & Ubeda, 2013), medicine (Salager-Meyer, 1990). More recently, the edition of a whole book on the subject (Herrmann & Berber-Sardinha, 2015) has given more prominence to the topic. The study of metaphor is undertaken from the perspective of specialist discourse as a whole and it is a first attempt to outline some of the main issues and methodological problems, irrespective of the particular specialist language studied. One of these issues had already been mentioned by Cameron when she contends that metaphor, or more precisely 'subtechnical metaphor', is often used to make "accessible the technical language of specialist groups to non-experts" (2008, p. 206).

In short, the study of metaphor requires the use of an appropriate corpus that facilitates the full understanding of the context and co-text of metaphors. In following this approach, the present book joins the group of studies where metaphor research relies on the use of compiled corpora (Berber-Sardinha, 2008; Charteris-Black, 2004; Deignan, 2005; Littlemore & MacArthur, 2012; Philip, 2008; Semino, 2006; Stefanowitsch & Gries,

2003). EuroCoAT (www.eurocoat.es), a sister corpus compiled to study metaphor in office hour consultations, was clearly a methodological choice of our first project and we intend to continue with this option by enlarging the corpus in the present study.

In this way the research on metaphor joins the *empirical turn* of the discipline within which it is integrated, namely Cognitive Linguistics, which started at the beginning of the twenty-first century and is now nearly a quarter of a century old:

> The introduction of corpus-based methods in usage-based cognitive linguistics, also described as its "empirical turn", can be traced back to the 2000's (Fanego 2004; Geeraerts 2003; Tummers et al. 2005; Gries & Stefanowitsch 2006; Gibbs 2007).
>
> (Rainieri and Debras, 2019, p. 1)

Main research perspectives to naturally occurring metaphors

According to Deignan (2015), there are two kinds of naturally occurring data one can turn to in the analysis of metaphor: corpus data and discourse data. In the first case, general patterns of meaning and metaphor emerge from the analysis of concordances of large corpora, which serve to establish connections between source and target domains in language. In the second case, researchers explore how metaphorical meaning is related to the communicative goals of the participants in specific communication events, an analysis which may not have such a broad validity but could help to understand how metaphor really works in context. In both cases, the understanding is that no invented data, however insightful a researcher might be, can substitute for the exploration and study of real language use.

These two approaches are not incompatible with each other, and on the contrary, they can be supportive of each other:

> There is some crossover between the corpus and discourse approaches, where scholars compile relatively small datasets examined using a combination of corpus and discourse methods. This hybrid approach is often used in the analysis of metaphor of specific genres and registers, for instance in the studies described by Deignan et al.. (2013).
>
> (Deignan, 2017, p. 104)

Corpus data

In the article by Kövecses et al. (2019) cited above, there is a summary of the advantages of using what the authors call the *corpus-linguistic method* in metaphor analysis, which they oppose to the traditional CMT approach that they call the *lexical method*. These advantages are the following:

1   The corpus-linguistic method allows us to find both conventional and non-conventional metaphors and is therefore more exhaustive when identifying the whole range of metaphors.

2   The corpus-linguistic method makes it possible to determine both metaphor types and tokens, which the usage-based literature has repeatedly linked to concepts such as conventionalisation and entrenchment.

The authors realise that the difference between methods is not so much a question of efficiency, but also one of perspective and general approach. Thus, the lexical method operates best at the supra-individual level, where metaphors lack specificity and richness (cf. also Kövecses, 2017), whereas the corpus method operates best at the individual level, "where speaker and hearer metaphorically conceptualize their experiences in a fully contextualized fashion" (Kövecses, 2017, p. 329). In what may perhaps be considered a simplification, given among other things the radically different approach to the conceptualisation of language, we could say that the lexical method would be appropriate for the study of the system as such, the Saussurean *la langue*, whereas the corpus-linguistic method would be consistent with the analysis of *la parole*.

However, for Semino (2017), whose starting point is linguistic metaphors, the main distinction should be made between, on the one hand, metaphor studies carried out on large corpora, which "tend to make or test generalisations about metaphor use in a whole (national) language, such as British English, or across two languages, such as English and Italian" and, on the other, specific studies, which would be concerned with "the forms, functions and implications of metaphor use in particular texts or text types" (Semino, 2017). In other words, it would be the size and representativeness of the corpus which allow us to make different types of claims regarding metaphor use and which would determine whether the conclusions are generally valuable or not.

According to Semino (2017), corpus linguistics, understood in its first sense, i.e., as the results of the analysis of large corpora, has had several important implications for CMT and for understanding the place of metaphor in language. These are, among others, the following:

1   Corpus analyses have allowed the provision of linguistic evidence, mostly related to token and type frequency, of conceptual metaphors. Metaphors arising from a single source or even a single linguistic metaphor are not enough to posit a conventional conceptual metaphor. For a conceptual metaphor to be considered as real, it would be necessary to show that there are different and frequent manifestations in a representative corpus.

2   Mappings between source and target domains are connected to specific linguistic forms, which makes it difficult to assume, as CMT sometimes implicitly did, that a mapping from source to target invariably affects all the forms related to a domain. Proof of this is found in:

a   certain animal metaphors that tend to occur as nouns (e.g., *he is a cow*), others only as verbs (e.g., *horsing around*) and yet others as both (e.g., *racist pigs* and *pigging*) (cf. Deignan, 2005).

b   Different morphological inflections (e.g., *rock* vs *rocks*) that may have different metaphorical interpretations (cf. Deignan, 2005).

3   A conceptual mapping should be subjected to the scrutiny of data: an analysis of an expression such as *rich life* in a large corpus resulted in the rejection of its association to the conceptual metaphor A PURPOSEFUL LIFE IS A BUSINESS (cf. Semino, 2008).

4   Words with similar literal meanings have been shown to have different metaphorical associations (e.g., *path* is usually associated with ways of living and potential difficulties, whereas *road* would indicate purposeful activities) (cf. Falck & Gibbs, 2012).

In other words, Corpus-Linguistic data has allowed us to rethink many of the tenets of CMT. The examples that CMT researchers provided off the top of their heads were simply that an ad hoc illustration needed to be checked against real data. Corpus linguistics provides the appropriate tools and techniques to carry out this analysis, which is mostly interested in the general functioning of the specific language being analysed.

Discourse data

The second perspective deals with what Deignan (2017) calls discourse data and has many points in contact with what the corpus-linguistic literature calls "specialised corpora" (See Koester, 2022). Semino refers to it as the research "concerned with the forms, functions and implications of metaphor in particular texts or text types" (Semino, 2017, p. 464). In this latter group of studies, to which the MetCLIL corpus presented here could be ascribed, Semino includes some studies like Skorczynska and Deignan (2006), who analyse a corpus of business language (popularisation vs research articles), Demmen et al. (2015), who study the language and metaphors dealing with cancer in three corpora obtained from people involved in this situation, or L'Hôte (2014) who focuses on political language by gathering corpora which include manifestoes and speeches of leaders.

The analysis of discourse data is also related, as already mentioned, to the perspective of complex dynamic systems mostly undertaken by Cameron and colleagues. Here the emphasis is on adopting a bottom-up approach where the metaphorical models are specifically connected to the discourse being analysed. In this process, contextual elements related to the place and time as well as the participants in the particular discourse take an important role. An early example of this approach would be Cameron's (2003) work on oral classroom discourse in primary education, where the exchanges between teachers and students are analysed from the perspective of metaphor. The book by Cameron is also one of the first examples focusing on the analysis of oral language, which up to that point had not been attended to in the same way as written language.

However, the method used by Cameron and colleagues is more qualitative than quantitative, although they also pay attention to quantitative aspects such as metaphor density, i.e., the number of metaphors per hundred words of running text found in a specific corpus. This exploration of discourse follows a procedure called Systematic Metaphor Research (Maslen, 2017), which intends to uncover the "systematicities arising out of numerous local discourse processes" (p. 91). Researchers annotate the metaphors that might be connected after a detailed analysis and in a second step they try to identify the topic that is being talked about, which is sometimes not a straightforward process when spoken language is analysed.

Using corpus linguistics to identify metaphor

The type of data used for metaphor analysis is only the first element that needs to be taken into account. A second element refers to how metaphors are going to be identified in the data. Berber-Sardinha (2012) refers to two main ways of metaphor identification, sample and census. In sample-based methods, only a portion of the metaphors that could be found in the data are analysed, whereas in census-based, all metaphors are under consideration as the goal is to provide a full picture of metaphorical meanings in the data. Both are dealt with in the following.

Sample identification methods

Since, as acknowledged already by Lakoff and Johnson (1980), conceptual metaphor is fairly pervasive, identifying all its linguistic manifestations in a large body of texts seems a rather Herculean task, as it may involve thousands of items. As a result, researchers normally undertake the more feasible task of searching for a specific sub-group of metaphors whose features are determined in accordance with the aims of the research to be carried out. In this case, corpus tools and procedures become of paramount importance as they make the process more expedient and less time consuming.

The procedure by which a small group is selected to represent a phenomenon is not new in the domain of social sciences and it is therefore no coincidence that Berber-Sardinha (2012) has chosen the expression "sampling technique". The implication is also self-evident: the findings obtained from a sample may be disproved with the results obtained from a different sample. This means that the selection of terms to be searched, which needs to be specified beforehand, has to be carefully crafted and that the sample has to be big enough in relation to the corpus study to be able to derive more definitive conclusions. In this way, we could term this as a semi-automatic process as the metaphor researcher still plays a central role in the selection of the units to be searched for in the corpus. This type of search should be distinguished from another process, still to be developed to its full potential, where human intervention is minimised and where the search tends to be fully automatised. This second procedure will be discussed in our next section. Meanwhile, in the present section I will explain and exemplify the main semi-automatic techniques identified by the literature so far (see Berber-Sardinha, 2012; Brdar et al., 2020), to which I will add some others recently used by researchers.

SEARCHING FOR PREDEFINED EXPRESSIONS

This technique is the simplest development of sampling and consists in elaborating a representative list of terms that are likely to yield good results in terms of metaphor identification. This list is then used to perform searches with the appropriate linguistic software to obtain concordances in which the predefined terms appear. The concordances are then individually analysed to ascertain whether they are metaphorically used or not.

There are different ways to determine the expressions used in the search, which differ in their complexity, ranging from very simple procedures to more complex ones, each of them drawing on a different linguistic concept to create the list of search terms:

a   Semantic field: A simple approach would be to "extract all instances of words from the field … and then discarding all cases that are not metaphorical" (Stefanowitsch, 2020, p. 117).

A sophisticated way of performing this technique is to use the semantic tagging tool developed by Rayson (2008) within the framework of the Wmatrix software tools for corpus linguistics (https://ucrel-wmatrix4.lancaster.ac.uk/wmatrix4.html). The semantic annotation tool is called USAS and allows words to be tagged into different semantic categories by using a previously compiled vocabulary list structured in 21 discourse domains and 453 semantic categories. Thus, after the semantic tagging process each word receives one or more semantic tags when analysed by the system. For example, MacArthur et al. (2015) used this procedure to search for words related to SIGHT. This meant they had to find words using the following tags: X3.4, which corresponds to "sensory: sight", X3.4+ to "seen", and X3.4- to "unseen". In this way, they obtained a preliminary list of concordance lines that were later on analysed to check whether they were used metaphorically or not. This was also the procedure used by Koller (2020) who mixes this technique with procedure 1c below: "I started with anecdotally established words that MPs and peers used to talk about the EU–UK relationship (e.g., 'trapped', 'shackles'). I then established what semantic domains these words belonged to and searched for other words with the same tags" (p. 88). The resulting list of terms was then used to produce a list of searching terms like the ones found in Table 1.1.

b   Metaphorical Pattern Analysis: Defined by Stefanowitsch (2004), this type of search differs from the previous one in that both items from the source and the target domains are used in the search. Thus, to find the patterns of ARGUMENT IS WAR the search would be performed by using terms from the source domain (*indefensible, target, shoot down*) within a specific window, to the right and to the left, of terms from the target domain (*claim, criticism, argument*) (Stefanowitsch, 2020). This means that the researcher has usually defined specific conceptual metaphors or specific source-target mappings that s/he would like to attend to.

c   Candidate identification: In this option, the researcher identifies all metaphors in a portion of the corpus to be analysed and then the metaphors identified would be used as a search list for the whole corpus. In this sampling technique, the idea is not to focus on specific domains but on finding all possible metaphors (cf. Berber-Sardinha, 2012, p. 28). This is the approach adopted by Lederer (2016), who read "a small portion of the restricted corpus" (p. 536) to scan it for frequent metaphors that were used to search the corpus. The only peculiarity is that this list was expanded by finding the collocates of these terms in a general corpus in a similar fashion to method (b) above, as it was hypothesised that these could also enlarge the source vocabulary used to talk about the target (see Table 1.2 for some of the search terms used by Lederer, which she made available in the Appendix of a related article [Lederer, 2019]). Thus, for example, if the word *ship* was found to be used metaphorically in the initial reading of a portion of the corpus, a search in COCA of the frequent collocates of *ship* was performed to "capture lexis representative of the discourse surrounding seafaring in general" (p. 537). A partial list of the resulting metaphorical combinations obtained by Lederer can be seen in Table 1.3. This list was published in the Appendix of her 2019 article (Lederer, 2019).

SEARCHING FOR METAPHOR CLUSTERS

This method is based on the propensity of metaphors to cluster together, i.e., to be used in the vicinity of other metaphors (cf. Alejo-González, 2022 or Cameron & Stelma, 2004). This is related to one of the typical patterning ways in which metaphor is used, repetition (Dorst, 2017). Thus, given that according to Berber-Sardinha's experimental data, a search for lexical items in a window of 5 to 10 words would retrieve up to 40% of the metaphors in the corpus, concordances of up to 10 words long, "may enable researchers to spot metaphors in the vicinity of node words" (2012, p. 35).

SEARCHING FOR POTENTIAL METAPHORS USING KEYWORDS

Well-known within corpus linguistics, keyword extraction is a procedure used to establish which words within a corpus are unusually frequent, i.e., their occurrence in the corpus is significantly (in statistical terms) higher than in another corpus used as a reference. Most corpus linguistics packages already incorporate a tool that can automatically extract the list of keywords in a corpus (e.g., WordsSmith Tools, Antconc, Sketch Engine or Wmatrix). The idea behind this technique is to identify the vocabulary that plays an important role in the corpus to be analysed. Frequently used words could be prone to metaphorical use given they are sometimes related to "textual properties such as aboutness, style, and textual salience, among other attributes" (Berber-Sardinha, 2012, p. 38).

Table 1.1 Example of search words in Koller (2020, p. 90)

Word stem	Word(s)	Example	Occurrences
b*nd*	binding, binds, bondage, bonds (noun), bound	[The withdrawal agreement] is a fully binding treaty with no exit clause.	10
block*	block (verb), blocking	It is unthinkable that the EU could impose laws on us … without our having some means of blocking it.	2
escape	escape (noun, verb)	The withdrawal agreement has no escape clause either.	2
free*	free, freedom, freedoms, freely, freer	How do we embrace the opportunities that freedom from the EU will give us?	19
hamstrings	hamstrings (verb)	The backstop … hamstrings negotiations on a trade deal.	1
limit	limit (verb)	[T]he Prime Minister will be involved in negotiations about … any terms that might be sought by the European Council to limit the extent to which we might be able to act in accordance with the result of the referendum.	1
lock*	lock (verb), locked, locking, locks (verb)	[T]his is a bad deal that could lock the UK indefinitely in a backstop for a very long time.	10
prison	imprisonment, prison	[T]here is a minimal legal risk of us being trapped in the prison of the backstop.	4
restrains	restrains	[T]he UK observes single market rules and customs duties and restrains our right to compete for a period of three years.	1
restrictions	restrictions	[T]here would be restrictions on the UK's ability to participate in some EU tools.	1
shackles	shackles (noun)	The people's vision … was that of a strong United Kingdom, holding its head high, free from the shackles of the European Union.	1
stuck	stuck	[W]e can have open and seamless trade without being stuck within the European orbit as a form of satellite state.	2

(Continued)

Table 1.1 Continued

Word stem	Word(s)	Example	Occurrences
tangle	disentangle, entangled, entanglement	Once free from our EU entanglement, we will be able to move forward.	3
tie*	ties (verb), tied	[T]he backstop … ties our hands for the future and sets us on a path to a subordinate relationship with the EU.	3
trap	entrapment, trap (verb), trapped	The idea that the EU wishes to trap us in the backstop is simply a wrong analysis.	22

Table 1.2 A subset of Lederer's (2019, Appendix A) search terms

Full list of source and target trigger lemmas

Target lemmas	Source lemmas		
BANK	*SHIP*	*WEATHER*	*BODY*
CAPITAL	AGROUND	ATMOSPHERE	AIL
DEBT	ANCHOR	BUBBLE	AUTOPSY
ECONOMY	BALLAST	CALM	CHEST PAIN
FINANCE	BOARD	CLIMATE	CIRCULATE
FIRM	BOAT	CLOUD	CLEANSE
GROWTH	BUOY	CONDITION	CODE BLUE
INVEST	CAPTAIN	COOLDAM	CONTAGION
MARKET	CHANNEL	DROUGHT	CURE
MONEY	CHOPPY	DRY	DISEASE
PRICE	CREW	EBB	EMERGENCY ROOM
RATE	CRUISE	FLOOD	EPIDEMIOLOGY
	FLOAT	FORECAST	FIZZLE
	FLOW	FREEZE	HEALTH
	FROTH	HOT	LIFE SUPPORT
	[…]	[…]	[…]

However, the results obtained in a test of this method by Berber-Sardinha point to the relatively low efficacy of this procedure: "About 53% of the metaphorically used words were not keywords at all…This suggests metaphorically used words are neither particularly frequent nor rare" (Berber-Sardinha, 2012).

SEARCHING FOR POTENTIAL METAPHORS BASED THE MEASURE OF MUTUAL
SEMANTIC RELATEDNESS

This is a technique that has not received a lot of attention, particularly from linguists as it is closely connected to automated metaphor retrieval and requires some skills in computer programming. Based on the idea that semantic incongruity between adjacent words is at the heart of metaphor use,

Table 1.3 List of source target metaphorical pairings (noun + noun) in Lederer (2019)

N(T)-N(S)

Tokens	Tokens	Tokens
1. bank freeze 1	22. economy recovery 2	43. market circulation 1
2. bank health 5	23. finance atmosphere 1	44. market drought 1
3. bank recovery 1	24. firm health 3	45. market bubble 53
4. bank wave 1	25. growth 2	46. market buoy 2
5. bank flow 1	26. growth conditions 3	47. market channels 9
6. capital bubble 1	27. growth forecast 33	48. market climate 5
7. capital channels 2	28. growth freeze 1	49. market conditions 349
8. capital circulation 1	29. growth pains 2	50. market contagion 1
9. capital conditions 1	30. growth wave 3	51. market cooling 1
10. capital flow 177	31. investment atmosphere 2	52. market float 1
11. capital stream 1	32. investment bubble 6	53. market flow 8
12. debt bubble 7	33. investment channel 1	54. market forecast 21
13. debt climate 1	34. investment climate 80	55. market freeze 1

this technique aims to find metaphors by spotting words that are semantically unrelated in comparison with their context (Brdar et al., 2020).

SEARCHING FOR SIGNALS OR MARKERS OF METAPHORICITY

This technique is based on the idea of finding metaphors by searching for the specific language that accompanies them. This language has been called "metaporicity signals" (cf. Wallington et al., 2003) or tuning devices (Cameron & Deignan, 2003). Brdar et al. (2020) make a useful list of these signals:

- Explicit signals that are not metaphorical:
  - Adverbs: *metaphorically speaking, figuratively, symbolically, etc.*
  - Nouns: *picture, image, model, copy, caricature, etc.*
  - Verbs: *think of … as, consider … as, seem like …*
- Explicit signals that are metaphorical:
  - Verbs: *look, sound, taste like …*
  - Expressions: *in another sense, in a sense, in a way*
  - Metalinguistic signals: *so to speak, say, in a manner of speaking*
- Other signals:
  - Bogus signal of reality: *literally, actually, simply put*
  - Signals of (near-)equivalence: *no different to/from, amount to*
  - Approximate categorizers: *a kind/sort/type of, a bit of a, the NP of …*
  - Signal of quasi-extremity: *absolutely, … a tiny/gigantic NP*
  - Contrasters: *if not …, not so much as …*
  - Commonisation of proper names: genitives (e.g., *this country's Picasso*)

Table 1.4 Metaphor signal categories (Skorczynska & Ahrens, 2015)

Category	Metaphor signal
Explicit signals	*Metaphor*
Intensifiers	*Just, really, literally*
Symbolism forms	*Symbol*
Superordinate terms	*Sort of, kind of*
Copular similes	*Like, as*
Clausal similes	*As if*
Perceptual processes	*Look*
Verbal processes	*Say, call*
Modals and conditionals	*May, could, would*

This method was used by Skorczynska and Ahrens (2015), who report how they used it in the following way: "The concordances of the words and phrases previously selected as potential metaphor signals can be manually analysed for the cases of metaphor signalling. In this study, WordSmith Tools 5 (Scott, 2008) was used to electronically query the three corpora for the use of the words and phrases in Table 1.1. Thereafter, the concordances obtained were manually examined for signalled metaphors. Three analysts independently conducted the manual analysis of the concordances" (p. 366).

However, the selection of signalling words used by Skorczynska and Ahrens (2015) is an adaptation of Goatly (1997) and is more restrictive in its scope (see Table 1.4).

The importance of choosing an adequate list of signalling words is emphasised by Stefanowitsch (2020), who claims that certain signals like *a kind/type/sort of, not so much NP as NP* do not necessarily associate with metaphorical language all the time. This is not the case of other signals that seem to be more strongly connected with accompanying metaphorical language. This is the case of expressions like *metaphorically speaking* or *figuratively speaking*, which in a case study analysis are shown to be used with metaphors with a probability above chance.

Automated metaphor searching

In this section, we are not concerned with how we can actively search for metaphors in a corpus, but with how, and to what extent, we can leave the task of finding metaphors in the hands of a computer or a computer system. This means that I will be dealing, briefly, with an area clearly situated within the limits of Natural Language Processing (NLP).

To understand the performance of metaphor identification by an automated system, it is important to start by defining two fundamental concepts in NLP studies, i.e., precision and recall. In its specific application to the field of metaphor, Stefanowitsch (2020) defines precision as the proportion of correctly identified instances of metaphor calculated in relation to the whole number metaphors identified by the system. In other words, if the system identifies many more metaphors than there actually are, it will have low precision rate, i.e., it will not be accurate in metaphor recognition as it includes many instances of not metaphorically related words. Recall, for its part, refers to the proportion of metaphors identified in comparison to the total number of metaphors. This means that the system needs to have a good predictive ability in identifying all the metaphors that can be found in a corpus. These measurements are typically compared to gold standards, where specialised human judgement is included.

The main aim of NLP systems is therefore to improve the results in both precision and recall, something that has progressively been achieved by the growing amount of research using automated systems, or Artificial Intelligence, to extract metaphors from texts. However, the application of computational processes to metaphor is far from reaching the efficacy and results of other areas such as part-of-speech tagging, syntactic structure parsing or automatic summarisation (cf. Shutova, 2010). Thus, although the different approaches to metaphor processing summarised by Veale et al. (2016) in their book – corrective, analogical and schematic – are progressively achieving higher precision and recall rates, they are still far from the numbers obtained by part-of-speech tagging, for example, which as reported by Rayson (2008) can achieve 96–97% accuracy.

In a survey article on metaphorical metaphor processing Rai and Chakraverty (2020) report that the precision and recall of methods studying what they call Metaphor II and III, where the target domain of the metaphor is implicit, show values between 60 and 70%. For his part, Gibbs (2017) also reports the results obtained by Neuman et al. (2013) in their use of an automatic identification algorithm called the "concrete overlap algorithm" (COO). The algorithm obtained notable success rates as it was able to recognise 71% of metaphors. However, in his summary of automatic systems for metaphor identification, Gibbs (2017) acknowledges, that only "a subset of the complex reality of metaphorical language" (p. 79) was submitted to COO and that their findings are far from being generalisable in any way. It seems, once again, that different metaphor types may require different methods and that the number of metaphorically used words also has an impact on their success rate. A major issue of some of these studies relates to the difficulty of establishing a gold standard corpus annotated by humans as some of them report the lack of agreement of researchers when determining words undisputedly used metaphorically. Neuman et al. (2013) state that "despite the specific and detailed instructions given to the annotators, the decision whether a phrase is metaphorical is highly controversial" (p. 7).

An important aspect to consider has to do with David and Matlock's (2018) claim that these computational approaches "may not be ideal when a metaphor researcher has specific questions about functions of metaphor in a particular language context or cognitive and social domain, or seeks a bird's-eye view of metaphor distribution within that domain" (p. 469). In other words, these automated systems are far removed from what the applied linguist might expect in terms of output. In this respect, a new important avenue has opened with the most recent automated system, MetaNet.

MetaNet (Sweetser et al., 2019) stands out both in its conception and in its applications, although it needs to be acknowledged that it is not a purely automated system given that it relies on a previously elaborated metaphor repository. The main advantage of MetaNet lies in that it has been developed by an interdisciplinary group of researchers, some of whom have a solid background in Cognitive Linguistics and Metaphor research. This has resulted in two major key developments (cf. David, 2017): 1. the adoption of a fundamentally conceptual approach to metaphor, which would be the basic structure of the system to which linguistic metaphors are linked; and 2. The rejection of a pre-existing list of "every possible target domain source domain word combination" and the incorporation of a smaller set of categories, organised in *cascades*, which consist in a predefined hierarchy of relations, which correspond to "the semantic frames that feed the source and target domains of metaphors ... enriched with specific lexical information" (p. 579). In other words, the system incorporates the most recent developments in metaphor research (e.g., Sullivan, 2013), whereby metaphor use is connected to specific constructions or frames. As David and Matlock (2018) explain, the specific consequence of this approach is that "MetaNet models metaphor as frame-to-frame mappings, and therefore uses frames, frame elements, and lexeme-to-frame evoking patterns" (p. 472).

This is how they explain the way MetaNet works:

> lexical items are associated with frames, which in turn are associated with metaphors; the metaphoricity of a phrase is determined by a cascade exploiting frame inheritance networks, metaphor inheritance networks, and frame-to-metaphor relationships, while mediating via the grammatical constructions in which the candidate expression appears (Dodge et al., 2015). The same lexical item, e.g., *cancer*, can be metaphoric in one sense (*poverty is a cancer in our society*) and literal in another (*a tough battle with cancer*), and the system can determine which is which.
>
> (David & Matlock, 2018, p. 479)

The potentiality of this approach lies in providing interesting results in certain topic areas of interest to society. Some of the analyses carried out using MetaNet refer, for example, to the analysis of the poverty or to taxation. David and Matlock (2018) compared the metaphors of poverty in the Spanish and English Gigacorpus and found the prevalence of different metaphors, POVERTY IS A CHANGING (GROWING) ENTITY in Spanish (e.g., *aumentar la pobreza extrema*) versus the preference for POVERTY IS A DISEASE more typical of English (e.g., *poverty infected the city*). Other researchers analyse a conceptual metaphor related to politics and the economy, i.e., TAXATION IS A BURDEN (Sweetser et al., 2019).

Census identification methods: corpora fully tagged for metaphor

All the metaphor identification methods discussed so far rely on computer tools, either through partial or sampling searches or through automatic identification. However, as indicated by Berber-Sardinha, there is a second approach to metaphor identification that he calls the census approach, which involves that "researchers would have to analyse each token in the corpus" (2012, p. 22).

A good example of this type of approach is the Vrije Universiteit Amsterdam Corpus (VUAMC), which intended to carry out "an encompassing comparison between various registers that considers *all* metaphor in language" (original emphasis) (Krennmayr & Steen, 2017, p. 1054). The goal of this important project was to determine the metaphors used in four registers of the English language (academic, conversation, fiction and newspapers) by identifying this figure of speech in a corpus of around 200,000 words derived from BNC-Baby, an equally representative sub-corpus of the British National Corpus (BNC), the best-known and more widely used corpus when the VUAMC project started. In terms of metaphor identification, this project gives rise to Metaphor Identification Procedure Vrije Universiteit (MIPVU), an evolution or extension of the already existing Metaphor Identification Procedure (MIP) (Pragglejaz Group, 2007), which I will carefully analyse in Chapter 5.

In the project developed in this book, we continue with the research on the use of metaphor in spoken academic contexts by L2 users, already undertaken in the EuroCoAT project (MacArthur et al., 2014; www.eurocoat.es), which is another important example of a census approach to metaphor identification. In that project, the mobility of Spanish students abroad provided the basic framework for a research project aimed at analysing the difficulty students might find in the interpretation and production of metaphors, a skill considered particularly important as these academic encounters were, in some cases, the only opportunity students had to talk to their teachers (cf. Alejo-González, 2022; MacArthur, 2016, 2020).

MetCLIL continues the work by EuroCoAT by applying a census approach to L2 metaphor use. The main difference between the two projects lies in the different speech event analysed – office hour consultations in EuroCoAT vs. discussion seminars in MetCLIL – and the change in the contextual framework of analysis. The change of framework was required as the academic speech event targeted in MetCLIL not only involves Erasmus students but also home students who are enrolled in undergraduate programmes usually taught in English. As can be understood, while it was possible to single out Erasmus students in the study of academic consultations, it is unreasonable to expect that other oral academic genres would solely involve students enrolled in this European programme. This means that, for the MetCLIL project, we had to choose between the context provided by British universities and that of other European universities where English is used as a Medium of Instruction (EMI) or, as other researchers call it (Fortanet, 2013) Content and Language Integrated Learning (CLIL) in Higher Education or Integrating Content and Language in Higher Education (ICLHE; Wilkinson & Walsh, 2015).

Conclusion

In this chapter, the objective has been to introduce the primary theoretical foundation of this book by presenting key approaches to the study of metaphor. To start, a brief exploration of the historical origins of contemporary metaphor analysis from a conceptual perspective was undertaken, providing a very brief outline of Conceptual Metaphor Theory's major contributions, responsible for much of the current surge in metaphor research. This new approach to metaphor has been complemented by a more linguistic perspective in the analysis of this figure of speech, whose discursive status began to be emphasised by some authors at the turn of the century. It is within this last strand of research where corpus linguistics emerged as a valuable instrument for analysing the utilisation of metaphor in authentic language. Hence, this discipline has provided researchers with the tools to explore the nuances of linguistic metaphors more profoundly, revealing previously overlooked patterns within extensive textual passages originating from specific contexts. In the forthcoming chapter, we will introduce the specific usage context of the metaphors at the heart of this book: English as a Medium of Instruction (EMI), a development driven by the growing use of English in higher education in non-English-speaking countries.

Note

1 I will expand on the different terms and acronyms related to academic contexts – CLIL, EMI, etc. – but when the project first started it was thought safer to use CLIL in the acronym given its wider currency and its higher level of generality in comparison to English as Medium of Instruction.

References

Alejo-González, R. (2010). Where does the money go? An analysis of the container metaphor in economics: The market and the economy. *Journal of Pragmatics*, 42(4), 1137–1150.

Alejo-González, R. (2011). The container schema in economics and its discourse. *International Journal of Innovation and Leadership in the Teaching of Humanities*, 1(1), 64–79.

Alejo-González, R. (2022). Metaphor in the academic mentoring of international undergraduate students: The Erasmus experience. *Metaphor and Symbol*, 37(1), 1–20. https://doi.org/10.1080/10926488.2021.1941969

Arleo, A. (2000). Life cycles, chaos and zoom lenses: A comparative analysis of some conceptual metaphors in the discourse of entrepreneurship theory. *Anglais Scientifique*, 27(30), 19–31.

Berber-Sardinha, T. (2008). Metaphor probabilities in corpora. In M. S. Zanotto, L. Cameron, & M. Cavalcanti (Eds.), *Confronting metaphor in use: An applied linguistic approach* (pp. 127–148). John Benjamins.

Berber-Sardinha, T. (2012). An assessment of metaphor retrieval methods. In F. MacArthur, J. L. Oncins-Martínez, M. Sánchez-García, & A. M. Piquer-Píriz (Eds.), *Metaphor in use: Context, culture, and communication* (pp. 21–49). John Benjamins.

Brdar, M., Brdar-Szabó, R., & Perak, B. (2020). Separating (non-) figurative weeds from wheat. In A. Baichi (Ed.), *Figurative meaning construction in thought and language* (pp. 46–70). John Benjamins.

Caballero, R. (2003). Metaphor and genre: The presence and role of metaphor in the building review. *Applied Linguistics*, 24(2), 145–167.

Caballero, R. (2006). *Re-viewing space: Figurative language in architects' assessment of built space*. Mouton de Gruyter.

Caballero, R. (2007). Manner-of-motion verbs in wine description. *Journal of Pragmatics*, 39(12), 2095–2114.

Caballero, R. (2017). Genre and metaphor: Use and variation across usage events. In E. Semino & Z. Demjén (Eds.), *The Routledge handbook of metaphor and language* (pp. 193–205). Routledge.

Cameron, L. (2003). *Metaphor in educational discourse*. Continuum.

Cameron, L. (2008). Metaphor and talk. In R. Gibbs (Ed.), *The Cambridge handbook of metaphor and thought* (pp. 197–211). Cambridge University Press.

Cameron, L. J., & Deignan, A. (2003). Combining large and small corpora to investigate tuning devices around metaphor in spoken discourse. *Metaphor and Symbol*, 18(3), 149–160. https://doi.org/10.1207/s15327868ms1803_02

Cameron, L. J., & Deignan, A. (2006). The emergence of metaphor in discourse. *Applied Linguistics*, 27(4), 671–690.

Cameron, L. J., & Stelma, J. H. (2004). Metaphor clusters in discourse. *Journal of Applied Linguistics*, 1(2), 107–136.

Charteris-Black, J. (2004). Why "an angel rides in the whirlwind and directs the storm": A corpus-based comparative study of metaphor in British and American political discourse. *Language and Computers*, 49, 133–150.

Chomsky, N. (1957). *Syntactic structures*. Mouton.

Croft, W., & Cruse, A. (2004). *Cognitive linguistics*. Cambridge University Press.

David, O. (2017). Computational approaches to metaphor: The case of MetaNet. In B. Dancygier (Ed.), *The Cambridge handbook of cognitive linguistics* (pp. 574–589). Cambridge University Press.

David, O., & Matlock, T. (2018). Cross-linguistic automated detection of metaphors for poverty and cancer. *Language and Cognition*, 10(3), 467–493. https://doi.org/10.1017/langcog.2018.11

Deignan, A. (2005). *Metaphor and corpus linguistics*. John Benjamins.

Deignan, A. (2015). Figurative language and lexicography. In P. Hanks & G.-M. de Schryver (Eds.), *International handbook of lexicography*. Springer.

Deignan, A. (2017). From linguistic to conceptual metaphors. In E. Semino & Z. Demjén (Eds.), *The Routledge handbook of metaphor and language* (pp. 102–116). Routledge.

Deignan, A., Littlemore, J., & Semino, E. (2013). *Figurative language, genre and register*. Cambridge University Press.

Demmen, J., Semino, E., Demjén, Z., Koller, V., Hardie, A., Rayson, P., & Payne, S. (2015). A computer-assisted study of the use of violence metaphors for cancer and end of life by patients, family carers and health professionals. *International Journal of Corpus Linguistics*, *20*(2), 205–231.

Dodge, E., Hong, J., Stickles, E., & Oana, D. (2013, June 26). *The MetaNet Wiki: A collaborative online resource for metaphor and image schema analysis*. Paper presented at the ICLC-12, Edmonton, AB. Online access to the Wiki. https://metaphor.icsi.berkeley.edu/pub/en/index.php/category:metaphor

Dodge, E. K., Hong, J. & Stickles, E. (2015). MetaNet: deep semantic automatic metaphor analysis. *Proceedings of the Third Workshop on Metaphor in NLP* (pp. 40–49). Denver, Colorado, 5 June 2015. Association for Computational Linguistics. Online: http://www. aclweb.org/anthology/W15-1405

Dorst, A. G. (2017). Textual patterning of metaphor. In E. Semino & Z. Demjén (Eds.), *The Routledge handbook of metaphor and language* (pp. 178–192). Routledge.

Fanego, T. (2004). Is Cognitive grammar a usage-based model? Towards a realistic account of English sentential complements, *Miscelánea. A Journal of English and American Studies 29*. 23–58.

Fortanet, I. (2013). *CLIL in higher education: Towards a multilingual language policy*. Multilingual Matters.

Friginal, E. (2018). *Corpus linguistics for English teachers*. Routledge.

Friginal, E., & Hardy, J. A. (Eds.). (2020). *The Routledge handbook of corpus approaches to discourse analysis*. Routledge.

Friginal, E., Lee, J. J., Polat, B., & Roberson, A. (2017). *Exploring spoken English learner language using corpora: Learner talk*. Palgrave Macmillan.

Geeraerts, D. (2003). 'Usage-based' implies 'variational': On the inevitability of Cognitive Sociolinguistics. Paper presented at the 8th International Cognitive Linguistics Conference 2003. Logrono, Spain, July 20–15.

Gibbs, R. W. (1994). *The poetics of the mind: Figurative thought, language, and understanding*. Cambridge University Press.

Gibbs, R. W. (2007). Why cognitive linguists should care more about empirical methods. In M. Gonzalez-Marquez, I. Mittelberg, S. Coulson, & M. J. Spivey (eds.), *Methods in Cognitive Linguistics* (pp. 2–18). John Benjamins.

Gibbs, R. W. (Ed.). (2008). *The Cambridge handbook of metaphor and thought*. Cambridge University Press.

Gibbs, R. W. (2017). *Metaphor wars: Conceptual metaphors in human life*. Cambridge University Press.

Goatly, A. (1997). *The language of metaphors*. Routledge.

Grady, J. (1997). *Foundations of meaning: Primary metaphors and primary scenes* (Ph.D. dissertation). University of California, Berkeley.

Grady, J. (1998). The "Conduit" metaphor revisited: A reassessment of metaphors for communication. In J.-P. Koenig (Ed.), *Discourse and cognition: Bridging the gap* (pp. 205–218). CSLI Publications.

Gries, S. Th. & Stefanowitsch, A. (eds.). (2006). Corpora in Cognitive Linguistics. *Corpus-Based Approaches to Syntax and Lexis*. Mouton De Gruyter.

Herrmann, J. B., & Berber-Sardinha, T. (Eds.). (2015). *Metaphor in specialist discourse*. John Benjamins.

Johansson Falck, M., & Gibbs, R. (2012). Embodied motivations for metaphorical meanings. *Cognitive Linguistics*, *23*(2), 251–272.

Koester, A. (2022). Building small specialised corpora. In A. O'Keeffe & J. McCarthy (Eds.), *The Routledge handbook of corpus linguistics* (pp. 48–61). Routledge.

Koller, V. (2020). Analysing metaphor in discourse. In C. Hart (Ed.), *Researching discourse: A student guide* (pp. 77–96). Routledge.

Kövecses, Z. (1990). *Emotion concepts.* Springer-Verlag.

Kövecses, Z. (2000). *Metaphor and emotion.* Cambridge University Press.

Kövecses, Z. (2005). *Metaphor in culture: Universality and variation.* Cambridge University Press.

Kövecses, Z. (2010). *Metaphor: A practical introduction.* Oxford University Press.

Kövecses, Z. (2017a). Conceptual metaphor theory. In E. Semino & Z. Demjén (Eds.), *The Routledge handbook of metaphor and language* (pp. 13–27). Routledge.

Kövecses, Z. (2017b). Levels of metaphor. *Cognitive Linguistics, 28*(2), 321–347.

Kövecses, Z., Ambrus, L., Hegedűs, D., Imai, R., & Sobczak, A. (2019). The lexical vs. the corpus-based method in the study of metaphors. In M. Bolognesi, M. Brdar, & K. Despot (Eds.), *Metaphor and metonymy in the digital age: Theory and methods for building repositories of figurative language* (pp. 149–172). John Benjamins.

Krennmayr, T., & Steen, G. (2017). VU Amsterdam metaphor corpus. In N. Ide & J. Pustejovsky (Eds.), *Handbook of linguistic annotation* (pp. 1053–1071). Springer.

L'Hôte, E. (2014). *Identity, narrative and metaphor: A corpus-based cognitive analysis of New Labour discourse.* Palgrave Macmillan.

Lakoff, G. (2006). The contemporary theory of metaphor. In D. Geeraerts (Ed.), *Cognitive linguistics: Basic readings* (pp. 185–238). Mouton de Gruyter.

Lakoff, G., Espenson, J., & Schwartz, A. (1991). *Master metaphor list, second draft copy.* University of California at Berkeley. http://araw.mede.uic.edu/~alansz/metaphor/metaphorlist.pdf

Lakoff, G., & Johnson, M. (1980). *Metaphors we live by.* University of Chicago Press.

Lakoff, G., & Turner, M. (1989). *More than cool reason: A field guide to poetic metaphors.* Chicago University Press.

Lange, C., & Leuckert, S. (2020). *Corpus linguistics for world Englishes: A guide for research.* Routledge.

Lederer, J. (2016). Finding source domain triggers: How corpus methodologies aid in the analysis of conceptual metaphor. *International Journal of Corpus Linguistics, 21*(4), 527–558.

Lederer, J. (2019). Lexico-grammatical alignment in metaphor construal. *Cognitive Linguistics, 30*(1), 165–203.

Lee, D. (2001). *Cognitive linguistics. An introduction.* Oxford University Press.

Littlemore, J., & MacArthur Purdon, F. (2012). Figurative extensions of word meaning: How do corpus data and intuition match up? In D. Divjak & S. T. Gries (Eds.), *Frequency effects in language representation* (pp. 195–233). Vol. 2. Mouton De Gruyter.

MacArthur, F. (2016). Overt and covert uses of metaphor in the academic mentoring in English of Spanish undergraduate students at five European universities. *Review of Cognitive Linguistics, 14*(1), 23–50.

MacArthur, F. (2020). Rock bottoms, juggling balls and coalprints. Exploring the metaphor L2 speakers of English produce in face-to-face interaction. In J. Barnden & A. Gargett (Eds.), *Producing figurative expression: Theoretical, experimental and practical perspectives* (pp. 331–361). John Benjamins.

MacArthur, F., Alejo-González, R., Piquer-Píriz, A. M., Amador-Moreno, C., Littlemore, J., Ädel, A., Krennmayr, T., & Vaughn, E. (2014). *EuroCoAT. The European corpus of academic talk*. http://www.eurocoat.es

MacArthur, F., Krennmayr, T., & Littlemore, J. (2015). How basic is understanding is seeing when reasoning about knowledge? Asymmetric uses of sight metaphors in office hours' consultations in English as academic lingua franca. *Metaphor and Symbol*, *30*(3), 184–217.

Maslen, R. (2017). Finding systematic metaphors. In E. Semino & Z. Demjén (Eds.), *The Routledge handbook of metaphor and language* (pp. 88–101). Routledge.

Mio, J. S. (1996). Metaphor, politics, and persuasion. In J. S. Mio & A. N. Katz (Eds.), *Metaphor: Implications and applications* (pp. 127–146). Erlbaum.

Morgan, G. (1996). *Images of organization*. Sage Publications.

Neuman, Y., Assaf, D., Cohen, Y., Last, M., Argamon, S., & Newton, H. (2013). Metaphor identification in large texts corpora. *PLoS One*, *8*(4). https://doi.org/10.1371/journal.pone.0062343

O'Keeffe, A., & McCarthy, M. (Eds.). (2022). *The Routledge handbook of corpus linguistics*. Routledge.

Ortony, A. (Ed.). (1979). *Metaphor and thought*. Cambridge University Press.

Paquot, M., & Gries, S. T. (Eds.). (2020). *A practical handbook of corpus linguistics*. Springer Nature.

Pérez-Paredes, P. (2021). *Corpus linguistics for education: A guide for research*. Routledge.

Philip, G. (2008). Metaphorical keyness in specialised corpora. In M. Bondi & M. Scott (Eds.), *Keyness in texts* (pp. 185–203). John Benjamins.

Pragglejaz Group. (2007). MIP: A method for identifying metaphorically used words in discourse. *Metaphor and Symbol*, *22*(1), 1–39. https://doi.org/10.1080/10926480709336752

Rai, S., & Chakraverty, S. (2020). A survey on computational metaphor processing. *ACM Computing Surveys (CSUR)*, *53*(2), 1–37.

Rainieri, S., & Debras, C. (2019). Corpora and representativeness: Where to go from now? *CogniTextes*, *19*. Retrieved May 27, 2022, from https://journals.openedition.org/cognitextes/1311

Rayson, P. (2008). From key words to key semantic domains. *International Journal of Corpus Linguistics*, *13*(4), 519–549. https://doi.org/10.1075/ijcl.13.4.06ray

Ricoeur, P. (1977). *The rule of metaphor: Multidisciplinary studies of the creation of meaning in language* (2nd ed.). Taylor and Francis.

Roldán-Riejos, A., & Úbeda, P. (2013). Metaphor in the ESP engineering context. *Ibérica: Revista de La Asociación Europea de Lenguas Para Fines Específicos*, *25*, 107–126.

Salager-Meyer, F. (1990). Discoursal flaws in medical English abstracts: A genre anaylsis per research-and text-type. *Text-Interdisciplinary Journal for the Study of Discourse*, *10*(4), 365–384.

Scott, M. (2008). *WordSmith tools version 5*. Lexical Analysis Software.

Semino, E. (2006). A corpus-based study of metaphors for speech activity in contemporary British English. In S. T. Gries & A. Stefanowitsch (Eds.), *Corpora in cognitive linguistics: Conceptual metaphors* (pp. 36–63). John Benjamins.

Semino, E. (2008). *Metaphor in discourse*. Cambridge University Press.

Semino, E. (2011). *Metaphor, creativity, and the experience of pain across genres*. Palgrave Macmillan.

Semino, E. (2017). Corpus linguistics and metaphor. In B. Dancygier (Ed.), *The Cambridge handbook of cognitive linguistics* (pp. 463–476). Cambridge University Press.

Shutova, E. (2010). Models of metaphor in NLP. In J. Hajič, S. Carberry, S. Clark, and J. Nivre (eds.). *Proceedings of the 48th annual meeting of the association for computational linguistics* (pp. 688–697). Association for Computational Linguistics.

Skorczynska, H., & Ahrens, K. (2015). A corpus-based study of metaphor signaling variations in three genres. *Text & Talk, 35*(3), 359–381.

Skorczynska, H., & Deignan, A. (2006). Readership and purpose in the choice of economics metaphors. *Metaphor and Symbol, 21*(2), 87–104.

Stefanowitsch, A. (2004). HAPPINESS in English and German: A metaphorical-pattern analysis. In Michel Achard & Suzanne Kemmer (eds.), *Language, culture, and mind* (pp. 137–149). CSLI.

Stefanowitsch, A. (2006). Words and their metaphors: A corpus-based approach. In A. Stefanowitsch & S. Th. Gries (Eds.), *Corpus-based approaches to metaphor* (pp. 61–105). Mouton de Gruyter.

Stefanowitsch, A. (2020). *Corpus linguistics: A guide to the methodology*. Language Science Press.

Stefanowitsch, A., & Gries, S. T. (2003). Collostructions: Investigating the interaction between words and constructions. *International Journal of Corpus Linguistics, 8*(2), 209–243.

Sullivan, K. (2013). *Frames and constructions in metaphoric language*. John Benjamins.

Sullivan, K. (2016). Integrating constructional semantics and conceptual metaphor. *MetaNet, 8*(2), 141–165. https://doi.org/10.1075/cf.8.2.02sul

Sweetser, E., David, O., & Stickles, E. (2019). Automated metaphor identification across languages and domains. In M. Bolognesi, M. Brdar, & K. Despot (Eds.), *Metaphor and metonymy in the digital age: Theory and methods for building repositories of figurative language* (pp. 23–47). John Benjamins.

Szudarski, P. (2018). *Corpus linguistics for vocabulary: A guide for research*. Routledge.

Tracy-Ventura, N., & Paquot, M. (Eds.). (2020). *The Routledge handbook of second language acquisition and corpora*. Routledge.

Tummers, J., Heylen, K., & Geeraerts, D. (2005). Usage-based approaches in Cognitive Linguistics: A technical state of the art. *Corpus Linguistics and Linguistic Theory 1*(2), 225–261.

Veale, T., Shutova, E., & Beigman Klebanov, B. (2016). *Metaphor: A computational perspective*. Morgan & Claypool Publishers.

Wallington, A. M., Barnden, J. A., Barnden, M. A., Ferguson, F. J., & Glaseby, S. R. (2003). *Metaphoricity signals: A corpus-based investigation*. School of Computer Science, University of Birmingham.

Wilkinson, R., & Walsh, M. L. (Eds.). (2015). *Integrating content and language in higher education: From theory to practice*. Peter Lang.

2 English as a Medium of Instruction

In Chapter 1, the main language-internal aspect of the Metaphor Production in Content and Language Integrated Learning seminars corpus (MetCLIL), metaphor, was introduced. In this chapter, the focus will shift towards the language-external factor that influenced the construction of the corpus, specifically the area of English as a Medium of Instruction (EMI). EMI refers to the use of English as the language of teaching and learning in non-English-speaking countries, particularly at the university level. To fully understand EMI, it is important to also consider its integration within the broader context of English as a Lingua Franca (ELF).

English as a lingua franca

In her book on bilingualism, which she uses as a synonym for multilingualism, Carol Myers-Scotton, a specialist in sociolinguistics, enumerates a series of situations in which the learning and use of second languages is promoted. Among them, she refers to contexts such as living in a bilingual country, migrations, living in border areas or marrying outside one's ethnic group (Myers-Scotton, 2006, pp. 45ff.). Some of these situations, like engaging in occupations involving contact with out-groups, already point towards a phenomenon that she touches on at the end of her book, globalisation and its impact on language policies. Another researcher on bilingualism, Ofelia García (2009), summarises, citing Fettes, this new contact situation in vivid way:

> National economies have become far more integrated in the global economy; money and workers have become much more mobile; the pace of technological change has accelerated to an unbelievable extent; and the explosive growth of communication and information networks is on the verge of "annihilating space."
>
> (2003, p. 37)

The consequences of this process, which is still developing and whose limits are as yet unknown to us, may be termed as unprecedented given that it has given a language, English, a predominant position that no other language has enjoyed in history:

DOI: 10.4324/9781003400905-2

it [English] has spread around the globe like no other language before, and ... it is spoken by people for whom it is a second or additional language more than by those for whom it is a first language.

(Mauranen, 2018, p. 7)

The situation of using a third language to communicate by people who do not have the same first language is not new in history (see, e.g., Latin) and this third language is normally referred to as a lingua franca. What seems to be new is the scale of the phenomenon, which has progressively led to an increasing research interest in this emerging reality and finally to the establishment of a new research area, English as a Lingua Franca (ELF), which has seen a progressive expansion in the twenty-first century (Jenkins, 2000; Mauranen, 2003; Seidlhofer, 2011).

The emergence of ELF as a research area has not only established a field of study that addresses the unique characteristics and communicative practices of non-L1 speakers of English, but it has also sparked discussions on important issues that have a significant impact on the discipline of linguistics and related fields. These issues include:

- The recognition that the current reality in the world is not limited to communication among monolingual speakers but rather encompasses multilingualism. This has challenged the traditional view that monolingualism is the norm and has highlighted the prevalence of multilingual communication, as is increasingly evident through the study of English in lingua franca contexts. This consideration of multilingualism both at a psycholinguistic and sociolinguistic level, i.e., those involving the cognitive and social aspects of language use, has led ELF researchers to progressively broaden their initial definitions of ELF to also include L1 speakers of English when interacting with non-natives. Thus, the definition of English as a lingua franca (ELF) has evolved over time given that, initially, ELF was conceptualised as a form of English used by non-native speakers as a common language to facilitate communication among themselves, with the assumption that native speakers of English would not be included (House, 1999). However, some scholars have argued that native speakers of English also use the language in ELF communication, and therefore should not be excluded. This means, as will be shown later when delimiting the actual extent of English as Medium of Instruction (EMI), that the context, not only the speakers, may also have an important role to play and that, as a consequence, majority English language contexts should not be considered as EMI and therefore as ELF.
- The concept of English as a Lingua Franca (ELF) as language use, rather than as a linguistic variety, has increasingly become widely accepted among linguistics scholars and researchers. Thus, the corpus-based descriptions of English as a Lingua Franca (ELF) in linguistic, discursive, or pragmatic terms provided by studies of major ELF corpora (such as Mauranen, 2012

or Seidlhofer, 2011) should not be understood as the characterisation of a variety. Rather, they should be seen as tendencies, subject to great variability. Björkman puts it this way:

> ELF is not a variety nor does it need to be a variety to be studied separately from World Englishes, creoles and learner languages. It is the largest use of the English language today by legitimate discourse communities, and that fact on its own suffices for ELF settings to be investigated thoroughly.
>
> (2013, p. 172, cit. in Pitzl, 2018, p. 15)

- As a consequence of the above, some of the main features of ELF as language use are linguistic, but perhaps the most important ones are pragmatic. Thus, ELF is characterised by simplified grammar, high-frequency vocabulary, repetition, reduced use of idiomatic expressions, and increased use of discourse markers such as "you know" or "I mean". It also prioritises communicative effectiveness, often applying the "let it pass" principle to overlook or tolerate language errors or deviations to maintain the flow of communication and achieve mutual understanding. ELF is dynamic and continuously adapting to the specific needs of its users (cf. Jenkins, 2015).

As suggested above, in establishing ELF as a research area, it has been important to delimit its distinctive features from other research areas with which it has close links. The first of these neighbouring areas is World Englishes, understood as those varieties of English (e.g., Indian English) that have developed outside the contexts where this language is mostly used by native speakers (e.g., British English). As explained by Jenkins and Mauranen (2019), ELF shares with World Englishes its detachment from nativist approaches to language, which consider "native English speakers ... [as] global owners ... [or] arbiters of its use and development" (Jenkins & Mauranen, 2019, p. 4), but at the same time it realises that the distinctive features of ELF do not depend so much on the L1 of the speakers but on the roles of the speakers and the features of interaction involved in the communication. ELF is not just the result of "a typical contact situation, where speakers of two different languages use one of them in communication" (cf. Mauranen, 2012, pp. 29–30). Instead, ELF is the result of:

> a multitude of different L1s [that] come into contact with English simultaneously and, in turn, these L1-based lects are in contact with each other, making ELF what Mauranen (2012) defines as a second-order language contact between "similects".
>
> (Mauranen et al., 2015, p. 402)

The second research area that ELF needs to be separated from is that of English as Foreign Language (EFL) and more precisely the sub-area of Learner Language and the recent developments in what is called Learner Corpus Research (LCR). In contrast to learner corpora, an ELF corpus seeks to include speech in a natural, often complex mix, rather than selecting for given L1 backgrounds and comparable proficiency levels.

(Mauranen et al., 2015, p. 404)

In other words, ELF is not concerned with phenomena such as language transfer, either in the form of errors or otherwise, and the language level or proficiency of the participants. Besides, from a strictly sociolinguistic perspective, the focus on learner language is more closely related to classroom settings, where the main goal is for the learner to align to native speaker models. For ELF, the participants recorded in the interaction are not language learners, but language users. This is also related to how data are obtained since the most important element for an ELF corpus is the authenticity of communication being recorded, whereas in particular when we deal with spoken language, language corpora do not usually respond to everyday normal spoken interactions, but rather to contrived interviews that intend to elicit the language learners would use in an invented situation.

English taught programmes in higher education

The transposition of globalisation into university contexts has usually received the name of internationalisation. This process is defined by the Report on Internationalization of Higher Education written for the European Parliament's Committee on Culture and Education in the following way:

the intentional process of integrating an international, intercultural or global dimension into the purpose, functions and delivery of post-secondary education, in order to enhance the quality of education and research for all students and staff, and to make a meaningful contribution to society.

(De Wit et al., 2015, cit. in Bowles & Murphy, 2020, p. 4)

The fact that the word "intentional" and the connection with quality assurance is incorporated into the definition clearly indicates that, probably in contrast with globalisation, internationalisation is the result of particular policies adopted by the different stakeholders involved at different levels of decision ranging from the local level (e.g., the specific university) to the wider level (e.g., transnational institutions like the European Union). For universities, internationalisation is the strategic way these institutions have responded to the challenges posed by a competitive and knowledge-based economy which requires students' competencies and skills allowing them to participate in the developments of this new society. It is the means to achieve success in the middle of the socio-political changes imposed by a new global educational and economic context (Wadhwa, 2016).

In the specific case of Europe, internationalisation is also inevitably connected to the process of political integration, which undoubtedly has an educational dimension. Thus, the European Union has adopted a series of policies in education that have promoted the internationalisation of higher education institutions. This is the case of the so-called Bologna process, which received the name of the city where the agreement to integrate the higher education systems of European countries was signed and gave rise to the European Higher Education Area (EHEA), or the launching of the Erasmus programme, subsidising the mobility of students and teachers, which has greatly contributed to the internationalisation of European universities (cf. Sursock, 2015).

Other internationalisation policies, seeking to attract students from different countries, include the increasing provision of courses and programmes taught in English in higher education. By offering courses and programmes in English, universities are thus able to expand their areas of influence and to boost the number of students. Using Beelen and Jones' words (2015), it could be said that, while the Erasmus programme deals with "internationalisation abroad", English taught programmes are the result of "internationalisation at home" efforts.

The importance of these other less institutional policies, as they usually involved decision of individual universities, was recognised by the literature very early on (Doiz et al., 2013). In Spain, one of the countries lagging behind other North European countries in the provision of English Taught Programmes (ETP), the numbers are certainly striking. According to this survey carried out by Wächter and Maiworm (2014), there were a total of 36 Spanish universities providing at least one ETP, which represents 20.3% of higher education institutions in our country, and they were offering 417 ETP programmes, which amounted to 2.3% of all the programmes offered.

The result of these policies has been obvious: the role of English as a lingua franca has been reinforced given that, using Smit's words, ETP is "the prototypical ELF scenario" (2018, p. 387, cit. in Jenkins & Mauranen, 2019, p. 6). English has established itself as the language that is used by default for communication in academic contexts even in countries where this language is not an official language. English is the academic lingua franca par excellence in universities.

However, the weight that this new context has acquired is so considerable that a separate research area referred to as English as Medium of Instruction (EMI) has gradually emerged. The more recent evidence of the growth of this area is the creation of a journal issued by a prestigious publishing house entitled *English Medium of Instruction*, which saw the light in 2022. Some of the topics of interest in EMI relate to questions like the lecturers' and students' attitudes to the implementation of bilingual degrees (Aguilar & Rodríguez, 2012; Dafouz et al., 2007; Doiz et al., 2011; Fortanet, 2012), teacher discourse and metadiscursive strategies (Dafouz, 2011; Dafouz & Núñez, 2010), language policies implemented at the university level (see part 1 of

Carrio-Pastor, 2020 or Doiz et al., 2013), teacher training issues (see part II of Carrió-Pastor, 2020 or Lasagabaster, 2022), academic literacies (Richards & Pun, 2022), or language use and interaction in EMI (Lasagabaster & Doiz, 2021; Macaro, 2018).

This rapidly expanding phenomenon has, however, not been sufficiently analysed in terms of the linguistic, cultural and academic implications that may be derived from the teaching/learning of disciplinary contents in English as an academic lingua franca. Unlike in the Primary and Secondary educational stages, where a considerable number of studies have been carried out (Alejo-González & Piquer-Píriz, 2016a, 2016b; Cenoz, 2009; Llinares et al., 2012; Lorenzo et al., 2009; or Pérez-Cañado & Lancaster, 2017 among others) studies focused on higher education are still scarce.

Defining EMI: distinctive traits

The importance of defining and delimiting EMI responds to two fundamental aspects. On the one hand, there has been a certain controversy regarding the scope of ELF, a field within which, as we have seen above, EMI is integrated, which meant that this dispute was also extended to the definition of EMI, although in a different sense. On the other, the empirical work involved in the compilation of a corpus entails understanding the phenomenon to be studied.

As regards the definition of ELF, Mauranen presents the debate as follows:

> Two kinds of widespread definitions of ELF circulate in the field of applied linguistics, one that takes it to apply only to people for whom it is not a first language, to the exclusion of native speakers (e.g. Firth, 1996; House, 1999), and another that accepts native speakers as parts of the mix (e.g. Jenkins, 2007; Mauranen, 2012; Seidlhofer, 2004, 2011).
>
> (Mauranen, 2018, p. 8)

As explained by Mauranen, the first definition is very restrictive and involves a distinction between native and non-native speakers that the research in Second Language Acquisition and Bilingualism has put into question. For our purposes, adopting the second definition is important because in some of the seminars recorded there were L1 users of English, which would have meant discarding that particular event as not falling within the phenomenon we intended to study.

The second controversy is more specific to EMI and has to some extent been overlooked by the specialised literature until a recent paper (Rose et al., 2021). In this paper, the question of the definition is not referenced to the people participating in the interaction, but to the actual context where the interaction takes place as becomes clear from the definition Macaro had previously given: "the use of the English language to teach academic subjects (other than English itself) *in countries or jurisdiction where the first language (L1) of the majority of the population is not English*" (Macaro, 2018, p. 19) (My emphasis).

This means that experiences found in British, American, Australian universities or in universities in other English-speaking countries, where both L1 and L2 users of English share the same class, are not included under EMI as they are considered to be of a different nature. We could say that those experiences are part of ELF, since they involve the interaction in English as an L2, but they are not EMI properly speaking. The reasons offered for this separation have to do with the different educational contexts and the language policies involved in the universities and with the importance of acknowledging the differences established by the SLA literature between "Foreign Language Contexts" and "Second Language Contexts" or between "naturalistic" and "instructed" experiences (cf. among others Ortega, 2009).

The implication of adopting Macaro's understanding of EMI for the gathering of our corpus is evident. All our recordings were made in universities located in countries where English was not a dominant language. MetCLIL is thus an EMI corpus in this restrictive sense and therefore separates itself from other existing ELF corpora like ELFA or VOICE, whose definition of the phenomenon is broader.

It is also important to note here that the definition used here also separates MetCLIL from learner language. EMI, perhaps unlike CLIL, and other contexts of learner interaction, has a specific status:

> ELF data clearly distinguishes itself from both Content and Language Integrated Learning (CLIL) settings, where speakers typically share a first language, and learner corpora, which are compiled from students of English. It is also important to note that ELFA corpus differs radically from learner or CLIL data in not taking note of speaker proficiency. It is easy to see that the speakers' proficiency levels vary, but no attempt was made to control, measure or code this. It is a normal part of lingua franca encounters that speaker proficiencies are different in the vehicular language, and it is important to capture this reality in its everyday manifestation.
>
> (Mauranen et al., 2010, p. 185)

The corpus that is introduced in the present book, MetCLIL, shows the degree of internationalisation of EMI classes is high. None of the groups of students recorded consists exclusively of local students.

Metaphor in EMI

Based on our understanding of how metaphor is utilised in other contexts, we can anticipate its significance in English as a Medium of Instruction (EMI) despite the limited research specifically devoted to this topic. Metaphor can be expected to facilitate the expression of abstract concepts in a clear and concise manner, making them more concrete and easier to understand. It can also make new or unfamiliar concepts more relatable and accessible. The use of metaphor in teaching through English can add interest and engagement, which can enhance the learning experience. Furthermore, metaphor is likely to play a crucial role in cross-cultural communication as it is a universal language feature. The following sections will examine the areas that may help us gain a deeper understanding of the role and function of metaphor in different related contexts and how it may be applied in EMI.

Metaphor in academic English

The most systematic approach to the use of metaphor in academic contexts was addressed by the Vrije Universiteit Amsterdam Metaphor Corpus (VUAMC) team (Dorst, 2011; Herrmann, 2013; Kaal, 2012; Krennmayr, 2011, 2015; Steen et al., 2010), already cited above. By using texts from the BNC-Baby corpus and coding them using the MIPVU (Steen et al., 2010), they calculated the density of metaphor in four main registers (conversation, fiction, news texts and academic writing) with the aim of establishing whether there were any differences in terms of metaphor use between these four registers. Curiously enough, and contrary to expectations, they found that metaphor is more frequent in academic writing (18.6%) and news texts (16.4%), whereas it is less extensively used in fiction (11.8%) and conversation (7.7%). But this is not the only surprising result; academic writing is also the register with the lowest number of direct metaphors, i.e., those metaphors that are lexically signalled or flagged by words or expressions indicating the target domain of the metaphor, a fact that can be explained in terms of the need that specialist subjects have of "demarcating meanings, while allowing for the construction of abstractness and complexity of content" (Herrmann, 2015, p. 185).

It is important to note that the VUAMC team use register as their framework of analysis and that their work is closely linked to the dimensions proposed by Biber and colleagues in their corpus analysis of discourse (cf. Biber, 2006; Biber & Conrad, 2009). Thus, metaphor becomes incorporated to the host of linguistic elements that can help us categorise a text according to certain functional dimensions of language. This would mean that certain linguistic features (e.g., use of nouns) could be demonstrated to co-occur with metaphors and are therefore related to the dimension of language (e.g., informational, involved, etc.) Biber and colleagues had defined. Already mentioned in the research published by the VUAMC team, this enterprise is taken up again by Berber-Sardinha (2015), who sought to apply a Multidimensional Analysis to the same corpus, the BNC-Baby, in order to incorporate metaphor to the functional dimensions of discourse. The conclusion is straightforward: "a high score on the 'information' side of dimension [1] would predict a large number of metaphors in the text, whereas a large score on 'involvement' would indicate few metaphors" (Berber-Sardinha, 2015, p. 27). Thus, the higher density of metaphors found in academic texts can be understood in relation to the lower scores of linguistic markers of involvement, such as personal pronouns and demonstratives.

Another group of researchers who study metaphor in academic discourse adopt a different approach. They rely more on the study of genre and typically focus on academic lectures, as they hold a prominent position in the network of oral academic genres. The main references in this field are Corts and Pollio (1999), Littlemore et al. (2011), Low (2010) and Low et al. (2008) and their findings can hardly be considered as conclusive as these studies only analyse a few lectures. The preliminary conclusions from the study of lectures are diverse and sometimes far from straightforward. Thus, for example, a gross estimate of the density of university lectures would place them between the 11–13% range (Low, 2011), which compared with the density of academic texts seems to indicate that oral, in contrast with written, academic language tends to be less metaphorically dense. Also, the genre can be characterised by the use of clusters at key moments of the discourse of the lecturer (Corts & Pollio, 1999), although Low et al. (2008) did not find such conclusive evidence and were only able to identify the presence of a final cluster with the clear rhetorical objective of ending the lecture on a high note. Moreover, the use of personification seems to be widespread, as in all academic discourse, and its main function aims "to make the argument more interesting, or to allow access to everyday terminology and thus condense the argument, or make it conceptually more accessible" (Low, 2011, p. 13). Finally, university lecturers do not make use of many similes (Low, 2010, 2011; Low et al., 2008) and this finding would be related to the fact the teachers may want to preserve this figure of speech for special cases where they really want to signal the mapping, usually with a didactic purpose.

One may surmise that that the way metaphor is used in general, academic contexts would be transferred to EMI contexts. However, given the peculiarities of this context, where English has a different status and the participants are in their majority L2 speakers, it is only reasonable that this preliminary conclusion awaits empirical confirmation and takes into consideration research dealing with metaphor use in educational contexts by L2 learners.

Metaphor in language teaching

Another context where the role of metaphor has been considered refers to the use of metaphor in foreign language teaching. Connected to the wider framework of Applied Cognitive Linguistics (Holme, 2004; Littlemore, 2009; Piquer-Píriz & Alejo-González, 2016, 2020; Tyler, 2012), within which it is clearly integrated, it shares with it the basic understanding that language cannot be considered as separated from cognition and that some of these cognitive mechanisms have an important role in how we use language (Tyler,

2012). Thus, attention to metaphor, and more precisely to conceptual metaphor, would become an important resource that language teachers could use in facilitating the learning of foreign languages (see Low, 1988, 2020).

A specific area that could benefit from this approach is vocabulary teaching. This is how Hoang and Boers explain it:

> Quasiexperimental studies within this strand (see Boers, 2013 for a review) have produced rather compelling evidence that helping learners to appreciate the connection between established figurative uses of word or phrases (e.g., the use of weed in We need to weed out corruption) and their original, literal meanings (e.g., the use of weed in the context of gardening) renders these words or phrases more memorable.
>
> (Hoang & Boers, 2018, p. 2)

Naturally, this would need to have teachers and lecturers ready to raise students' awareness of the potential of metaphor to boost their learning (cf. Low et al., 2008; MacArthur, 2017) and the creation of materials that respond to this approach. So far, phrasal verbs (cf. Rudzka-Ostyn, 2003) seem to have been the area where this approach has more readily been applied, but more general textbooks used in school contexts still seem to disregard any contributions made from this linguistic perspective (cf. Alejo-González et al., 2010).

Metaphor in L2 acquisition

The role of metaphor in language teaching cannot be fully understood if it is not placed in the more general framework where it belongs, i.e., Second Language Acquisition. In other words, using metaphor in teaching is a way of acknowledging that metaphor is a vital element of the language competence that needs to be acquired by L2 speakers. Although there has been some literature on the subject (Danesi, 1992, 2008; Littlemore, 2001; Littlemore & Low, 2006; Low, 1988, 2020), mostly concerned with its definition and integration with other competences, the attempts to operationalise the concept, for example in the same way that written competence has taken shape in the form of written tests, and to develop an empirical measure have been really scarce (Castellano-Risco & Piquer-Piriz, 2020; O'Reilly & Marsden, 2021 as exceptions).

Until tests to measure metaphorical competence become standard and are implemented regularly in tests assessing L2 linguistic competence, the analysis of the metaphors produced by L2 speakers has concentrated on written production, even if we have to acknowledge together with Nacey (2020) that both comprehension and production are connected. In the research carried out in this area, corpus-based analyses are the norm. In some cases, a great majority, existing learner corpora are used and exploited, while in others, corpora, like in the present book, are specifically compiled for metaphor analysis. In the following, I summarise some of the most relevant research.

The first example is the book-length analysis carried out by Susan Nacey (2013), who compared the production of metaphors in written essays by Norwegian speakers of English with that of native speakers of English. To this end, she undertook the analysis of metaphor use in both the Norwegian subcorpus of the International Corpus of Learner English (NICLE), and its comparable British English counterpart from the Louvain Corpus of Native English Essays (LOCNESS). Contrary to expectations, the levels of metaphor use in both corpora were very high and not significantly different, which indicates that second language learners do not necessarily lag behind native speakers in metaphor use. Naturally this would need to be confirmed for other L2 speakers with a different L1.

In another analysis of written production, Littlemore et al. (2014) examined data of a different kind. In this case, the corpus was made up of the examination texts included in the Cambridge Learner Corpus (CLC), which has been compiled on the basis of the official Cambridge examinations of English to speakers of other languages (ESOL). This allowed the researchers to select texts produced at the different proficiency levels and to analyse them for metaphor use. The speakers selected belonged to only two different L1 backgrounds, Greek and German, in order to account for the possible influence of transfer from the L1. The results obtained go in the direction of enforcing the link between metaphor use and proficiency level as it was found that the higher the level of the learner, the greater the number of metaphors used. The B2 level was shown to be a turning point in this respect as not only the number but also the type of metaphors used considerably changed at this level.

Finally, Hoang and Boers (2018) did a study similar to Littlemore et al.'s (2014), although with a slightly different methodology and in a different context. This time the corpus consisted of 72,122 words obtained from 396 Vietnamese learners of English doing a four-year degree in English Language who had to write an essay of at least 250 words, which was later graded by experienced teachers. The results also show a statistically significant correlation between the number of metaphors and the different grades of the BA, used as a proxy for proficiency level. Students in higher grades not only showed greater use of metaphor but were also more in line with the use of metaphorical conventions of English.

These three studies can indeed be described as robust research both in terms of their rigour and the depth of their analysis. However, it can clearly be seen that there is still a lot of ground to be covered in this area, given that many questions remain unanswered (e.g., What is the extent to which learners use conventional and unconventional metaphors?) and that the samples refer to very specific populations of L2 learners.

Regarding the research on metaphorical production in oral language, the state of affairs has been delineated in the following way:

there exist very few studies of how people expressing themselves in another language use metaphor in face-to-face conversation …[T]hese contexts of use are sufficiently different to encourage researchers to examine how L2 speakers express themselves metaphorically when their discourse is unplanned and produced in the oral mode … so we will expect that findings on the metaphors produced by L2 speakers in planned discourse (e.g. Littlemore et al., 2014; Nacey, 2013) may be somewhat different from those they use in spontaneous conversational interaction.

(MacArthur, 2020, pp. 331–332)

Two complementary elements may explain this situation. On the one hand, it is possible to connect it to the limited availability of spoken learner corpora and to the way these corpora are compiled by way of tasks (usually class-related and involving an arranged conversation with a native speaker teacher). This results in the production of language that is not completely authentic, in the sense of reproducing the conversations that L2 speakers would have in real contexts. On the other hand, the process of tagging metaphors in spoken conversation is a major challenge as meaning is much more context dependent and sometimes implicitly expressed.

A first attempt to overcome these difficulties has been made by the research on the role of metaphor in office hour consultations by Erasmus students (Alejo-González, 2022; MacArthur, 2016b). In this case, the research is clearly conducted within the parameters delineated by the citation above and attempts to confirm the significance of this figure of speech in the academic genres used in a context which is adjacent to, if not within, ELF (Alejo-González, 2022; MacArthur, 2015, 2016a, 2016b, 2017; MacArthur et al., 2015; Piquer-Piriz & Alejo-González, 2016). As also happens with academic lectures (see Low et al., 2008), office hour consultations show a low number of overt or direct uses of metaphors (cf. MacArthur, 2016b), which can be considered to facilitate students' understanding of the subject matter as they involve an explicit reference to source metaphoric domain thus helping them to make the appropriate connections.

The study of metaphor use in discussion seminars undertaken in the MetCLIL project means a move forward in the investigation of academic talk, an area still neglected if compared with academic writing (Biber, 2006 Swales, 2004). By analysing metaphor in real language use, this book will contribute to the study of how students and teachers communicate in the academic context provided by EMI programmes and Higher Education CLIL.

Metaphor in ELF

The research reviewed thus far may have provided some insights into the use of metaphor in contexts that have some connections with English as a Medium of Instruction (EMI), because the domain they explore, i.e., academic language, or the participants involved, i.e., learners, have something in common with it. However, as previously discussed in this chapter, EMI, as part of English as a Lingua Franca (ELF) research, has its own unique characteristics that distinguish it from both English as a Native Language (ENL) and English as a Foreign Language (EFL) contexts. Therefore, it is important to consider the specific needs and nuances of ELF communication when examining the use of metaphor in this context. We focus on ELF as, to the best of our knowledge, no research has specifically addressed metaphor in EMI and the scarce research dealing with academic language (e.g., Franceschi, 2013) has mostly done so to derive conclusions that are applicable to ELF in general.

When analysing metaphor in ELF interaction, researchers have mostly focused on two main aspects: idioms and creativity. The focus on idiomatic language can be explained in terms of the need to account for the difficulty that such language poses to L2 users. For its, part creativity and innovation are the linguistic consequence of the previous difficulty. L2 users adapt and modify their language use creatively in order to communicate effectively in a multilingual context. It is important to examine each of these aspects separately to gain a deeper understanding of how metaphor is used and perceived in ELF communication.

Regarding idioms, Seidlhofer (2002) has shown that phraseological expressions with a metaphorical meaning can be disruptive to ELF communication and sometimes give rise to what she calls "unilateral idiomaticity". She expands on it in a later article (Seidlhofer 2009), where she gives the following example used in a conversation between a BBC journalist and an interviewee, an L2 user: "but that makes it a criminal offense, in my book!" (p. 202). According to Seidlhofer, "it is clear that for his interlocutor this [the use of 'in my book'] causes difficulties that are very unlikely to have arisen had he said I think or in my opinion" (2009, p. 202). In other words, idioms sometimes go against the cooperative principle in ELF interactions and may be a source of difficulty in achieving mutual understanding.

However, 'unilateral idiomaticity' in ELF can often be compensated for by the use of strategies such as the 'let it pass' principle. These strategies allow for the maintenance of the flow of conversation despite the difficulties that idioms may create. For example, if a speaker uses an idiom that the listener does not understand, the listener may use a 'let it pass' strategy and move on to a different topic rather than halting the conversation. This approach allows the listener to accept the idiom without requiring the speaker to explain its meaning, which means that conversation can continue without disruption. The operation of this principle was proposed by Firth (1996) and was later confirmed by other researchers such as Franceschi (2013), who in her study on ELF interactions shows that 'let it pass' strategies can be used to overcome difficulties caused by idioms and to maintain a smooth conversation flow.

Another strategy used in ELF is what Seidlhofer (2009) calls 'idiomatizing', which she understands as the way ELF speakers make use of and adapt idiomatic expressions to communicate effectively or to build rapport with the person they are talking to. It would be as way of creating a sense of 'togetherness', i.e., "to identify speakers as members of the here-and-now group, as insiders in the conversation, and in this respect are also markers of shared territory, expressive of common understanding and attitude" (Seidlhofer, 2009, p. 205). According to this author, 'idiomatization' can also include the use of metaphorical language, where for example a word like *endangered*, typically used as a collocate of, for example, the word *species*, is "collaboratively broadened to include the nouns *activities, areas, disciplines, field(s), program and study*, and an in-group consensus is well and truly established" (Seidlhofer, 2009, p. 208).

The consequences of 'idiomatizing' are very similar to the process of accommodation, which has been defined as "the systematic use of the same or similar metaphor vehicles across turns" (MacArthur, 2020, p. 352). Its role in ELF can be anticipated by its attested status not only in L1 (cf. Cameron, 2008), but also in L2 contexts (cf. MacArthur, 2016a, 2016b; MacArthur & Littlemore, 2011). In the case of novel metaphors, this systematic use of similar metaphors has been described as a "temporary pact" (cf. MacArthur, 2020) made by interactants to refer to and convey certain concepts, ideas or attitudes that are important for the discourse. As suggested by Pitzl (2018), accommodation is essentially a "pragmatic process" (p. 166) in which interactants deliberately or unconsciously converge with their interlocutors in their use of metaphor.

Regarding the second relevant aspect of metaphor use in ELF, creativity, the primary reference is Pitzl (2018). Pitzl, in line with the ELF field, rejects the idea of unconventional language use as errors. Instead, she argues that the use of unconventional figurative language by ELF speakers merits analysis from a creativity perspective. She also provides a classification of the various types of variation (semantic, lexical, syntactic, or morphosyntactic) that ELF users incorporate into conventional idioms. Additionally, Pitzl introduces the concept of "re-metaphorization" in ELF contexts, which aligns with Müller's (2008) idea of "activated metaphoricity" or "waking metaphors". This concept is characterised by the formal variations (e.g., lexical substitution) introduced by ELF speakers to conventional idioms, which enhances their metaphorical value and makes them "semantically decomposed and rendered figuratively compositional" (Pitzl, 2018, p. 228). In Müller's terms, these formal variations in idioms can be considered as "contextual cues" that indicate the metaphorical activation of a word in ELF contexts.

Finally, the pragmatically oriented thrust of metaphor analysis in ELF has led to paying some attention to the functions of metaphor. Pitzl (2018) enumerates a series of functions which can be ascribed to two main groups: a) interpersonal/social, which would include rapport, solidarity, humour, mitigation or projecting stance; and b) ideational/transactional, which would comprise emphasising, summarising, discussing abstract concepts. These two groups of functions roughly correspond to the social and communication functions proposed by Franceschi (2013), which in turn allude to the broad Hallidayian ideational and interpersonal functions (cf. Pitzl, 2018, p. 155). However, as pointed by MacArthur (2020), these two main functions need to be completed with the textual function, also mentioned by Halliday (1994) and extensively substantiated in L1 discourse (cf. Herrmann, 2013).

It is important to note at the end of this chapter that the phraseological approach mostly adopted by the ELF literature is in contrast with the word level approach adopted by the researchers studying metaphor in academic English (see above). Thus, to cite a couple of examples from the ELF research, Pitzl (2018) explicitly excludes from her analysis "examples for (creative) use of ontological or spatial metaphors" (p. 90) and Franceschi (2013), although not excluding single words from her analysis (included when "based on an underlying metaphor" [p. 82]), seems to have disregarded most of them given their scarce density (0.22%) in her corpus. By contrast, metaphor identification procedures such as the Metaphor Identification Procedure (MIP, Pragglejaz, 2007) or Metaphor Identification Procedure Vrije Universiteit (MIPVU, Steen et al., 2010), use words or lexical units as the default unit of analysis and assume that even formulaic or idiomatic language are susceptible of being analysed into the different individual metaphors (cf. e.g., the analysis of "wear the mantle" in MIP, Pragglejaz Group, 2007, p. 8). This methodological approach is the one adopted here and will be developed more fully in chapter 5.

Conclusion

In this chapter, I have explored the emerging topic of English as a Medium of Instruction (EMI) as the primary communicative context where the metaphors, constituting the central focus of our linguistic analysis, have been gathered. This exploration has been accomplished through references to key conceptual elements drawn from the emerging literature on the subject particularly by paying attention to the burgeoning field of English as a Lingua Franca (ELF). ELF provides the broader theoretical framework within which EMI is situated and has allowed us to reach a more precise definition of EMI as a context. This means that it needs to be understood as a university context, situated in non-English-speaking milieus, where English is used to communicate by participants, regardless of their first language, which may also include some native speakers of English. In the last part of the chapter, I have provided a summary of the literature on English in academic and L2 acquisition contexts as an introduction to the scarce literature dealing with metaphor in ELF contexts, which can establish the foundation for the final three chapters of the book, where three different analyses employing various perspectives, ranging from qualitative to quantitative approaches, have been employed in the study of metaphor in EMI.

References

Aguilar, M., & Rodríguez, R. (2012). Lecturer and student perceptions on CLIL at a Spanish university. *International Journal of Bilingual Education and Bilingualism*, 15(2), 183–197.

Alejo-González, R. (2022). Metaphor in the academic mentoring of international undergraduate students: The Erasmus experience. *Metaphor and Symbol*, 37(1), 1–20. https://doi.org/10.1080/10926488.2021.1941969

Alejo-González, R., & Piquer-Píriz, A. (2016a). Measuring the productive vocabulary of secondary school CLIL students: Is Lex30 a valid test for low level school learners? *Vigo International Journal of Applied Linguistics*, 16, 31–53.

Alejo-González, R., & Piquer-Píriz, A. (2016b). Urban vs. rural CLIL: An analysis of input-related variables, motivation and language attainment. *Language, Culture and Curriculum*. https://doi.org/10.1080/07908318.2016.1154068

Alejo-González, R., Piquer-Píriz, A., & Reveriego, G. (2010). Phrasal verbs in EFL course books. In S. De Knop, F. Boers, & A. De Rycker (Eds.), *Fostering language teaching efficiency through cognitive linguistics* (pp. 59–78). Mouton de Gruyter.

Beelen, J., & Jones, E. (2015). Redefining internationalization at home. In R. Pricopie, J. Salmi, P. Scott, & A. Curai (Eds.), *Redefining internationalization at home* (pp. 67–80). Springer.

Berber-Sardinha, T. (2015). Register variation and metaphor use: A multi-dimensional perspective. In J. B. Herrmann & T. Berber Sardinha (Eds.), *Metaphor in specialist discourse* (pp. 17–52). John Benjamins.

Biber, D. (2006). *University language: A corpus-based study of spoken and written registers*. John Benjamins.

Biber, D., & Conrad, S. (2009). *Register, genre, and style*. Cambridge University Press.

Boers, F. (2013). Cognitive linguistic approaches to teaching vocabulary: Assessment and integration. *Language Teaching*, 46(2), 208–224.

Björkman, B. (2013). *English as an academic lingua franca: An investigation of form and communicative effectiveness*. Mouton de Gruyter.

Bowles, H., & Murphy, A. C. (2020). EMI and the internationalization of universities: An overview. In H. Bowles & A. C. Murphy (Eds.), *English-medium instruction and the internationalization of universities* (pp. 1–26). Palgrave Macmillan.

Cameron, L. (2008). Metaphor and talk. In R. Gibbs (Ed.), *The Cambridge handbook of metaphor and thought* (pp. 197–211). Cambridge University Press.

Carrió-Pastor, M. L. (2020). *Internationalising learning in higher education: The challenges of English as a medium of instruction*. Palgrave Macmillan.

Castellano-Risco, I., & Piquer-Píriz, A. M. (2020). Measuring secondary-school L2 learners vocabulary knowledge: Metaphorical competence as part of general lexical competence. In A. M. Piquer-Piriz & R. Alejo-González (Eds.), *Metaphor in foreign language instruction* (Vol. 42, pp. 199–220). Mouton de Gruyter.

Cenoz, J. (2009). *Towards multilingual education*. Multilingual Matters.

Corts, D. P., & Pollio, H. R. (1999). Spontaneous production of figurative language and gesture in college lectures. *Metaphor and Symbol*, 14(2), 81–100.

Dafouz, E. (2011). English as the medium of instruction in Spanish contexts: A look at teacher discourse. In Y. Ruiz de Zarobe, J. M. Sierra, & F. Gallardo del Puerto (Eds.), *Content and foreign language integrated learning: Contributions to multilingualism in European contexts* (pp. 189–209). Peter Lang.

Dafouz, E., & Núñez, B. (2010). Metadiscursive devices in university lectures: A contrastive analysis of L1 and L2 teacher performance. In C. Dalton-Puffer, T. Nikula, & U. Smit (Eds.), *Language use and language learning in CLIL classrooms.* (pp. 213–232). John Benjamins.

Dafouz, E., Núñez, B., Sancho, C., & Foran, D. (2007). Integrating CLIL at the tertiary level: Teachers' and students' reactions. In D. Wolff & D. Marsh (Eds.), *Diverse contexts converging goals: Conten)t and language integrated learning in Europe.* (pp. 91–102). Peter Lang.

Danesi, M. (1992. Metaphorical competence in second language acquisition and second language teaching: The neglected dimension. In J. E. Alatis (Ed.), *Language communication and social meaning (Georgetown University round table on languages and linguistics)* (pp. 489–500). Georgetown University Press.

Danesi, M. (2008). Conceptual errors in second-language learning. In S. De Knop & A. De Rycker (Eds.), *Cognitive approaches to pedagogical grammar* (pp. 231–256). Mouton de Gruyter.

Doiz, A., Lasagabaster, D., & Sierra, J. M. (2011). Internationalisation, multilingualism and English-medium instruction. *World Englishes, 30*(3), 345–359.

Doiz, A., Lasagabaster, D., & Sierra, J. M. (Eds.). (2013). *English-medium instruction at universities. Global challenges.* Multilingual Matters.

Dorst, A. G. (2011). *Metaphor in fiction: Language, thought and communication.* Box Press Uitgeverij.

Fettes, M. (2003). The geostrategies of interlingualism. In J. Maurais & M. Morris (Eds.), *Languages in a Globalising world* (pp. 37–46). Cambridge University Press.

Firth, A. (1996). The discursive accomplishment of normality: On 'Lingua Franca' English and conversation analysis. *Journal of Pragmatics, 26*(2), 237–260.

Fortanet, I. (2012). Academics' beliefs about language use and proficiency in Spanish multilingual higher education. *AILA Review, 25,* 48–63.

Franceschi, V. (2013). Figurative language and ELF: Idiomaticity in cross-cultural interaction in university settings. *Journal of English as a Lingua Franca, 2*(1), 75–99.

García, O. (2009). *Bilingual education in the 21st century: A global perspective.* Wiley-Blackwell.

Halliday, M. A. K. (1994). *An introduction to functional grammar.* Edward Arnold.

Herrmann, J. B. (2013). *Metaphor in academic discourse: Linguistic forms, conceptual structures, communicative functions and cognitive representations* (Dissertation). LOT Dissertation Series, Utrecht.

Herrmann, J. B. (2015). High on metaphor, low on simile? An examination of metaphor type in sub-registers of academic prose. In J. B. Herrmann & T. Berber-Sardinha (Eds.), *Metaphor in specialist discourse* (pp. 163–190). John Benjamins.

Hoang, H., & Boers, F. (2018). Gauging the association of EFL learners' writing proficiency and their use of metaphorical language. *System, 74,* 1–8.

Holme, R. (2004). *Mind, metaphor and Language Teaching.* Palgrave Macmillan.

House, J. (1999). Misunderstanding in intercultural communication: Interaction in English as *lingua franca* and the myth of intelligibility. In C. C. Gnutzmann (Ed.), *Teaching and learning English as a global language* (pp. 1–19). Stauffenburg.

Jenkins, J. (2000). *The phonology of English as an international language.* Oxford University Press.

Jenkins, J. (2007). *English as a Lingua Franca: Attitude and Identity.* Oxford University Press.

Jenkins, J. (2015). Repositioning English and multilingualism in English as a Lingua Franca. *Englishes in Practice*, 2(3). 49–85.

Jenkins, J., & Mauranen, A. (2019). Researching linguistic diversity on English-medium campuses. In J. Jenkins & A. Mauranen (Eds.), *Linguistic diversity on the EMI campus: Insider accounts of the use of English and other languages in Universities within Asia, Australasia, and Europe* (pp. 3–20). Routledge.

Kaal, A. A. (2012). *Metaphor in conversation*. Uitgeverij BOX Press.

Krennmayr, T. (2011). *Metaphor in newspapers* (Dissertation). LOT Dissertation Series, Utrecht.

Krennmayr, T. (2015). What corpus linguistics can tell us about metaphor use in newspaper texts. *Journalism Studies*, 16(4), 530–545.

Lasagabaster, D. (2022). Teacher preparedness for English-medium instruction. *Journal of English-Medium Instruction*, 1(1), 48–64.

Lasagabaster, D., & Doiz, A. (Eds.). (2021). *Language use in English-medium instruction at university: International perspectives of teacher practice*. Routledge.

Littlemore, J. (2001). Metaphoric competence: A possible language learning strength of students with a holistic cognitive style? *TESOL Quarterly*, 35(3), 459–491.

Littlemore, J. (2009). *Applying cognitive linguistics to second language learning and teaching*. Springer.

Littlemore, J., Chen, P., Barnden, J., & Koester, A. (2011). Difficulties in metaphor comprehension faced by international students whose first language is not English. *Applied Linguistics*, 32(3), 408–429.

Littlemore, J., Krennmayr, T., Turner, J., & Turner, S. (2014). An investigation into metaphor use at different levels of second language writing. *Applied Linguistics*, 35(2), 117–144.

Littlemore, J., & Low, G. (2006). *Figurative thinking and foreign language learning*. Palgrave Macmillan.

Llinares, A., Morton, T., & Whittaker, R. (2012). *The roles of languages in CLIL*. Cambridge University Press.

Lorenzo, F., Casal, S., & Moore, P. (2009). The effects of content and language integrated learning in European education: Key findings from the Andalusian bilingual sections evaluation project. *Applied Linguistics*, 31(3), 418–442.

Low, G. (1988). On teaching metaphor. *Applied Linguistics*, 9(2),125–146.

Low, G. (2010). Wot no similes? The curious absence of simile in university lectures. In G. D. Low, Z. Todd, A. Deignan, & L. Cameron (Eds.), *Researching and applying metaphor in the real world* (pp. 291–308). John Benjamins.

Low, G. (2011). "Pin me down a bit more." Researching metaphor in university lectures. *International Journal of Innovation and Leadership in the Teaching of Humanities*, 1(1), 6–22.

Low, G. (2020). Taking stock after three decades: 'On teaching metaphor'revisited. In A. M. Piquer-Piriz & R. Alejo-González (Eds.), *Metaphor in foreign language instruction* (pp. 37–56). Mouton de Gruyter.

Low, G. D., Littlemore, J., & Koester, A. (2008). Metaphor use in three UK university lectures. *Applied Linguistics*, 29(3), 428–455.

Macaro, E. (2018). *English medium instruction*. Oxford University Press.

MacArthur, F. (2015). On using a dictionary to identify the basic senses of words. *Metaphor and the Social World*, 5(1), 124–136.

MacArthur, F. (2016a). Beyond engaged listenership: Assessing Spanish undergraduates' active participation in academic mentoring sessions in English as academic lingua franca. In J. Romero-Trillo (ed.). *Yearbook of corpus linguistics and pragmatics 2016: Global implications for culture and society in the networked age* (pp. 153–178). Springer.

MacArthur, F. (2016b). Overt and covert uses of metaphor in the academic mentoring in English of Spanish undergraduate students at five European universities. *Review of Cognitive Linguistics, 14*(1), 23–50.

MacArthur, F. (2017). Using metaphor in the teaching of second/foreign languages. In E. Semino & Z. Demjén (Eds.), *The Routledge handbook of metaphor and language* (pp. 413–425). Routledge.

MacArthur, F. (2020). Rock bottoms, juggling balls and coalprints. Exploring the metaphor L2 speakers of English produce in face-to-face interaction. In J. Barnden & A. Gargett (Eds.), *Producing figurative expression: Theoretical, experimental and practical perspectives* (pp. 331–361). John Benjamins.

MacArthur, F. & Littlemore, J. (2011). On the repetition of words with the potential for Metaphoric extension in conversations between native and non-native speakers of English. *Metaphor and the Social World, 1*, 201–38.

MacArthur, F., Krennmayr, T., & Littlemore, J. (2015). How Basic Is "UNDERSTANDING IS SEEING" When Reasoning About Knowledge? Asymmetric Uses of Sight Metaphors in Office Hours Consultations in English as Academic Lingua Franca, Metaphor and Symbol. 30:3, 184–217, DOI: 10.1080/10926488.2015.1049507.

Mauranen, A. (2003). The corpus of English as a lingua franca in academic settings. *TESOL Quarterly, 37*(3), 513–527.

Mauranen, A. (2012). *Exploring ELF: Academic English shaped by non-native speakers*. Cambridge University Press.

Mauranen, A. (2018). Conceptualising ELF. In J. Jenkins, W. Baker, & M. Dewey (Eds.), *The Routledge handbook of English as a lingua franca* (pp. 7–24). Routledge.

Mauranen, A., Carey, R., & Ranta, E. (2015). New answers to familiar questions: English as a lingua Franca. In D. Biber & R. Reppen (Eds.), *The Cambridge handbook of English corpus linguistics* (pp. 401–417). Cambridge University Press.

Mauranen, A., Hynninen, N., & Ranta, E. (2010). English as the academic lingua franca- the ELFA project. *English for Specific Purposes, 29*, 183–190.

Müller, C. (2008). *Metaphors dead and alive, sleeping and waking: A dynamic view*. University of Chicago Press.

Myers-Scotton, C. (2006). *Multiple voices: An introduction to bilingualism*. Blackwell.

Nacey, S. (2013). *Metaphors in learner English [metaphor in language, cognition, and communication 2]*. John Benjamins Publishing Company.

Nacey, S. (2020). Metaphors in high-stakes language exams. In G. B. Steien & L. A. Kulbrandstad (Eds.), *Språkreiser–festskrift til Anne Golden på* (pp. 287–308). Novus Forlag.

O'Reilly, D., & Marsden, E. (2021). Eliciting and measuring L2 metaphoric competence: Three decades on from low (1988). *Applied Linguistics, 41*(2), 24–59.

Ortega, L. (2009). *Understanding second language acquisition*. Routledge.

Pérez-Cañado, M. L., & Lancaster, N. K. (2017). The effects of CLIL on oral comprehension and production: A longitudinal case study. *Language, Culture and Curriculum, 30*(3), 300–316.

Piquer-Píriz, A. M., & Alejo-González, R. (2016). Applying cognitive linguistics. *Review of Cognitive Linguistics, 14*(1), 1–20.

Piquer-Píriz, A. M., & Alejo-González, R. (Eds.). (2020). *Metaphor in foreign language instruction* Mouton de Gruyter.

Pitzl, M. L. (2018). *Creativity in English as a lingua franca: Idiom and metaphor.* Mouton de Gruyter.

Pragglejaz Group. (2007). MIP: A method for identifying metaphorically used words in discourse. *Metaphor and Symbol, 22*(1), 1–39. doi:10.1080/10926480709336752

Richards, J. C., & Pun, J. (2022). *Teaching and learning in English medium instruction: An introduction.* Routledge.

Rose, H., Macaro, E., Sahan, K., Aizawa, I., Zhou, S., & Wei, M. (2021). Defining English medium instruction: Striving for comparative equivalence. *Language Teaching, 56*, 1–12.

Rudzka-Ostyn, B. (2003). *Word Power: Phrasal Verbs and Compounds. A Cognitive Approach.* Mouton de Gruyter.

Seidlhofer, B. (2002). The shape of things to come? Some basic questions about English as a lingua franca. In K. Knapp & Ch. Meierkord (Eds.), *Lingua franca communication* (pp. 269–302). Peter Lang.

Seidlhofer, B. (2004). Research perspectives on teaching English as a lingua franca. *Annual review of applied linguistics, 24*, 209–239.

Seidlhofer, B. (2009). Accommodation and the idiom principle in English as a lingua franca. *Intercultural Pragmatics, 6*(2), 195–215. https://doi.org/10.1515/IPRG.2009.011

Seidlhofer, B. (2011). *Understanding ELF.* Oxford University Press.

Steen, G. J., Dorst, A. G., Herrmann, J. B., Kaal, A. A., & Krennmayr, T. (2010). Metaphor in usage. *Cognitive Linguistics, 21*(4), 765–796.

Sursock, A. (2015). *Trends 2015: Learning and teaching in European universities.* European University Association.

Swales, J. M. (2004). *Research genres: Explorations and applications.* Cambridge University Press.

Tyler, A. (2012). *Cognitive linguistics and second language learning: Theoretical basics and experimental evidence.* Routledge.

Wächter, B., & Maiworm, F. (Eds.). (2014). *English-taught Programmes in European higher education: The state of play in 2014.* Lemmens.

Wadhwa, R. (2016). New phase of internationalization of higher education and institutional change. *Higher Education for Future, 3*(2), 227–246.

3   Introducing the MetCLIL corpus

As already explained, the main goal of this book is to provide a comprehensive overview of the process of creating a corpus, the MetCLIL corpus (Alejo-Gonzalez et al., 2021), which is designed to examine the use of metaphor in academic seminars conducted in English as a Medium of Instruction (EMI) in Europe. The main idea is to cover the conceptual, methodological and analytical frameworks necessary for understanding the construction and analysis of such a corpus. The first two chapters have provided an introduction to the theoretical background by dealing with the most important research on metaphor use and on English as a Medium of Instruction as the main concepts shaping its final design. Before addressing the methodological decisions taken in the compilation and elaboration of the corpus, which will be done in Chapters 4 and 5, the present chapter argues for the need for a corpus such as MetCLIL and intends to familiarise the reader with the main objectives of the corpus and the decisions taken to meet them.

Explaining the need for MetCLIL

Compiling a corpus is not an easy task and, as shown by the literature (cf. e.g., Koester, 2022), it involves a great deal of collective effort by a research team. This is why it is important to analyse the existing resources available to explore the research questions to be addressed. Thus, the decision to design MetCLIL was taken after considering the corpora available and analysing whether they were suitable for our purposes.

A first step was to check whether the two English as a Lingua Franca (ELF) projects in Europe, whose scope is broader than the one adopted here, could be used for our purposes. These two corpora, each of them comprising one million words, are VOICE (Vienna-Oxford International Corpus of English, VOICE, 2009/2018) and ELFA (English as a Lingua Franca in Academic settings, cf. Mauranen, 2012). Both corpora focus on representing speech events naturally occurring in settings where speakers do not share a first language and as a consequence have to resort to English as a medium for communication (cf. Seidlhofer, 2011). However, while ELFA concentrated on academic settings, VOICE had a wider range and covered other contexts such as leisure or business.

ELFA and VOICE are reliable and solid sources for any corpus-linguistic work on the phenomenon of English as a Lingua Franca. However, the need to compile MetCLIL was felt for a number of reasons:

DOI: 10.4324/9781003400905-3

1 VOICE only provides a limited number of academic events connected to the traditional university genres (lectures or seminars) and, although ELFA does indeed cover many monologic and speech events at a higher education institution, it only includes one seminar dealing with the domain the research project was focused on, i.e., business and marketing (economics and administration seminars only represent 5% of the ELFA corpus, cf. Mauranen et al., 2010). MetCLIL selected this topic domain as the literature has shown that this is an area where metaphors are frequent (cf. Alejo-González, 2010; Koller, 2003).

2 Even if the ELFA corpus is more closely connected to university settings, it mostly followed MICASE (Simpson-Vlach et al., 2002) methodology in attempting to reproduce the different speech events taking place at a single place, the University of Tampere, Helsinki. This meant that the academic conventions were those of Finland, or at least of a Northern European country, and that the number of participants from certain first languages was skewed towards both the home country of the university or to the surrounding countries. ELF speakers from Southern countries such as Spain, Italy and Portugal only represent 2.0%, 2.9% and 1.8% respectively.[1] One of the goals of the project was precisely to be able to compare whether the North/South divide (cf. Maiworm & Wächter, 2014) established for EMI in Europe had an effect on metaphor use and this will have an effect in the structure of the corpus, as we will see later.

3 What is most important, VOICE and ELFA were intended as resources for the description of language used in ELF contexts in general, whereas MetCLIL was designed to compare the use of metaphor in EMI contexts. This meant restricting the selection of the topic areas covered, in our case business and management, so that the specific metaphors used by speakers could be compared. At the same time, given the work-intensive task of manual annotation of metaphor needed, since automatic tagging for this figure is far from being achieved, reducing the corpus size to make this work manageable was important.

Within this context, MetCLIL intended to contribute a corpus which represented the more varied nature of business and management seminars taught in Europe in the first quarter of the twenty-first century. Thus, the MetCLIL corpus contains data transcription of 116 EMI participants (110 students and 6 lecturers), comprising 110,493 words and amounting to a total of 15 hours and 32 minutes of transcription.

A particular feature of MetCLIL that needs to be highlighted has to do with the number of settings, i.e., countries, where the data were obtained. Unlike existing corpora, MetCLIL recorded seminars from six different countries. This approach may not be a comprehensive solution, but it helps to alleviate some of the problems that Mauranen (2012) points out in dealing with the disciplinary divide in universities:

> Disciplines constitute important dividing lines and territorial bounda-
> ries in the academia, and must somehow be taken on board in a corpus.
> It is not unproblematic to capture the right balance between them, and
> it may well not even be worth trying, in view of their divergences across
> universities. In a single-university approach, achieving a representative
> sample is a feasible task, because we can list all its departments, for
> example, but even there its benefits might not be very high, given that
> universities have their local profiles. The findings from a corpus that is
> perfectly representative of a particular university in terms of discipli-
> nary distribution may not be valid or interesting more widely.
>
> (Mauranen, 2012, p. 76)

In other words, despite the relatively modest size of MetCLIL, the inclusion
of a variety of countries constituted a decision in the right direction. This
and other decisions taken in its design will be explained in more detail in the
remainder of the chapter.

Structure of the corpus: description of recorded events

The MetCLIL corpus was intended to offer valuable insights for studying
English-medium instruction in European tertiary education. However, it
should be noted that MetCLIL, rather than a general corpus with a broad
scope, is instead a specialised corpus with a specific focus, very much in line
with Koester's (2022) concept of 'small specialised corpora'. The specifica-
tion of this focus was clear from the inception of the project and related
to the exploration of metaphorical language in interactive academic spoken
contexts in business and marketing in tertiary education across Europe. As
a consequence, apart from the specific attention to metaphor, three main
language-external aspects were key in its design:

a. A coverage of tertiary EMI provision in Europe which went beyond the
    single institution approach adopted by other academic corpora.
b. An emphasis on the more interactive side of academic spoken language
    used in university contexts.
c. A focus on business and marketing topics.

The importance of clearly defining the objectives that the corpus aims to
achieve cannot be emphasised enough as it impinges on its structure and final
outcome. Specifically, the objectives guide the selection of speech events to
be recorded and determine the type of information that was to be included in
the corpus. Additionally, having a clear understanding of the research questions that the corpus will be used to answer helps ensure that the corpus is
designed in a way that is most useful for the intended research purpose.

In this sense, a first key feature of MetCLIL was intended to fill a specific gap in the existing corpus landscape by providing a broad description

of metaphorical language in EMI in Europe, which meant incorporating more countries than the existing ELF corpora cited above. To achieve this aim, the corpus was structured to focus on the genre of academic seminars and to include countries from both sides of what Maiworm and Wächter (2014) term as the "North-South divide",[2] which refers to the quantitative differences in EMI provision between the North and South of Europe. This specialisation allows for a deeper understanding of the use of metaphorical language in EMI in Europe, and how it may differ across different contexts and regions. Thus, the overall structure of the corpus was devised to capture this fundamental difference between Northern and Southern provision of EMI by selecting countries that could be considered as representative of these experiences. This is reflective in the two sections making up MetCLIL (see Figure 3.1) and also in the balanced representation of tokens they have in the corpus (see Table 3.1).

Other important aspects of the MetCLIL corpus were its emphasis on interactive academic events, as the aim was to investigate the use of metaphor in spoken academic contexts where students are actively engaged, together with the selection of a specific topic domain, business and marketing. To this end, it was important to make sure that the specific interactions recorded met these requirements.

In the following, a summary of the interactions and topics covered in each of the seminars recorded is provided. To supplement this description, a broad linguistic characterisation including the number of tokens and turns in each seminar is also presented. This information can be used to assess the level of

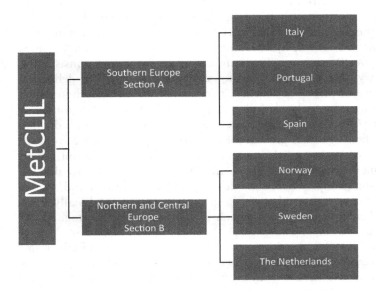

Figure 3.1 Overall structure of the MetCLIL corpus

Table 3.1 The MetCLIL corpus

Country	# Seminars	Tokens
Spain (3 seminars)	Sem 1	12,039
	Sem 2	12,085
	Sem 3	10,200
Italy	Sem 4	8,674
Portugal	Sem 5	8,681
Total Section A: Southern Europe EMI		51,679
Norway	Sem 6	14,854
Sweden (2 seminars)	Sem 7	10,708
	Sem 8	12,135
The Netherlands	Sem 9	21,117
Total Section B: Northern and Central Europe EMI		58,814

interaction and participation by the students. In order to maintain the anonymity of the participants, no identifying information about the university or specific course is included.

Section A: EMI provision in Southern Europe

Seminars 1, 2 and 3: Spain

Seminars 1–3 were held at a small to medium-sized university situated in one of the most populous cities in Spain, where there is a wide range of bachelor and master's degrees taught in English. They were designed to provide hands-on experience and supplement the theoretical knowledge taught in a Digital Marketing course, by breaking the class down into small groups of no more than 20 students. The seminars were structured consistently, with the primary objective of instructing students in the skill of delivering an effective 'elevator pitch' – a succinct, persuasive business speech in which they showcase their specialised skills, interests and career aspirations in a short timeframe (30 or 90 seconds). Each seminar follows a process divided into two steps: first, students present their 30-second pitch and receive feedback from the instructor and their peers (whole group presentation); then, after completing their individual 30-second pitches, the students are divided into two working groups where they deliver a 90-second pitch and receive feedback from the group members (split group presentations). Finally, each group selects their preferred pitch, which is then presented on stage at the end of the class.

As shown in Table 3.2, the three seminars are nearly identical in the number of turns devoted to whole-group work. In contrast, substantial variations are found in the distribution of split groups. This may be an indicator of the determining role of the lecturer, who mainly guides and intervenes in the whole group task, as a conductor of the lesson.

Table 3.2 A summary of the structure of Spanish seminars

Degree	Seminar	Whole group		Split group			Total duration
		Duration	*Task*	*Duration*	*Task*		
BA	1	50"	Presentation & Feedback	20' group A 20' group B	Presentations & Feedback		90'
BA	2	50'	Presentation & Feedback	20' group A 20' group B	Presentations & Feedback		90'
BA	3	50'	Presentation & Feedback	20' group A 20' group B	Presentations & Feedback		90'

Table 3.3 Linguistic make-up of Spanish seminars

	Tokens	Lemmas	Types	Turns
Seminar 1	12,039	1,102	1,389	374
Seminar 2	12,085	1,104	1,349	309
Seminar 3	10,200	950	1,167	398

The linguistic structure of the three seminars is highly consistent, as demonstrated by the similar number of tokens, types and lemmas observed in the data (Table 3.3). The only seminar that presents a slight deviation is seminar 3, which is slightly shorter in terms of lexical content. This discrepancy is likely due to the number of participants in that particular seminar.

Seminar 4: Italy

Recorded from a medium-sized university of around 17,000 students located in a town not exceeding 50,000 inhabitants, the seminar was one of the final lessons of a 54-hour module on Place Branding and Rural Development (1st year Magistrale, i.e., fourth year of university study) within the taught MA programme in International Tourism and Marketing, an International MA delivered exclusively in English. The seminar can be divided into three phases. In the first, the lecturer returns to a point discussed in previous lessons, i.e., the marketing of typical products and the wicked problems that are associated with the green economy, reducing the carbon footprint, and related environmental concerns. The lecturer raises numerous points for discussion but gets relatively little in return from the students. In the second part (after a break), he shows video material (in Italian, with English subtitles) to illustrate a case study; in this part, two students engage to some extent in debate. The third part is dedicated to revising and troubleshooting for a forthcoming end-of-module test. This part includes a high proportion of citations read out directly from the set texts, with commentary from the lecturer, and the odd request for clarification from some students. Despite many attempts by the lecturer to engage students in discussion and debate, the vast majority of the recorded text was monologue, with only five or six students speaking at any point during the course of the seminar.

The seminar comprises 8,674 tokens (5,569 types and 1,157 lemmas). Although the duration of the seminar is relatively long (Table 3.4), the instructor is the dominant speaker, resulting in a less interactive seminar as indicated by the number of turns (as can be seen from Table 3.5).

Seminar 5: Portugal

This seminar is a practical session complementing the lectures given by the teacher in the course programme being taught at medium-sized

Table 3.4 Structure of the Italian seminar

Degree	Seminar	Whole group		Split group		Total
		Duration	Task	Duration	Task	
MA	Seminar 1	108'	Lecturer's explanation			108'

Table 3.5 Linguistic make-up of the Italian seminar

Time	Tokens	Lemmas	Types	Turns
108'	8,674	1,157	1,410	68

Table 3.6 Linguistic make-up of the Portuguese seminar

Time	Tokens	Lemmas	Types	Turns
80'	8,681	986	1,214	126

Table 3.7 Structure of the Portuguese seminar

Degree	Seminar	Whole group		Split group		Total
		Duration	Task	Duration	Task	
BA	1	20'	Presentation & Feedback			80'
		60'	Debate			

Table 3.8 Structure of the Norwegian seminar

Degree	Seminar	Whole group		Split group		Total
		Duration	Task	Duration	Task	
MA	Seminar 1	120'	Presentation Debate			120'

university in the South of Portugal. It constitutes an in-depth study of a specific topic – International Aid – which is supported by the reading of general and specific literature and materials selected by the lecturer. In the session, three students make a presentation followed by a debate that gives the class the opportunity to reflect on and discuss the assigned reading. During the presentation, the students elicited their colleagues' opinions on some of the issues presented. At the end of the session, the lecturer summarises and highlights some aspects of the topic presented. These comments fostered a general discussion and a debate with the participation of most students (see Table 3.7 for a summary).

With respect to the linguistic characteristics of the seminar, a total of 8,856 tokens (986 lemmas and 1,214 types) were spoken. These were distributed among 126 turns, which primarily consist of the lecturer's elaboration on the topic of Aid and Development, including summaries and expansions on the key points presented by three student speakers and the ensuing discussion among students.

Section B: EMI provision in North and Central Europe

Seminar 6: Norway

This seminar is part of a course taught at a medium-sized university in Norway with an important tradition in the Social Sciences. It is structured in two parts (see Table 3.8). First, two students present a case study to the class, which is then followed by a group discussion. In the second part of the lesson, the instructor explains key concepts from the case study, as well as strategies for effectively teaching the subject to achieve optimal learning outcomes. The session concludes with a self-assessment questionnaire for the students. The students are seated in rows of tables facing the front of the classroom. The discussion centres around two key terms: exploitation vs exploration in innovative project management, and makes use of specialised terminology such as the "diamond of innovation", "cookie dough", or "painting by numbers". The second half of the session is dedicated to providing guidance on how to write the final essay for the course, including an in-depth explanation of the purpose of learning and how grades are determined.

The seminar consists of 14,854 tokens distributed in 308 turns (see Table 3.9). Tokens are not equally distributed between the two activities performed in the seminar: the presentation of the three students is shorter in time and number of lexical units than the subsequent debate in which the lecturer clarifies some concepts. The students are given feedback on their presentation and there is a final discussion about the relevance of these activities for the final essay they have to hand in.

Seminars 7 and 8: Sweden

The two seminars recorded in Sweden were part of courses provided at a small to medium-sized university. The sessions were designed to facilitate discussion and interaction, with all participants seated around a large conference-style table. The seminars began with a few minutes of reading time before the teacher introduced discussion topics related to the day's reading, which focused on the interaction of marketing and culture (See

Table 3.9 Linguistic make-up of the Norwegian seminar

	Presentation	Debate	Total
Tokens	3,286	11,568	14,854
Lemmas	582	1,074	1,261
turns	68	240	308

Table 3.10 Structure of the Swedish seminar

Degree	Seminar	Whole group		Split group		Total
		Duration	Task	Duration	Task	
MA	1	8'	Reading articles for discussion			84
		76'	Debate based on the articles			
MA	2	2'	Reading articles for discussion			83
		81'	Debate based on the articles			

Table 3.9). The teacher's questions guided the discussion, but students were encouraged to contribute their own perspectives and insights. The discussions covered a range of topics, including the appropriateness of marketing strategies for different cultures, cultural adaptations of specific brands and stores, culturally appropriate behaviours, cross-cultural communication, and the media's role in shaping societal attitudes towards different cultures.

Both seminars were identical in duration and activities, but they differed in the number of turns and lexical information. In spite of having fewer participants, seminar 8 consists of a larger number of tokens, types and lemmas, and it is also characterised by a higher degree of interaction that becomes evident in a larger number of turns. Table 3.11 provides a summary of the main linguistic and lexical features of the two seminars.

Table 3.11 Description of the two Swedish seminars

Seminar	Duration (in ')	Tokens	Lemmas	Types	Turns
Seminar 7	84	10,708	1,098	1,308	826
Seminar 8	83	12,135	1,118	1,352	1,006

Table 3.12 A summary of the structure of the Dutch seminar

Degree	Seminar	Whole group		Split group		Total
		Duration	Task	Duration	Task	
MA	Seminar 1	156'	Lecturer's explanation	13'	Discussion in two groups	187'
			Debate	18'	Pair-work discussion	

Seminar 9: The Netherlands

The course within which the seminar is integrated is called Theory Building in Business and Management and is taught at a large university located in one of the largest cities in the Netherlands. It is part of the MA programme Business in Society. It is open to MA students and, upon approval, to PhD students. The topic of this particular seminar is how business management can be inspired by other fields. It discusses analogical reasoning, borrowing and blending as tools. The class consists of teacher-centred blocks of talk, group work, pair work and three student presentations (see Table 3.12). The student presentations are about assigned readings revolving around the class themes. They are given by pairs of students and are meant to spark discussion with the whole group. The students talk freely and do not read from their notes. The structure is as follows: teacher-centred talk, group work (two groups), discussion of group work led by the teacher, teacher-centred talk, student presentation plus discussion, teacher-centred talk, student presentation plus discussion, teacher-centred talk, pair work, discussion of pair work led by the teacher, student presentation plus discussion, teacher-centred talk, discussion of final assignment and answering student questions. It is a research methods seminar focusing on analogical and counter-intuitive reasoning. Metaphors and analogy are discussed far more than any business concepts.

Although the seminar includes whole group and split groups, due to the way in which it was recorded, only the whole-group work could be transcribed. The seminar is the longest in time and, consequently, it also presents the largest number of tokens (21,117), types (2,010) and lemmas (1,603) in the corpus. However, it is not the most interactional, as, according to the number of turns, there are other seminars (such as the Swedish ones) in which the participants show more interaction. Table 3.12 summarises the main linguistic features of the seminar.

Describing participants

To ensure the validity of the corpus as an instrument for research, it is crucial to not only align its architecture with the main research objectives, but also to provide comprehensive extralinguistic and contextual information about the corpus being gathered. This information is particularly important in the case of the study of a figure of speech, such as metaphor, as the context and extralinguistic factors can significantly influence the use and frequency of metaphor as we will see in the last chapters of the book. Therefore, in agreement with the following quote, it was thought that providing detailed extralinguistic information was methodologically sound:

> As language use is characterized by variability, factors which may have an impact on the way in which language is used should be recorded in some way—these may include demographic information about the speakers/writers, or situational information such as the purpose of the communication or the type of relationship between the discourse participants.
>
> (Ädele, 2020, p. 10)

In the case of MetCLIL, the information about the participants was gathered through a questionnaire that the participants filled in before the recording of each seminar (see Appendix F). This information allowed us to characterise the speech events recorded.

Number of participants

The overall number of participants is 147, which gives an average of 16 people per seminar, comprising lecturers. In fact, if we exclude seminar 4 (Italy), the number of participants in the seminars does not vary much as it ranges between 9 (seminar 7 in Sweden) and 19 (seminar 5, Portugal). Seminar 4 (Italy) is an exception as there are 38 participants, although only nine students engage in active participation. As already described above this seminar is the one where there is less interaction and is the most similar to a lecture even though it is part of a master's degree programme.

On the whole, the number of participants responded to the objective of MetCLIL to focus on small-size seminars where interaction (lecturer-student or student-student) was more likely to happen. The participants for Section A and B of the corpus (see Table 3.13) could be considered as balanced, although the interpretation of the data from the Italian seminar should take into account the particularities mentioned.

Table 3.13 Linguistic make-up of the Dutch seminar

Degree	Duration (in ')	Tokens	Lemmas	Types	Turns
MA	156'	21,117	1,603	2,010	419

Table 3.14 Number of participants in the seminars

	Country	Seminar	# Participants
Section A	Spain	sem 1	15
		sem 2	15
		sem 3	12
	Italy	sem 4	38 (7)[3]
	Portugal	sem 5	19 (10)
			99 (59)
Section B	Norway	sem 6	18(14)
	Sweden	sem 7	9
		sem 8	10
	The Netherlands	sem 9	11
			48 (42)

Demographic data

This section analyses demographic data of students and lecturers to provide a characterisation of the participants. Thus, the average age of students is 24.3, with a wide range of ages falling between 19 and 50. It must be noted that BA seminars (seminars 1–3 in Spain and seminar 5 in Portugal) show a significantly lower average age (21) than MA seminars (27.8), a difference also reflected in the average age of sections A and B of the corpus. The age range of lecturers goes from 32 (the Spanish lecturer of seminars 1–3) to 57 (Portuguese lecturer in seminar 4). However, in the majority of the six lecturers[4] involved in the recordings the average age falls between 40 and 50, which would point to a certain degree of experience.

The data related to the distribution by gender is not completely balanced as they are skewed towards a greater representation of female participants (61%). This is congruent with a recent report by Eurostat, which states that women accounted for a majority of the total number of students within the field of business, administration or law.[5] In the case of lecturers, the situation is the opposite as there is a majority of male (4) vs female (2) teachers.

Internationalisation

The composition of English-medium instruction (EMI) classes in terms of the international students attending them has been studied in a report by Ferencz et al. (2014). The report acknowledges that the data gathered by different studies is not stable, although, in most cases, foreign students enrolled in EMI programmes are usually a majority (usually over 50%). The seminars in MetCLIL comply with this trend, as more than half of the students – more specifically an average of 54% – are international. However, as can be seen from Figure 3.2, there is a high degree of variation between the seminars with the two Swedish seminars showing a high degree of internationalisation by contrast to the more domestic student population in seminar 6

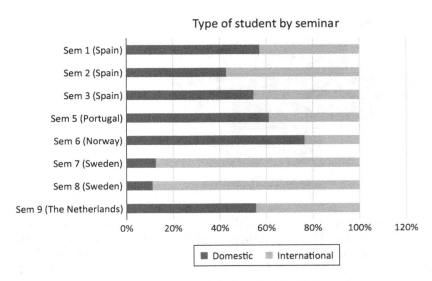

Figure 3.2 Domestic vs. international students in MetCLIL seminars

(Norway). This means that the tendency, also described in Ferencz et al's study cited above, that the higher degree of internationalisation is typical of Northern European countries does not completely hold in our corpus.

Many of these international students are European, enjoying an Erasmus stay abroad (31[6]). The rest of the students come from very different regions of the world. These include the United States, different Latin American countries (such as Brazil or Mexico), African countries (Kenya, Nigeria or Mozambique), or Asian countries (Bangladesh, Sri Lanka, India or China).

English proficiency

The questionnaire (see Appendix F) also incorporated questions regarding the participants' language background and proficiency, including their first language (L1) and any second languages (L2) they may have. Additionally, participants were asked to provide information about their prior experience with English-language instruction, specifically in Content and Language Integrated Learning (CLIL) programmes or similar. To further gauge their proficiency, participants were asked to self-assess their level of English proficiency using the Common European Framework of Languages (CEFR) scale (Appendix F), which ranges from A1 (beginner) to C2 (advanced).

Based on the responses to the final question, the proficiency level of 119 participants was available. The results show that the majority of students self-assess their English proficiency at the C1 (49%) and the B2 (27%) levels.

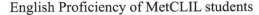

English Proficiency of MetCLIL students

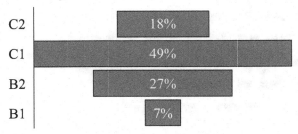

Figure 3.3 Proficiency level of MetCLIL students

A smaller proportion of students rated their skills at the C2 level (18% , and only a small minority (7%) placed themselves at the B1 level (see Figure 3.3). As for the lecturers, the distribution is as follows: only one (from Sweden) reported a B2 level, three (from Italy, Norway, and Portugal) reported a C1 level, and two (from the Netherlands and Spain) reported a C2 level.

As shown in Figure 3.4, there is a significant amount of variation between seminars. While seminars 4 (Italy) and 6 (Norway) have a majority of participants within the B1–B2 range, the remaining seminars have a larger proportion of participants within the more advanced levels, i.e., C1–C2. This variation cannot be attributed to a specific programme, as demonstrated by the analysis of the three Spanish seminars, which have differing proficiency levels among participants in different classes.

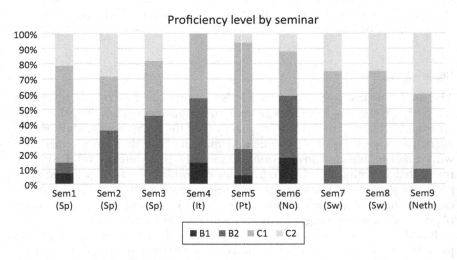

Figure 3.4 Proficiency level by seminar

Table 3.15 Age of participants: students

	Seminar	Avg.	Max.	Min.
BA programmes	Sems. 1–3 (Spain)	21.2	26	20
	Sem. 5 (Portugal)	20.8	26	19
Subtotal		21.2	26	19
MA programmes	Sem. 4 (Italy)	24.7	30	22
	Sem. 6 (Norway)	28.7	50	22
	Sems. 7–8 (Sweden)	28.2	42	20
	Sem. 9 (The Netherlands)	29.5	42	23
Subtotal		27.8	50	20
Total		25.5	50	19

Using MetCLIL online

The most effective way to become familiar with a corpus is through frequent use. While providing information about MetCLIL is helpful, it cannot substitute for the specific inquiries and investigations that researchers must conduct in order to fully explore and utilise the data it contains. To achieve this, the corpus must be accessible to researchers.

In recent years, there has been a significant increase in the availability of open data resources, including corpora that are increasingly made available to researchers for their own research purposes. These resources can save researchers time and effort in compiling their own data sets. In the case of MetCLIL, it was determined that the best option for accessibility would be through Sketch Engine (see Figure 3.5).

Sketch Engine is a cloud-based corpus management system that enables users to search, analyse and build text corpora. It offers a user-friendly interface and hosts a variety of monolingual, parallel and multilingual corpora, some of which require registration and payment. The MetCLIL corpus is available as an 'open corpus' and can be accessed without registration or payment[7].

The linguistic tools offered by Sketch Engine on its platform are certainly useful and include some of the most essential resources for researchers seeking to make their way into corpus linguistics. The *Word Sketch* tool is particularly useful as it allows users to obtain the most common grammar, lexical and phrase collocations of a word or phrase. The tool clusters collocations into different categories, known as 'grammatical relations', based on the relationship the collocation has with the searched word. The *Thesaurus* tool, on the other hand, automatically identifies lists of words that are used as synonyms in the corpus, making it useful for exploring the use of synonyms and related words. The *Word List* tool allows for frequency analysis by providing users with frequency lists that can be filtered by type of information, such as specific parts of speech, words starting or ending with certain words, etc. The tool also offers three types of lexical units: tokens, word forms and lemmas. Another useful tool is the *N-grams* feature, which provides users with

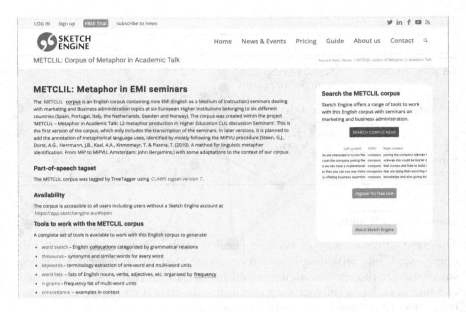

Figure 3.5 Accessing MetCLIL corpus information via Sketch Engine

frequency lists of multi-word expressions. Users can determine the number of tokens that must appear in the search and limit the search to specific parts of speech or lemmas, among other restrictions. Finally, the *Word Sketch Difference* tool offers users the possibility of comparing how two words are used in the corpus and the terms they collocate with. This can be useful for researchers to explore differences in word usage, such as how students with different L2 proficiency levels may differ in their use of words with similar senses. Overall, Sketch Engine provides a comprehensive set of tools that can aid researchers in exploring various linguistic features and facilitating METCLIL research.

The most valuable tool for researching metaphor on Sketch Engine is the *Concordance* tool (see Figure 3.6). Its user-friendly CQL language allows for easy searches for collocations of specific words or phrases, with the added capability to impose restrictions on parts of speech. Furthermore, the tool's ability to search for "structures" enables researchers to identify all lexical items tagged as metaphor in the corpus. This feature was implemented in the adaptation of MetCLIL to Sketch Engine as the most efficient way to include the tagging of metaphors. In this way, a search for a specific lexical unit or part of speech could be combined with a metaphor search.

One of the main advantages of using Sketch Engine to research MetCLIL is precisely the opportunity it provides to take advantage of the metadata about the participants and events that the corpus has incorporated. These metadata refer to the information about the participants in the speech

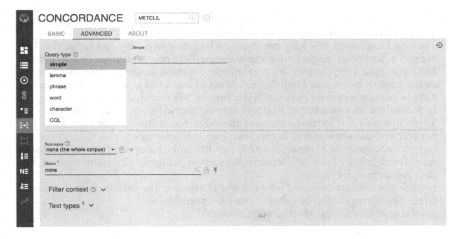

Figure 3.6 Concordance tool in Sketch Engine

events included in previous sections of the present chapter. In some of the tools, but particularly in *Concordance* and *Wordlist*, it is possible to restrict the results obtained by what the platform calls text types. This facility enables the user to identify the different metalinguistic tags incorporated into the corpus. In the case of MetCLIL, this allows identifying whether the specific language searched should be restricted to a specific seminar number, a type of activity (discussion, explanation, presentation, etc.), a particular speaker, a specific role (student or lecturer), or to characteristics related to the language background information of the speakers such as their L1 or their L2 level.

Conclusion

This chapter serves as a comprehensive introduction to the primary features of the corpus employed in the analysis of metaphors within the present book, MetCLIL. Key attributes, including its size and the nature of communicative events recorded, have been outlined. Furthermore, we have delved into the rationale behind the creation of this corpus, emphasising its distinctiveness in comparison to other available English as a Lingua Franca (ELF) corpora. The chapter also provides insights into the corpus's structure, with particular attention to addressing the unique demands posed by English-Medium Instruction (EMI) in both Northern and Southern Europe. Additionally, crucial demographic variables associated with the corpus, along with aspects related to participants' language proficiency, have been detailed. This chapter lays the foundation for the subsequent one, which offers a more in-depth exploration of the corpus construction methodology.

Notes

1 Data available at www2.helsinki.fi/en/researchgroups/english-as-a-lingua-franca -in-academic-settings/research/elfa-corpus#section-67034
2 They had explained this idea previously when they say: "By and large, the Alps are still a European 'English-medium watershed'. In most countries north of them, English-taught programmes are a relatively common feature, while those in the south seem to be almost 'English-free'. Most of countries in the centre and east of Europe occupy a middle position" (Wächter & Maiworm, 2008, p.26).
3 In parenthesis the number of students actively participating in the seminar.
4 There are only six lecturers because the three Spanish seminars only have one lecturer and the same is true for the two Swedish seminars.
5 Report accessed in January, 2023, at https://ec.europa.eu/eurostat/statistics -explained/index.php?title=Tertiary_education_statistics#Participation_in_ter- tiary_education_by_sex
6 English students are included here since at the time of the collection of the corpus Great Britain was still a member of the European Union.
7 Available at https://app.sketchengine.eu/#open

References

Ädel, A. (2020). Corpus compilation. In M. Paquot and S.T. Gries (Eds.). *A Practical Handbook of Corpus Linguistics* (pp. 3–24). Springer Nature.

Alejo-González, R. (2010). Where does the money go? An analysis of the container metaphor in economics: The market and the economy. *Journal of Pragmatics*, 42(4), 1137–1150.

Alejo-González, R., Piquer-Píriz, A.M., Castellano-Risco, I., Martín-Gilete, M., Fielden-Burns, L., MacArthur, F., Nacey, S., Philip, G., Krennmayr, T., Coelho, M., Littlemore, J., & Ädel, A. (2021). *The MetCLIL corpus*. v1. https://www. sketchengine.eu/metclil-corpus-of-metaphor-in-academic-talk.

Koller, V. (2003). *Metaphor clusters in business media discourse: A social cognition approach* (Ph.D thesis). University of Vienna, Vienna.

Ferencz, I., Maiworm, F., & Mitic, M. (2014). Traits and daily operation of ETPs. In F. Maiworm & B. Wächter (Eds.), *English-taught programmes in European higher education: The state of play in 2014*. ACA Papers on International Cooperation in Education (pp. 63–97). Lemmens.

Koester, A. (2022). Building small specialised corpora. In A. O'Keeffe & J. McCarthy (eds.), *The Routledge Handbook of Corpus Linguistics* (pp. 48–61). Routledge.

Maiworm, F., & Wächter, B. (Eds.). (2014). *English-taught programmes in European higher education: The state of play in 2014*. ACA Papers on International Cooperation in Education. Lemmens.

Mauranen, A. (2012). *Exploring ELF: Academic English shaped by non-native speakers*. Cambridge University Press.

Mauranen, A., Hynninen, N., & Ranta, E. (2010). English as the academic lingua franca- the ELFA project. *English for Specific Purposes*, 29, 183–190.

Seidlhofer, B. (2011). *Understanding ELF*. Oxford University Press.

Simpson-Vlach, R. C., Briggs, S. L., Ovens, J., & Swales, J. M. (2002). *The Michigan corpus of academic spoken English*. The Regents of the University of Michigan.

VOICE. (2009/2018). *The Vienna-Oxford International Corpus of English* (version 1.0/3.0 online). https://voice.acdh.oeaw.ac.at (versioin 3.0 Accessed 7th Nov. 2023)

Wächter, B., & Maiworm, F. (Eds.). (2008). *English-Taught Programmes in European higher education. The Picture in 2007*. Bonn: Lemmens.

4 Building MetCLIL

Criteria used in building METCLIL

The building of a corpus should be based on the sound principles that have been described by the literature. The recent volume *A Practical Handbook of Corpus Linguistics* (Paquot & Gries, 2020), particularly in its first part, is a good example of a publication focusing on making the criteria of sound corpus design and compilation explicit. However, general criteria need to be assessed in specific contexts, especially if the corpus does not intend to be of a general nature. In other words, some key words mentioned in the literature dealing with corpus design such as authenticity, representativeness, size and balance are important, and I will deal with each of them individually later on, but perhaps the most decisive element is to understand and to conceptualise the type of corpus that is being built.

In this sense, it is relevant to read the following quotation from McEnery and Brookes:

> Once we are clear about our purpose in using a corpus, the distinction between specialised and general corpora becomes relevant. Specialised corpora are designed to represent a particular genre or variety of language, usually within a specified context and/or time frame (e.g. Brookes and Baker's [2021] corpus of newspaper articles mentioning *obesity*). General corpora, meanwhile, represent language use on a broader scale, often whole languages (e.g. the BNC), and tend to be much larger than specialised corpora.
>
> (2022, p. 36)

It was clear from the beginning that MetCLIL should be a specialised corpus, both in the sense that it should deal with the language of Business and Marketing and in so far as it intended to represent a very specific genre, discussion seminars, whose precise definition will be dealt with later, in a very specific context, that of EMI programmes in Europe. Taking this into account, the whole process of building a corpus becomes a completely different matter. The questions of size, representativeness, authenticity and balance take on a different perspective.

DOI: 10.4324/9781003400905-4

Size

As we have seen above, MetCLIL contains 110,493 running words and can be considered as a small corpus if we compare it to one of today's most representative corpora like COCA or the enTenTen family of corpora, which consist of a billion words. Naturally, large corpora are the ones which are most useful if the main purpose is for it describe a language in its different dimensions and with a higher level of refinement if one wants to study low frequency linguistic phenomena.

However, Koester (2022) advocates the use of small corpora and Vaughan and Clancy (2013), also cited by Clancy (2022), concur with this view when they argue that small corpora in the range between 20,000 and 200,000 words can be useful to investigate context and genre-related phenomena. Some of the reasons for the preference of small corpora in the case of MetCLIL follow.

Factors relating to the study of metaphor

As we will see later, we have adopted a census approach to the study of metaphor, which means that all instances of metaphor use were targeted, which involved manually tagging them by the group of researchers integrating the project (See Appendix J). Our rationale for this approach aligns with certain strategies employed in the field of corpus linguistics applied to Pragmatics, where emphasis is placed on the function rather than the form of linguistic elements (O'Keeffe, 2018). However, this task is time and labour intensive and would be unthinkable to be carried out with a large corpus. Although there has been significant progress in the automatised tagging of metaphor, the systems developed still show certain limitations. For example, David and Matlock (2018) explain how a metaphor like *give cancer the boot* could not be detected by MetaNet given that ditransitive constructions had not yet been integrated into the system and Dodge et al. (2015) also indicate that the system wrongly identified as metaphorical expressions such as *government building* and *government house,* in some cases used literally, because of the very often used conceptual metaphor GOVERNMENT IS A PHYSICAL STRUCTURE.

Factors relating to the spoken mode

In the same way as the focus on metaphor made it necessary to keep the size of the corpus manageable, the same could be said of the fact that the targeted mode was not writing but speech. For obvious reasons, which include the wide availability of written texts, compiling a corpus of spoken language is far more difficult than it is to collect a corpus of written language. This difficulty makes it advisable to keep the corpus within manageable size limits. In fact, if one looks at the available spoken discourse corpora one can see that a corpus of over a million words can already be considered a big corpus for general purposes and as already mentioned, a specialised corpus of more than 100,000 running words seems already an appropriate size.

Factors relating to the ecology and context of the corpus

Another important element to be considered has to do with the importance for the metaphor researcher of understanding the context where the corpus is being gathered. This is particularly the case of a corpus involving the compilation of materials in different countries, where different academic cultures may be at work. Even if, as is the case with MetCLIL, the researchers involved in its compilation are not specialists in the topic area targeted, i.e., business and marketing, understanding the context and the language typically used by students constitutes an essential advantage in corpus linguistic research in general, but in metaphor analysis in particular given that the interpretation of unconventional metaphors may be reliant on these contextual factors. Koester summarises this in the following way:

> Where large corpora, through their decontextualization, give insights into lexico-grammatical patterns in the language as a whole, smaller, specialised corpora give insights into patterns of language use in particular settings. With a small corpus, the corpus compiler is often also the analyst and therefore usually has a high degree of familiarity with the context.
>
> (2022, p. 49)

In MetCLIL, this was definitely the case as the corpus was recorded and also tagged for metaphor by a researcher connected to the country and, in some cases, to the university where the recording was made.

Representativeness

Representativeness is considered by corpus linguistics as a key element in the compilation of a corpus. The texts selected need to be good representatives of the type of discourse that is being studied. The best way to think about representativeness is to use the idea of sampling in statistical terms, i.e., compiling a corpus is obtaining "a maximally representative—in practice, this translates into acceptably representative—sample of a population of language users, a language variety, or a type of discourse" (Ädel, 2020, p. 4).

The question that arises with specialised corpora is that of the unit of counting. In other words, when conducting the sampling, it is important to bear in mind the type of 'population' to be represented. Using Ädel's citation, one could ask if the population to be represented is a population of speakers or a population of discourse events, for example. In the case of MetCLIL, one of the obvious targets is the population of metaphors, but of course it would be impossible to use sampling techniques as it is precisely this population that the project wanted to establish.

Table 4.1 EMI programmes in Europe (by subject area) (Wächter & Maiworm, 2014, p. 68)

	Bachelor	Master	Total
Agriculture	2	2	2
Education	3	1	2
Engineering, manufacturing and construction	19	18	18
Health and welfare	6	5	5
Humanities and arts	10	7	7
Sciences	11	26	23
Services	3	1	2
Social sciences, business and law	42	34	35
Other subject area	3	6	5
Total	100	100	100
Count (n)	(175)	(725)	(900)

In our case, the population that is to be used as a reference has to do with the EMI programmes taught in Europe, and more precisely with those related to Business and Marketing, which is the topic area we focused on. The problem with this 'population' is that there is no census in Europe of registered EMI programmes. However, we do have an alternative that, while not flawless, can at least provide some assistance. I refer to the study carried out by Wächter and Maiworm (2014), based on a survey that gives us the most accurate estimate of the number of programmes that may exist and to which different topic areas they belong (see Table 4.1). If we do the maths, since the numbers for each area express percentages, this means that there were approximately 315 EMI programmes dealing with Social Sciences, Business and Law. Obviously, not all these programmes would be related to business or marketing, which will probably mean a lower number. In this sense, although the number of programmes used in our corpus (6) could seem low, it is not so low if one considers that there may be no more than 200.

It is also important to acknowledge in the compilation of our corpus that practical reasons relating to convenience also intervened. However, this is nothing new as "the principles of corpus design interact with practical considerations relating to the nature of the data collected and how limitations regarding sampling can be dealt with" (Koester, 2022, p. 53).

Authenticity

The question of authenticity was also key in the elaboration of MetCLIL as it affected the type of data considered as acceptable to be incorporated into the corpus. Would mock seminars, arranged especially for the occasion even if using real lecturers and students, be acceptable to be included in the corpus? This would seem a naïve question, but it actually becomes a real one when it is difficult to find participants, either lecturers or students, willing to give their consent to be recorded. In other words, when it is difficult to find natural data.

The answer to the question was clearly negative and in this respect the project followed the guidelines generally adopted by ELF corpora, which are to opt for recording only naturally occurring seminars. This position seems straightforward but at the same time needs some explanation since learner corpora adopt a similar stance, although with some important nuances worth considering.

Starting with learner corpora researchers, the attitude they generally adopt is summarised by the following quotation:

> [T]he term near-natural is used to highlight the "need for data that reflects as closely as possible "natural" language use (i.e. language that is situationally and interactionally authentic) while recognizing that the limitations facing the collection of such data often obligate researchers to resort to clinically elicited data.
>
> (Granger, 2008, p. 337)

In other words, LC researchers do not reject elicited data.

Now compare this approach to the one adopted by VOICE:

> [I]t is the aim of the VOICE project to collect naturally occurring ELF speech, i.e., interactions which are not elicited or set up for research purposes, but "talk that would have happened anyway, whether or not a researcher was around to record it (Cameron, 2001:20)"
>
> (Breiteneder et al., 2006, pp. 164–165)

It is true that later the authors acknowledge the possibility of incorporating additional quasi-natural conversations, which they say are a minority in the corpus, but the main aim of the corpus is precisely that of capturing and recording something that would have happened anyway. In MetCLIL, this was also the case. All seminars would have occurred even if they had not been transcribed.

Balance

According to McEnery and Hardie (2012), balanced corpora contain "relative sizes of each of [the subsections that] have been chosen with the aim of adequately representing the range of language that exists in the population of texts being sampled" (p. 239, cit. in Ädel, 2020, p. 5). In other words, balance is closely connected to the representativeness of a corpus and is dependent on adequate representation of the groups or sections identified in the population that wants to be sampled.

As already stated, the target 'population' that MetCLIL wanted to sample consisted of EMI programmes in Europe, which meant we needed to keep a balance between the main groups of programmes established. Since the classification of programmes according to subject area was ruled out, given that it had been decided that only discussion seminars covering business and marketing would be considered, the other important criterion left was that of the geographical location. This grouping criterion was of crucial interest given that it had been shown to be the main source of variation in EMI (cf. e.g., the initial reports on EMI programmes by Maiworm & Wächter, 2002; Wächter & Maiworm, 2008).

These reports on EMI programmes had clearly established a split between countries from the north and the south in Europe and it was important to ascertain whether the 2014 report confirmed the picture. This is what Wächter and Maiworm say:

> [O]ne must note that there are considerable regional differences in the spread of ETPs[1] and size of enrolment. Most common are ETPs in the Nordic region where 61% of institutions offer Bachelor and/or Master programmes completely taught in English, 20% of all programmes fall into this category and 5% of all students are enrolled in ETPs. Central West Europe and the Baltic states follow with a substantial proportion of institutions offering ETPs (44.5% and 38.7% respectively), a share of ETPs at about 10% of all study programmes and an enrolment share of about 2%. In all other regions at most one fifth of institutions are running ETPs, at most 5% of all programmes are ETPs and not more than 1% of students are enrolled. The North-South divide observed in the previous two studies clearly remains.
>
> (Wächter & Maiworm, 2014, p. 17)

In our case, a balanced corpus was interpreted as making sure that programmes from countries belonging to both North and Central West Europe would be represented, while at the same time recruiting the same amount of data, i.e., tokens, from countries belonging to South Europe.

Main design features: key MetCLIL variables

The main difficulty when compiling an EMI corpus lies in the need to find a workable definition of the phenomenon one wants to study. In the following, I will elaborate on the three most important external groups of variables that define the MetCLIL corpus: a) the spoken genre to which we limited our corpus, i.e., the discussion seminar; b) the geographical area covered by the corpus, in our case Europe, together with the two most important geographical subsections – North and Central West vs South – resulting from our approach; and c) the participants recorded.

Genre

The corpus comprises discussion seminars held in higher education institutions in the European Union. Their main feature is that they are interactive and that they involve the participation of both students and teachers. The main aim of the corpus was to gather a representative sample of the spoken interaction that takes place in English as a Medium of Instruction programmes, which is the target of our study. The seminars can be classified within the Social Sciences as a general area of knowledge, and their more specific focus is related to business and marketing.

The discussion seminar is an academic speech event that, in contrast to lectures or offices-hours consultations, is given different names in higher education institutions. Jordan (1997) already mentions this problem and cites how 'seminars' or 'tutorials' are also sometimes used with the same meaning. The use of the different terms and the meaning with which they are used may be susceptible to variation depending on the discipline or the academic culture of the country considered. Even chronological aspects may play a role. This is the case, for example, of Spain, where the word 'seminario' (literal translation of 'seminar') has gained currency of use ever since the enforcement of the European Higher Education Area (EHEA) agreements (Bologna declaration of 1999).

This is why it seems more important to specify its main objectives so that, when we use the name of 'discussion seminars', it becomes clear what we are referring to. To do this, we will borrow the definition from Beard and Hartley, who refer to it as "group discussion" and summarise its main goals as follows: "The objectives of group discussion range widely. The objective which outweighs all others in importance [...] is that students should be helped to discuss and to clarify difficulties arising from lectures or other teaching sessions" (Beard & Hartley, 1984 cit. in Jordan, 1997, p. 10).

According to Furneaux et al. (1991), a possible list of seminar types would include student group work (for example, a problem-solving exercise); lessons where students would go over answers to case studies; discussion of materials previously read by the whole group; or presentations (students reporting on readings or research they have done) (cit. in Jordan, 1997, p. 196).

We have also taken into account within the label of 'discussion seminar' what, with some adjustments, Morell and others call "the interactive lecture" (cf. Morell, 2004, 2007). This is typical of some programmes where there is not a clear separation between practical and theoretical work. She draws on a definition given by Northcott:

> a classroom learning event for a ... group of students primarily controlled and led by a lecturer and including subject input from the lecturer but also including varying degrees and types of oral participation by students.
>
> (Northcott, 2001, pp. 19–20, cit. in
> Morell, 2007, p. 223)

We have taken out of this definition the reference to the size of the group (large – more than 20 students) as this is one of the aspects that may be conflicting with the definition of seminars that is normally accepted under EHEA, at least in Spain.

As a summary, the main features of what we call seminars are: 1) it is a genre designed to be supplemental or additional to the explanations provided in lectures; 2) the number of students involved is relatively small, usually resulting from the breakup of a larger group; 3) it is characterised by a certain amount of interaction; 4) the presence of a teacher or assistant teacher is required and, although the teacher may lead the session, his/her role is different from that of a teacher-fronted lesson.

Institutions and countries

As already made explicit, incorporating seminars from different European countries was important in terms of the corpus representativeness of the targeted phenomenon, i.e., EMI at a European level. It must be stressed here that the corpus was not intended to characterise the features of EMI in other parts of the world, given mostly the great educational differences between the systems. Thus, we made sure that countries and institutions experiencing a different moment in the expansion and, most probably, the culture of EMI were represented in the corpus.

This general idea was transformed into the following criteria:

- The data collection would be restricted to European universities offering Economic and Business courses in English.
- Only programmes from public institutions would be contacted.
- The courses selected to be recorded would be the final years of BA degrees or first year in MA degrees.
- A balanced distribution between Northern and Southern European higher education Institutions would be sought.

Table 4.2 summarises the main features of the institutions and courses taking part in the project and some key features of the place where the institutions are situated.

This summary of the institutions covered in our project indicates that MetCLIL has been able to address the two main types of EMI institutions identified by Rose et al. (2021) as typical categories within the globalisation process driving these programmes. Thus, the Spanish and Dutch institutions could be identified as *Internationalised EMI programmes,* given that both the size of the cities in which they are located and the general policies the universities followed are more oriented towards attracting international students. The rest of the universities are not incompatible with this characterisation, but their outlook could be characterised as *Glocalised EMI programmes* in so far as they could be said to be oriented towards the home students interested in developing a wider knowledge base.

Table 4.2 Institutions' information

Country	Spain	Portugal	Norway	Italy	Sweden	The Netherlands
Department	Economics and Business	Social Sciences	Economics, Management, & Innovation	Education, Cultural Heritage & Tourism	–	School of Business and Economics
Programme	BA International Business Economics	BA Development Economics	Master in Project Management in Innovation Processes	Master in International Tourism and Marketing	Master Program in Business Studies with an International Focus	Master in Theory Building in Business and Management
Number of students in the institution	11,698	9,000	13,000	11,213	12,000	26,500
Inhabitants of the city	1.6 million	56,600	30,100	42,200	37,300	821,700

Participants

As already discussed, MetCLIL cannot be strictly defined as a learner corpus; this is why this variable group is more adequately referred to as participants or L2 users, as ELF theoreticians do (cf. Mauranen, 2012). At the same time, while this is our general approach, the corpus gathered information regarding the status of the participants as L2 learners, since in the analysis of metaphor use variables such as proficiency level or amount of exposure to the L2 could certainly not be disregarded.

General information

The first layer of information gathered from the participants would be like the one obtained by any corpus. We could refer to this kind of data as demographic and it would include elements such as age, gender, country of birth or mother tongue. Taking this into account, the data in MetCLIL show that 116 people participated in the seminars recorded, 67 of whom were women and 49 men, and their average age is 25.6 years old. The participants come from 28 different home countries and have 27 mother tongues, with only seven participants speaking English as their L1, all of them students.

Academic information

The second data source is related to the academic context where the corpus has been recorded. It has to be remembered that the participants in this project are connected to Marketing and Business programmes in their last year BA or first year MA courses. This implied that it was important to separate the roles of the students, which make up the bulk of the participants, 110, and the lecturers, 6 (see Table 4.3 for a summary). At the same time, the status of the students as either home or international was also considered an important piece of information as there was a high number, 44, which belonged to the second group. It should not be forgotten that one of the goals of EMI programmes is to attract students from other universities.

Learner information

Regarding learner variables, the level of English is obviously the first one that should be taken into consideration as it has been shown that the speaker's level determines the use of language. Measuring the level would have involved a great deal of time and effort; it was decided that the levels would be established by the information self-reported by the participants on the questionnaire (Appendix F).

The English level was described following the Common European Framework of Reference for Languages (CEFRL). Almost half of the participants have a C1 level (47.27%). Around one-fourth of the participants present a B2 level (25.45%), and one fifth show a C2 level (17.27%). Only

Table 4.3 A summary of participants' information

			Number	*In percentage*
Students	Number		110	
	Origin	Home students	66	60
		International students	44	40
	Mother tongues		27	-
	Home countries		28	-
	Personal features	Average age	25.6	-
	English Level	B1	8	7.27
	(CEFRL)	B2	28	25.45
		B2 – C1	2	1.83
		C1	52	47.27
		C1-C2	1	0.91
		C2	19	17.27
Lecturers	Number		6	
	Mother tongues		6	
	Home countries		6	
	Average age		45.5 years	
	Teaching experience	Average teaching experience	16.75 years	
		Average teaching experience in English	5.3 years	
	English Level	B2	1	17
	(CEFRL)	C1	3	50
		C2	2	33

7.27% of the participants state that their level is a B1. Table 4.4 provides a summary of lecturers' and students' main features. This information was contrasted with other more objective information that could account for their English level such as the number of years of English at school (9.6) or years attending a content subject taught in English (2.9).

Summary

Obviously, the information above concerns the characterisation of the whole corpus. More detailed information by seminar and country can be found in Table 4.4. From this table we can see that the averages provided for the corpus do not vary greatly.

Data collection

In his book on the compilation of the 2014 BNC spoken corpus, Robbie Love (2020) establishes three main components of spoken data collection: speaker recruitment, metadata and audio data. In this section, I will only deal with the first and third components as the second has already been touched upon in the previous section.

Table 4.4 Learners' information (summary by country)

Country	Seminar	Participants	Home country	International students	Mother tongues	Gender	Average age	English level
Spain	Seminar 1	14	6	6	8	7 F 7 M	21	C1 (9), C2 (3) B2 (1) and B1 (1).
	Seminar 2	14	7	6	8	11 F 3 M	21.1	B2 (5), C1 (5), C2 (4).
	Seminar 3	11	6	4	5	7 F 4 M	21.6	B2 (5), C1 (4), C2 (2).
Italy	Seminar1	39 (9)	4	1	4	4 F 5 M	25.7	B2 (4), C1 (4), B1 (1)
Portugal	Seminar1	18	7	6	4	14 F 4 M	21.2	C1 (12). B1 (2), B2 (3) and C2 (1).
Norway	Seminar1	17	4	3	5	8 F 9 M	28.8	B2 (7), C1 (5), B1 (3) C2 (2).
Sweden	Seminar 1	8	8	7	8	6 F 2 M	28.8	C1 (3), B2-C1 (2), C2 (2), B2 (1).
	Seminar 2	9	8	8	9	2 F 7 M	32.5	C1 (4) C2 (2), B2 (1) and B1 (1).
The Netherlands	Seminar 1	10	4	3	5	6 F 4 M	29.5	C1 (5), C2 (3), C1-C2 (1) and B2 (1).

Recruitment

As already mentioned, the aim of the project was not to obtain a representative sample of the population of students and lecturers in European EMI. MetCLIL adopted what is called an "opportunistic approach" (cf. Love, 2020, p. 52) to the recruitment of participants. The reason for this type of approach is the difficulty involved in obtaining speech data that are at the same time representative of the population of speakers.

Contacting classes: lecturers and students

Given the inherent difficulty of the task of collecting spoken data and at the same time representing the different EMI situations in Europe, the starting point in the project was to use the group of researchers involved in the project as the main collaborators and initiators of the data collection process. In our case an opportunistic approach was also used and these researchers, with their expertise and knowledge of the situation in the country where they work, were given the responsibility to contact lecturers and students who would be willing to participate in the recording. Obviously, the first contact would be with the lecturers, but it was also considered important to have a first meeting with the students to explore their readiness to participate and the practical problems that the recording might pose.

Ethics approval

After this first contact, or even simultaneously, the researchers gave the necessary steps to ask for permission from the different institutions from which they intended to gather the data. It is interesting to note here a difference, at least at the moment that the project started, between institutions where the process of ethics approval was not only established for sciences and disciplines like biology or medicine, but also for social sciences project like ours, and those where this was not the case. In any case, we followed the standard procedure which involved:

- Giving lecturers and students an information sheet (see Appendix D) with the main details of the project and the name of the person they could contact in case they had any doubt or wanted to withdraw their consent for the project to use their data.
- Asking participants to sign a consent form (see Appendix E) where they expressed their agreement to be recorded under the conditions expressed, which included not making available images or personal data.

Recording

The recording phase could be considered one of the most vital phases in the development of the project as a failure in this phase could not be easily repaired. Here again the activities were divided into three different steps:

- Pre-recording activities: apart from preparing and printing a presentation letter (see Appendix A), mostly consisted in anticipating problems and having everything ready for the recording. To this effect, a checklist of materials and actions was prepared for all researchers involved in data collection (see Appendix B).
- Activities at the moment of the recording, which mostly consisted in first passing the participants the consent form (Appendix E) and the questionnaires to be filled in (Appendices F and G), in placing the two cameras – one towards the front of the classroom and one towards the desks – so that all intervening participants could be adequately recorded.
- After-recording activities, which involved:
  - asking students and lecturers to complete follow-up questionnaires on naturalness (see Appendices H and I)
  - filling in a template for video recording (see Appendix C) with important information from each seminar. Participants were identified in the video or pictures from the sessions, and the videos were transcribed taking into account the different turns and the participants.

Results of data collection

The seminars making up the MetCLIL corpus were recorded in six different European countries: Spain (3 seminars), Portugal (1 seminar), Norway (1 seminar), Italy (1 seminar), Sweden (2 seminars) and The Netherlands (1 seminar). The setting and duration of the seminars were different, as can be seen from Table 4.5.

The seminar recorded in Italy is 108 minutes long and consists of a lecturer explaining the importance of designation of origin and project a positive image for rural brands.

In The Netherlands, the seminar is related to debating how business management can learn from other fields. It is 187 minutes long, and two main tasks are performed: lecturer's explanation and debate in the whole group (156 minutes long) and pair-work and discussion in split groups (31 minutes long).

The Norwegian seminar is, together with the Dutch seminar, one of the longest recordings (120 minutes), and it combines a presentation, group discussion and debate throughout the seminar. The content of the seminar is related to how to deal with and face organisational problems in business. As explained in the previous chapter, a group of students is asked to present a case study on a specific enterprise having some managing problems and they must provide possible solutions. After that, there is a debate on the key ideas of the case study linking it with the theoretical papers students have been asked to read.

In Spain, the three seminars have a similar setting, structure, and duration as they are different subgroups of students taking the same subject. The main objective of the seminar is to help students learn to deliver an elevator pitch, a business genre in which speakers have a concise amount of time (usually

Table 4.5 Data collected: Duration in minutes by country

Country	Duration in minutes (Total)	In %
Spain	270	29
Portugal	80	8
Norway	120	13
Italy	108	12
Sweden	167	18
The Netherlands	187	20
TOTAL	932	100%

30–90 seconds) to introduce themselves and set themselves apart to spark interest in who they are and what they do and/or offer. In each seminar, 50 minutes are devoted to 30-second presentations and feedback in the whole group and 40 minutes to the same task in split groups (group A and group B) which makes a total of 90 minutes per seminar.

In the case of Portugal, the seminar is about 'International Aid and Development'. Data consists only of one seminar, which starts with a 20-minute presentation followed by a 60-minute debate. This makes a total of 80 minutes.

Finally, in Sweden, two seminars of similar characteristics were recorded. Seminar 1 and seminar 2 were 83 and 84 minutes long respectively. Both seminars started with questions on articles previously read by students (2 minutes and 8 minutes), followed by a debate on marketing strategies and cross-cultural communication.

In Table 4.5 above, a summary of the length by country (in minutes) is presented. The total amount of time recorded adds up to 932 minutes which is translated into 15 hours and 32 minutes.

Besides, Table 4.6 shows detailed information on seminars recorded in the different countries, including duration (in minutes) and the type of activities performed.

Transcription

Introduction

According to Weisser (2016), the term transcription can be defined as "converting spoken data into a written form, either rendering it orthographically or phonetically/phonemically" (p. 276). This process is not simple because it depends on the quality of the recordings to be transcribed and what is more important, on the way the transcriber, who needs to be as faithful as possible to what is being said, interprets the utterances. In most cases the text can be easily transcribed and there is no ambiguity. However, there are other cases where the transcriber has to interpret what the speaker intends to say.

Table 4.6 A summary of the duration and the kind of activities performed per seminar

Country	Degree	Seminar	Whole group		Split group		Total
			Duration	Task	Duration	Task	
Spain	BA	Seminar 1	50'	Presentations & Feedback	20' group A 20' group B	Presentations & Feedback	90'
		Seminar 2	50'	Presentations & Feedback	20' group A 20' group B	Presentations & Feedback	90'
		Seminar 3	50'	Presentations & Feedback	20' group A 20' group B	Presentations & Feedback	90'
Portugal	BA	Seminar 1	20' 60'	Presentation & Feedback Debate			80'
Norway	MA	Seminar 1	120'	Presentation Debate			120'
Italy	MA	Seminar 1	108'	Lecturer's explanation			108'
Sweden	MA	Seminar 1	8' 76'	Reading articles for discussion Debate based on the articles			84'
		Seminar 2	2' 81'	Reading articles for discussion Debate based on the articles			83'
The Netherlands	MA	Seminar 1	156'	Lecturer's explanation Debate	13' 18'	Discussion in two groups Pair-work discussion	187'

Table 4.7 Adaptations in the transcription process and cleaning

Element	TAG	Examples from the corpus
Unintelligible speech	<un> xxx </un>	everyone <un> xxxx </un> and then
Unidentified speaker(s)	SX	<s turn="u_0291" speaker=SX> okay </s>
Short pauses (less than one second)	(.)	some topics that are relevant nowadays (.) sustainability (.) food sector (.) sustainable tourism (.)
Long pauses (the approximate number of seconds in parenthesis)	(5)	and there was a very nice speech *from* that entrepreneur (2) </s>
Lengthening	:	u:h (.) okay (.)
Speaker noises	<coughs> <clears throat> <smacks lips>	<s turn="u_0451" speaker="SPF"> hahaha but <sighs>
Word fragment	--	e supervisor or whe-- where she stands
Polywords and compounds[2]	Marked with a hyphen "-"	there is a trade-off between
Laughter	transcribed as 'ha'. Utterances spoken laughingly between <@> </@>	let's work @@ because it was my mistake
Uncertain transcription	put in parentheses ( )	so it's (like) if i help you
Coinages, i.e., unconventional words used by L2 users	<pvc> </pvc>	to appreciate the <pvc> indigens </pvc> like
Onomatopoeic noises	<ono> </ono>	very early okay okay <ono> shhh </ono> if you have
First language speech	Marked with L1 and then the initials of the L1 (it=Italian; sp= Spanish; sw= Swedish)<L1sp> </L1sp>	six nine twelve <L1sp> perdon </L1sp> fourteen
Spelling out	<spel> </spel>	<spel> G E </spel> so <i> in
Proper names	<propername> </propername>	this is the case of <propername> nutella </propername>
Acronyms	<acronym> </acronym>	a percent of the <acronym> gdp </acronym> now
Speaking modes	<reading> </reading>	to <reading> enable diversity members to grasp one-another's perspective and productively share their insights </reading> and i think
Contextual information	added between { }	this is this blend here <{pointing at the screen}>

Given the general research area where this project is integrated, i.e., English as a Lingua Franca, we decided to rely on the general criteria used for the transcription process of the corpus VOICE, which can be checked in the following link: www.univie.ac.at/voice/page/transcription _general_information.

Some adaptations were carried out during the transcription process to the VOICE convention. These adaptations were similar to the ones used in the previous project EuroCoAT (for more information see: www.euro-coat.es/web_sections_1/the_corpus_eurocoat_the_european_corpus_ of_ academic_talk_12).

However, we thought it was necessary to provide a detailed explanation of the most important elements and criteria included in the transcription of the corpus. The idea is to make our decisions as explicit as possible and to group them according to the issue addressed.

Non-verbal data

Unlike VOICE, which "is based on audio-recordings" (cf. Breiteneder et al., 2006, p. 170), MetCLIL was recorded making use of cameras. The main reason behind this decision is related to the possibility of analysing gestures in the interpretation of metaphors, as this is a growing area of research in the field (Cienki & Müller, 2008) and it was considered appropriate to leave open the possibility for researchers to go back and analyse non-verbal behaviour. However, given the difficulty of such an enterprise, both in terms of technical knowledge and of the amount of work this would entail, the project did not plan to include gestures in the transcription of text.

Other non-verbal data (see Appendix K for transcription sample) were taken into account and transcribed:

1) Speaking modes. Utterances that are spoken in a particular mode and are notably different from the speaker's normal speaking style are marked accordingly. The list of speaking modes is not established beforehand. The beginning and the end of the mode used are marked by an opening and a closing tag, for example, <reading> </reading> or <whispering> </whispering>. The case of the 'reading' mode, i.e., when the lecturer or the students were reading from a text, was particularly important for metaphor analysis. It is not hard to hypothesise that the type of metaphor or even the number of metaphors used may be different as what participants are reproducing is a written text and not speaking off the top of their heads in 'online speech' production.
2) Speaker noises. Noises produced by the speakers are transcribed whenever possible. The list of speaker noises is also open (e.g., <coughs>).
3) Pauses. Short pauses, i.e., stretches of the video where no words are uttered, are indicated by (.). Long pauses are pointed out by providing the number of seconds they last approximately. For example, (4) would indicate that there is a pause of 4 seconds.

4) Uncertain transcription. Utterances written between conventional brackets – '(is free to loan)'– indicate that the transcriber is not completely certain whether this is the correct transcription.
5) Unintelligible speech. Fragments that are not understandable are marked by the convention <un> xxx </un>, in which each of the 'x' approximately represents a syllable of the unintelligible speech. If there are several words, there must also be different representations of words. E.g.: <un> xxxx xxx xxxx </un> for a fragment of 3 words.
6) Laughter. Laughter is transcribed as 'ha ha'. Utterances spoken laughingly are put between <@> </@> tags.

Verbal data

One of the key elements in the success of the compilation of a corpus is to adapt all the different steps to the planned objectives and to the resources available. This is particularly relevant in the case of the transcription of verbal data, which represent one of the most labour-intensive activities in corpus linguistics as tested in other projects:

> According to Ballier and Martin (2013, p. 33), it is estimated that one word of "simple" orthographic transcription costs about one euro. In terms of time, it was calculated within the framework of the LINDSEI project that each minute of learner speech requires some 20 to 30 minutes for transcription (including post-transcription checks).
>
> (Gilquin, 2015, p. 20)

The transcription of verbal data was therefore carried out following the principle that what was most important for the project was what students said and not how students said it. In other words, we followed what Leech (1997) call orthographic transcription, which is nothing other than an "orthographic rendering of written or spoken language, with or without punctuation" (cit. in Weisser, 2016, p. 228). The other possibility, i.e., a phonetic/phonemic transcription, was discarded as not important to the analysis of metaphor, the main objective of the corpus (cf. Gilquin, 2015 for a similar opinion on lexical analysis). Phonemic transcription was sometimes used in the very few instances where participants mispronounced and failed to reproduce the phonetic shape of a word. Only in this case is the orthographic transcription followed by a phonetic rendering of the pronunciation between /.

The use of orthographic transcription did not mean, however, that we did not attempt to be as faithful as possible in what refers to the rendering of non-standard forms. It was considered important to transcribe contractions such as *won't* or *hasn't* but also other forms that the guidelines of VOICE advise transcribing in their non-standard form: "With the exception of four wide-spread lexicalized phonological reductions (*cos, gonna, gotta, wanna*) and all standard contractions, words are represented in full standard orthographic form" (Breiteneder et al., 2006, p. 175).

As is usual in spoken corpora, other features which have a role in interaction were also transcribed. I refer here to hesitation markers ('*erm*' or '*em*' depending on their lengthening), backchannels, that typically inform the speaker of a listening attitude.

In some cases, the transcription of words is not straightforward as there are different spelling possibilities for a word. Thus, the project in the first place had to choose which spelling norm, British or American (e.g. *colour* vs *color*), would be used. This question was settled on the grounds that MetCLIL was a European project and that therefore the most appropriate decision would be to choose the British norm. However, as sometimes dictionaries differ in the way they transcribe certain words, most notably compounds such as, for example, *role-play*, *role play* or *roleplay*, it was thought important to establish a dictionary as a reference to decide on how to transcribe these words. The obvious choice, given that we have opted for a British standard, was the *Oxford English Dictionary* (OED), and this was the choice made by a previous related project, EuroCoAT, but in MetCLIL it was considered important to make use of the same dictionary that was used in the process of metaphor tagging (see Chapter 5). This dictionary is the Macmillan online dictionary (macmillandictionary.com), although in cases of doubt the OED was referred to.

Finally, in the few cases where it was necessary to transcribe code-switches from other languages, this was carried out by the researcher based on the country where the language was spoken according to the standards of that language. For example, to transcribe Spanish the norm of the *Real Academia de la Lengua* was adopted.

The main decisions taken in the project regarding transcriptions (see an example in Appendix K) are the following:

a   Contractions. One of the main criteria of the transcription process is to render the spoken language as it is actually produced by speakers. This means that reduced forms such as *gonna* and *wanna* were included without modification. The same happens with standard contractions. Forms like *he'd*, *I'll* or *she's* are included in the corpus as a way of representing what is being said as faithfully as possible.

b   Backchannels. The same principle as (a) above applies in the case of backchannels. Thus, for example, when the participants affirm, express understanding or agreement, or want to show they are listening to the person who is talking they can either use 'yes' or more often 'yeah'.

c   Hesitation markers. When speakers express hesitation, they use different sounds that the transcription has attempted to render. The most frequent ones are 'erm' or 'em'.

d   Repetitions. In spoken language, certain words are sometimes repeated for emphasis or as an indication of hesitation. These repetitions are transcribed.

e   Lengthening. When the speakers in the interaction lengthen a sound, this is marked with a colon ':'.

f   Onomatopoeic noises. When speakers produce sounds in order to imitate something instead of using words, these words are represented in spelling according to general principles of English orthography between <ono> </ono> tags.

g   Word fragments. Sometimes speakers interrupt their speech in the middle of a word. In this case, two hyphens mark the part of the word missing. For example, 'ca—' indicates that the speaker did not pronounce the whole of the word 'capabilities'. Polywords and compound words are marked with a single hyphen.

h   Capital letters. Capital letters are avoided in the representation of speech.

i   Non-English speech. Whenever speakers used their first language, codeswitching or codemixing, tags indicating the speaker's L1 were included before and after: '<L1sp> xxx </L1sp>'.

j   Overlaps. Unlike EuroCoAT, MetCLIL did not transcribe overlaps. Here we followed the advice by Atkins et al. (1992, pp. 11–12, cited in Love, 2020) to give

> careful thought about the extent to which punctuation should represent written conventions, and suggest that faithful and precise transcription of overlapping speech is costly; thus, an evaluation of the value and utility of including both punctuation and overlaps should be made before transcription begins.
>
> (p. 128)

It was decided that, at least initially, overlaps would not be marked.

Added information: contextual and structural mark-up

From the perspective of a small, specialised corpus like MetCLIL, adding too much information to the transcription or adopting already existing annotating schemes was not considered feasible. In this respect, we followed the advice given by Weisser when referring to the Text Encoding Initiative (TEI):

> following these guidelines [TEI's or other] and including all the mark-up required to comply with them represents a kind of overhead that may not be warranted for smaller research projects and may also make reading and processing the materials to be annotated more difficult
>
> (Weisser, 2015, p. 86).

1) Contextual information
   a   At the beginning of the text, a short description of the context of the class is provided between curly brackets (i.e., {}). The idea behind this is to provide the reader with information that can help him/her understand the interactions happening in that particular event.
   b   Clarifications about particular contextual circumstances are sometimes necessary in order to be able to understand the transcription. These comments are also included between {} brackets.
2) Seminar structure. Specific tags were used to identify each of the seminars recorded as well as the turns and the grouping activities within each of the seminars.
   a   Seminar identification. All seminars include a tag indicating the beginning of the seminar with the following structure <t information=" "> and another tag indicating the end (</t>). Thus, the seminar recorded in Italy would be included between a tag such as <t information="ITALY, Seminar 1"> and a </t> tag indicating the end of the seminar.
   b   Utterances/turns. We indistinctly use both terms to avoid deciding on a unit of spoken discourse that remains controversial. Thus, we acknowledge the complexity of the concept as defined by Conversation Analysis (e.g., see Yngve, 1970), where backchannels or similar elements cannot interrupt a turn, but at the same time we are aware that other traditions make use of a different concept of turn: "any speaker change will be treated as a new turn" (Tao, 2003, p. 189, cit. in Csomay, 2007). Used also in other studies more closely related to the academic context (see, e.g., Csomay (2002, 2007), we decided to leave this question open and let researchers decide if the utterance used here can be equated to their understanding of turn, as we have done. The identification of each utterance, which begins with the tag '<s turn=', will also include information regarding the number of utterance ('u_#'), the identification of the speaker ('speaker='), the role of the speaker, i.e., student or teacher, the L1 of the speaker, and the level of English following the Common European Framework of Reference for Languages. All this information is combined as shown in the following example: <s turn="u_0002" speaker="ELO" role="student" L1="Spanish" L2level="C1"> </s>.
   c   Grouping. The corpus includes tags indicating whether the transcribed extract involves the participation of the whole group of students in a particular seminar (<p GROUP="WHOLE">) or whether the methodology used implies some sort of grouping (<p GROUP="SPLIT">). The end of the extract is marked by </p>.
   d   Activity. Whenever possible, information is given about the type of activity carried out in class, for example: <ACTIVITY="PRESENTATION & FEEDBACK">.

Anonymisation

As is customary in the design and implementation of linguistic corpora, anonymisation was considered an important issue. On the one hand, the intention was to provide as much information about the context and participants as possible, as the interpretation of linguistic data is sometimes dependent on these external factors. On the other, participants in the seminars recorded were assured, via information sheets signed by the person responsible for the project, that no personal information would be used.

As a result, each of the names of the participants were substituted by a three-character acronym (e.g.: PPF). It should be noted that all of them begin by the letter of the country in question (e.g.: P = Portugal). The two following letters have been chosen to represent the full names that we invented for each of the participants. This means that when a participant's name was mentioned in the interaction, her/his real name was not used, but instead a name taking into account the speaker's home country was invented. For example, if the name of the real participant was Luis Orts, the acronym used within the turn tag would be ELO.

Tokenisation

Tokenisation decisions

The process of tokenisation is crucial for ensuring the comparability of results with other corpora. This is particularly important when studying metaphor density (cf. e.g., Nacey, 2013) since the calculation involves comparing the number of metaphors against the total number of words used in a text.

This process is not always straightforward as tokenisation involves important decisions. Thus, some researchers have pointed out that the token count of a well-known corpus like the BNC made with different criteria can fluctuate by 17% depending on the tokenisation criteria used (cf. Brezina & Temperley, 2017). The difference is explained as follows:

> Some tools (e.g. CQPweb, Sketch Engine) include punctuation in token counts. Others (e.g. #LancsBox) stay closer to the simple (surface) definition of the 'token' as presented in this book and do not count punctuation. In addition to punctuation, other sources of variation in token counting include: treatment of clitics (e.g. 'll in he'll) and hyphenated words (well-known).
>
> (Brezina, 2018, p. 39)

Given the importance of the tokenisation process for the project, we decided to make explicit how problematic cases should be counted. Table 4.8 provides a summary of the most important decisions.

Table 4.8 A summary of the most important tokenisation decisions

Problems	Examples	Decision
Clitics	we'll / you'd/ i'm	Two tokens
Abbreviations and acronyms	<spel> S A A R T </spel>	One token
Hyphenated-words, usually compound adjectives and nouns	start-up	One token (hyphenated words should have an entry in the reference dictionary used, i.e., MacMillan Dictionary)
Proper nouns	<propername> oliver </propername>	One token
Polyword conjunctions and prepositions	In front of	One token (phrases receiving a single part of speech tag and included in the BNC list of multiword units)
Quantity expressions	a bit/ a lot/	Follow Wmatrix, i.e. one token
Fixed expressions	for instance/ of course/ instead of	One token (expressions included in the BNC list of multiword units)
Phrasal, prepositional and phrasal prepositional verbs	look up/ look for/ look forward to	Two tokens (or three in the case of phrasal prepositional verbs)
Semi modals (as defined by Biber et al., 1999)	have to/used to/going to	One token

Part of speech mark-up

Procedure

The identification of the part of speech (PoS) was made using Wmatrix (https://ucrel-wmatrix4.lancaster.ac.uk/), following what was done in the sister project (EuroCoAT). Wmatrix identifies the part of speech using the tags proposed in the BNC list on the part of speech (see the following link: www.natcorp.ox.ac.uk/docs/c5spec.html). The reported accuracy of the tagger used by Wmatrix lies within the 96–97% range (cf. https://ucrel-wmatrix4.lancaster.ac.uk/cgi-bin/wmatrix4/help.pl#annotate). However, during the process of metaphor tagging, the automatically assigned PoS tags were manually revised and corrected when needed.

Results

The process of tokenisation was carried out using the database after the transcription and cleaning process were finished. In Table 4.9, detailed information on the number of tokens in each seminar is presented. Results show

Table 4.9 Number of tokens in each seminar

Seminar	Tokens
Italy	8,674
Norway	14,854
Portugal	8,681
Spain: Seminar 1	12,039
Spain: Seminar 2	12,085
Spain: Seminar 3	10,200
Sweden: Seminar 1	10,708
Sweden: Seminar 2	12,135
The Netherlands	21,117

that the seminar recorded in The Netherlands is the one with the larger number of tokens (21,117), followed by Norway (14,854). After that, there are three seminars with around 12,000 tokens (Sweden 2: 12,135; Spain 1: 12,039; Spain 2: 12,085). The next ones would be Sweden 1 (10,708), Spain 3 (10,200), Portugal (8,861) and lastly Italy (8,674). The total amount of tokens in each seminar can be clearly seen in the following table.

Conclusion

The current chapter has embraced a comprehensive methodological approach, intending to offer valuable insights into the various criteria and choices involved in crafting a specialised corpus like MetCLIL. In the forthcoming chapter, I will delve deeper into the methodological considerations pertaining to the identification of metaphors within the corpus. This will entail a thorough exploration of the specific decisions and intricacies associated with the most frequently employed metaphor tagging schemes found in the existing literature on the analysis of metaphor from a corpus linguistics perspective.

Notes

1 ETP stands for English Taught Programme. It is an equivalent term of EMI and is mostly used as a general term by those who are not concerned with the language-related aspect of the experience.
2 The definition of these words will be explained in the next chapter.

References

Ädel, A. (2020). Corpus compilation. In M. Paquot & S. T. Gries (Eds.), *A practical handbook of corpus linguistics* (pp. 3–24). Springer Nature.

Ballier, N. & Martin, P. (2013). Developing corpus interoperability for phonetic investigation of learner corpora. In N. Ballier, A. Diaz-Negrillo, & P. Thompson, (Éds.), *Automatic treatment and analysis of learner corpus data* (pp. 33–64). John Benjamins.

Beard, R., & Hartley, J. (1984). *Teaching and learning in higher education*. Harper & Row.

Biber, D., Johansson, S., Leech, G., Conrad, S., & Finegan, E. (1999). *The Longman grammar of spoken and written English*. Longman.

Breiteneder, A., Pitzl, M.-L., Majewski, S., & Klimpfinger, T. (2006). VOICE recording – methodological challenges in the compilation of a corpus of spoken ELF. *Nordic Journal of English Studies*, 5(2), 161–187. http://doi.org/10.35360/njes.16

Brezina, B. (2018). *Statistics in corpus linguistics: A practical guide*. Cambridge University Press.

Brezina, V., & Timperley, M. (2017). *How large is the BNC? A proposal for standardized tokenization and word counting*. CL2017. Retrieved March 31, 2023, from https://www.birmingham.ac.uk/Documents/college-artslaw/corpus/conference-archives/2017/general/paper303.pdf

Brookes, G. & Baker, P. (2021). *Obesity in the news: Language and representation in the press*. Cambridge University Press.

Cameron, D. (2001). *Working with Spoken Discourse*. Sage Publications.

Cienki, A., & Müller, C. (Eds.). (2008). *Metaphor and gesture*. John Benjamins.

Clancy, B. (2022). Building a corpus to represent a variety of language. In A. O'Keeffe & M. J. McCarthy (Eds.), *The Routledge handbook of corpus linguistics* (pp. 62–74). Routledge.

Csomay, E. A. (2002). *Episodes in university classrooms: A corpus linguistic investigation*. Northern Arizona University.

Csomay, E. A. (2007). A corpus-based look at linguistic variation in classroom interaction: Teacher talk versus student talk in American University classes. *Journal of English for Academic Purposes*, 6(4), 336–355.

David, O., & Matlock, T. (2018). Cross-linguistic automated detection of metaphors for poverty and cancer. *Language and Cognition*, 10(3), 467–493. https://doi.org/10.1017/langcog.2018.11

Dodge, E. K., Hong, J., & Stickles, E. (2015, June 5). MetaNet: Deep semantic automatic metaphor analysis. In E. Shutova, B. Beigman Kebanov, P. Lichtenstein (Eds.), *Proceedings of the third workshop on metaphor in NLP* (pp. 40–49). Association for Computational Linguistics.

Furneaux, C., Locke, C., Robinson, P., & Tonkyn, A. (1991). Talking heads and shifting bottoms: The ethnography of academic seminars. In P. Adams, B. Heaton, & P. Howarth (Eds.), *Socio-cultural issues in English for academic purposes* (pp. 74–85). Macmillan.

Gilquin, G. (2015). From design to collection of learner corpora. In S. Granger, G. Gilquin, & F. Meunier (Eds.), *The Cambridge handbook of learner corpus research* (pp. 9–34). Cambridge University Press.

Granger, S. (2008). Learner corpora in foreign language education. In N. Van Deusen-Scholl & N. H. Hornberger (Eds.), *Encyclopedia of language and education* (Vol. 4, pp. 337–351). Springer.

Jordan, R. R. (1997). *English for academic purposes: A guide and resource book for teachers*. Cambridge University Press.

Koester, A. (2022). Building small specialised corpora. In A. O'Keeffe & J. McCarthy (Eds.), *The Routledge handbook of corpus linguistics* (pp. 48–61). Routledge.

Leech, G. (1997). Introducing corpus annotation. In R. Garside G. Leech and T. McEnery (Eds.). *Corpus Annotation. Linguistic information from computer text corpora* (pp. 1–18). Routledge.

Love, R. (2020). *Overcoming challenges in corpus construction: The spoken British national corpus 2014*. Routledge.

Maiworm, F. & Wächter, B. (Eds.). (2002). *English-Language-Taught Degree Programmes in European Higher Education. Trends and Success Factors*. Lemmens.

Mauranen, A. (2012). *Exploring ELF: Academic English shaped by non-native speakers*. Cambridge University Press.

McEnery, T., & Brookes, G. (2022). Building a written corpus: What are the basics? In A. O'Keeffe & M. McMarthy (Eds.), *The Routledge handbook of corpus linguistics* (pp. 35–47). Routledge.

McEnery, T. and Hardie, A. (2012). *Corpus Linguistics: Method, Theory and Practice*. Cambridge University Press.

Morell, T. (2004). Interactive lecture discourse for university EFL students. *English for Specific Purposes*, 24, 325–338.

Morell, T. (2007). A presentation course design for academics of English as an additional language: A multimodal approach. In S. Burgess & M. Cargill (Eds.), *English as an additional language in research publication and communication* (pp. 237–253). Linguistics Insights Series, Peter Lang.

Nacey, S. (2013). *Metaphors in learner English [metaphor in language, cognition, and communication 2]*. John Benjamins Publishing Company.

Northcott, J. (2001). Towards an ethnography of the MBA classroom: a consideration of the role of interactive lecturing styles within the context of one MBA programme. *English for Specific Purposes*, 20, 15–37.

O'Keeffe, A. (2018). Corpus-based function-to-form approaches. In A. H. Jucker, K. P. Schneider, & W. Bublitz (Eds.), *Methods in pragmatics* (pp. 587–618). Mouton de Gruyter.

Paquot, M., & Gries, S. T. (Eds.). (2020). *A practical handbook of corpus linguistics*. Springer Nature.

Rose, H., Macaro, E., Sahan, K., Aizawa, I., Zhou, S., & Wei, M. (2021). Defining English medium instruction: Striving for comparative equivalence. *Language Teaching*, 56, 1–12.

Tao, H. (2003). Turn initiators in spoken English: A corpus-based approach to interaction and grammar. In P. Leistyna & C. Meyer (Eds.), *Language and computers: Studies in practical linguistics No. 46. Corpus analysis: Language structure and language use* (pp. 187–208). Rodopi.

Vaughan, E., & Clancy, B. (2013). Small corpora and pragmatics. *Yearbook of Corpus Linguistics and Pragmatics*, 1, 53–73.

Wächter, B., & Maiworm, F. (2008). *English-Taught, Programmes in European Higher Education. The Picture in 2007*. Lemmens.

Wächter, B., & Maiworm, F. (Eds.). (2014). *English-taught programmes in European higher education: The state of play in 2014*. Lemmens.

Weisser, M. (2015). Speech act annotation. In K. Aijmer & Ch. Rühlemann (Eds.), *Corpus pragmatics: A handbook* (pp. 84–114). Cambridge University Press.

Weisser, M. (2016). *Practical corpus linguistics: An introduction to corpus-based language analysis*. Wiley-Blackwell.

Yngve, V. H. (1970). On getting a word in edgewise. In *Chicago linguistics society, 6th meeting, 1970* (pp. 567–578). University of Chicago Press.

5 Metaphor tagging

Introduction to metaphor identification methods

The study of metaphor has a long tradition, which encompasses analyses that range from a more philosophical perspective to those of a more literary character, without leaving aside those concerned with a psychological approach. The majority of these studies either take for granted the identification of metaphors or rely on intuition. Obviously, none of these approaches is appropriate to the study of metaphor use from a CL perspective, which is not based on intuitions or preconceived notions about a linguistic phenomenon, but rather on empirical evidence obtained from the analysis of large-scale corpora. A corpus-based approach to metaphor will necessarily mean using annotation guidelines based on criteria that enable the systematic identification and categorisation of metaphorical language.

Annotating a corpus is a labour-intensive process because it involves manually identifying and tagging linguistic features in a large-scale dataset. This process, which is time-consuming and requires trained annotators, is even more challenging when the feature to be annotated is metaphor. The difficulty is mostly due to the highly contextual nature of this figure of speech, which may result in different annotators identifying metaphors differently. To ensure consistency in metaphor annotation, it is essential to develop clear and comprehensive annotation guidelines, which should specify the criteria for identifying and categorising metaphors, as well as provide examples and instructions for annotators. This would ensure that the annotation process is systematic, replicable and accurate.

The complexity of the tagging process is the explanation behind the limited number of corpora annotated for metaphor use, as well as their comparatively small size in relation to other more general-scope corpora. The only available corpus tagged for metaphor is the VUAMC corpus, which has a relatively small size of 200,000 words if we compare it with other general corpora. It was created using part of the BNC-Baby, a subcorpus of the British National Corpus, and tagging it for metaphor use. The corpus can be accessed through the Metaphor Lab website at the Vrije Universiteit in Amsterdam (http://metaphorlab.org/metaphor-corpus) where metaphors can be searched online.

DOI: 10.4324/9781003400905-5

Different proposals for metaphor identification have been made and most of them were developed when researchers began to address metaphor from a more linguistic and discursive perspective (described in Chapter 1). The present chapter will deal in detail with two of the most important ones – the Metaphor Identification Procedure (MIP) by the Pragglejaz group and its later development, the MIPVU, carried out by researchers from the Vrije Universiteit in Amsterdam. These two procedures constitute the base on which our identification method is founded, although as we will see some variations have been added.

Before dealing with MIP and MIPVU, it is right to acknowledge that other scholars have also made their own proposals. Identifying similarities and differences can help us understand the basic elements involved. One of these proposals is the Metaphor Identification procedure through Vehicle terms (MIV), developed by Cameron (1999). According to this author, MIV's main objective is to detect vehicles, i.e., words or phrases, whose meaning contrasts with the current topic of the text. Consequently, the first step is to identify those words or phrases that could create this incongruity or contrast. Next, the process involves the identification of the transfer of meaning to the topic. Sometimes this transfer is based on similarity between the vehicle and the topic, but at other times the incongruity between vehicle and topic, i.e., between the words being used and the matter talked/written about, can simply be explained as seeing something in terms of another.

Both these steps constitute the basic elements of any identification procedure and are also at the heart of the MIP and MIPVU procedures, but there is something where MIV and MIP/MIPVU differ: the unit of analysis. For MIV, individual words are not the only vehicles that can be considered metaphorical since longer stretches of languages can also be interpreted as one metaphorical vehicle. This can be considered to cause certain identification problems as Krennmayr (2011, p. 33) explains:

> For example, in a sample conversation Cameron (2006) identifies *at one point* in "I believed at one point" as a vehicle term, arguing that it "is a phrase with a meaning of physical location that is metaphorical when used to refer to a moment in time". In "Juliet is the sun", she identifies *the sun* as the vehicle and argues that the definite article is included because "it is the particular, specific sun that is being referred to and this is signalled with the definite article". It is less clear then, why in "(…), to politically and constitutionally, correct that situation", *that* is not included into the vehicle term *situation*.

Therefore, the primary issue for MIV, also recognised by Nacey et al. (2019), is rooted in the imprecise boundaries that metaphorical vehicles may have. This may not be a problem for the analysis of individual texts but is certainly more difficult to implement with large corpora. In fact, it seems very likely that this explains why both MIP and MIPVU have been more frequently used in the annotation of corpora and that MIPVU and the VUAMC corpus were chosen to illustrate metaphor tagging in the *Handbook of Linguistic Annotation* (cf. Krennmayr & Steen, 2017).

Metaphor Identification Procedure (MIP)

The origins of MIP date back to the year 2000, when a group of metaphor experts met in Amsterdam (cf. Steen, 2017 for a short account) to discuss the possibility of developing a widely accepted framework that would enable researchers with differing approaches to agree on which specific instances should be considered as metaphor. It is no mere coincidence that the meeting was held in Amsterdam. It was the research group led by Professor Steen (VUAMC team), which had shown the most interest in developing a metaphor identification procedure and which had continued to bring some discussion to the Researching and Applying Metaphor (RaAM) conferences (see Nacey, 2013). This ongoing discussion solidified when the Pragglejaz group, the group of ten metaphor researchers who met in 2000, produced the now famous article published in *Metaphor and Symbol* in 2007: "MIP: A method for identifying metaphorically used words in discourse". This is what we know as the MIP procedure and its application in the identification of metaphors in a text, in this or in the subsequent version called MIPVU that we will see later on, is referred to as mipping. It is important to note, however, that there are some differences, even though slight, between the publication by the Pragglejaz group and some of the initial proposals by the VUAMC group that constitute the origin of MIP. As Nacey (2013) explains, even though MIP and Pragglejaz show certain differences, most research refers to them as one procedure under the label of MIP.

The basic tenet for both MIP, which is also valid for MIPVU, is that the objective is to adopt a census methodology (cf. Chapter 1), where all the metaphors in the corpus will be identified. This involves adopting what Steen (2007) calls an inductive approach to metaphor. As a consequence, even if metaphors are understood as conceptual structures, the identification of metaphorically used words should proceed in a bottom-up way, i.e., considering case by case, and not assuming which metaphorically mappings these words entail.

The procedure described in the 2007 article follows four main stages in the identification of metaphor:

- Reading the whole text to be analysed for a general understanding of its meaning.
- Determining the lexical units involved.
- Establishing the contextual meaning of the units analysed and determining whether they have a more basic meaning. If they have a more basic meaning, determining if the contextual meaning can be understood in comparison with it.
- If yes, mark the unit as metaphorical.

In order to understand these four steps of the Metaphor Identification Procedure (MIP), it is important to recognise that, consistent with the principles of Conceptual Metaphor Theory discussed in Chapter 1, MIP views metaphors as conceptual structures, known as conceptual metaphors, which influence the way we think, reason and perceive the world. These conceptual metaphors can manifest in various forms of metaphorical expressions, and they provide a means of mapping abstract or unfamiliar domains of experience onto concrete or familiar ones. As such, MIP offers a systematic approach to identifying and analysing metaphorical language use in discourse, with the ultimate goal of uncovering the underlying conceptual mappings that structure our understanding of the world.

The first step involves reading and understanding the text in order to find out about its content. For example, in the three seminars recorded in Spain by the MetCLIL project, the topic of the seminar is Digital Marketing and more specifically the presentation or pitch that students are practising. As a consequence, the language used was mostly related to Digital Marketing and to the activity they are developing in the seminars, which consist in students giving short presentations and in providing feedback on them. It is only if we clearly identify the subject matter dealt with in the language that we can later realise that there are certain words that do not typically belong there.

The second step is also of importance as researchers must decide which lexical unit to include in their analysis. This step presupposes a decision about what the researchers consider a lexical unit, a controversial issue as we have already seen when explaining MIV. In the context of MIP, where the reference unit is the word,[1] it is necessary to identify the words that have the potential to be used metaphorically because of the context. This involves determining which words undergo a mapping process between the source and target domains, resulting in a metaphorical expression.

However, it is the third step that is key to the whole process. As pointed out by Nacey (2013, pp. 69–70), it involves several decisions:

- "Determination of the contextual sense
- Determination of the basic sense
- Deciding whether these two senses sufficiently differ, and if so, then
- Deciding whether these two senses are related by comparison."

If we consider a sample from MetCLIL, such as the feedback comment "it just needs to be condensed" given to a student after a presentation, each decision can be explained as follows:

- There are six words in the sentence which approximately have the following *contextual* meaning: 1. It: third-person singular pronoun used to refer to objects, animals or concepts; 2. Just: adverb meaning 'only'; 3. Needs: third person singular of the simple present of the verb 'need' with the meaning of 'require'; 4. To: infinitive marker; 5. Be: passive auxiliary; and 6. Condensed: participle of the verb 'condense' with the meaning of 'shorten'.

- Words 1–5 have a basic meaning which is similar to the one explained in the previous paragraph. However, when we check the differrent meanings of the word 'condense' in the Macmillan online dictionary (MM), its basic meaning is different from the contextual meaning identified above. This basic meaning of 'condense' would be 'changing into liquid' as it is more concrete than the contextual one identified.
- Since words 1–5 have the same contextual and basic meanings, the next step is not necessary. However, in the case of 'condense', the only candidate to be a metaphor, it is necessary to say whether its contextual meaning, 'shorten', is sufficiently different from its basic meaning. In my opinion, the answer is positive as no meaning overlap between 'changing into a liquid' and 'shorten' seems to be reasonable.
- The two senses are related by comparison since the source domain of NATURAL PROCESSES is being mapped into the target domain of SPEECH. The comparison seems clear: when the molecules of a gas or vapour condense, they move closer together and they take up less space. It seems logical to conclude that 'condense' is a metaphor.

One very important characteristic of MIP is that it is not designed to "identify similes as metaphoric" (Pragglejaz Group, 2007, p. 32). The reason is simple: when you employ a simile, the words are not actually used metaphorically. Nacey explains this with an example such as 'writing is like hiking': "we find no contrast between contextual and basic meanings; none of these words are metaphorically used. The insertion of the 'alien' domain of hiking as a means of explaining the writing process, however, clearly activates an underlying conceptual metaphor" (2013, p. 76). To express this idea in technical terms, MIP is only concerned with *indirect metaphor* and excludes other types of metaphorical language such as *direct metaphor*, which is however incorporated by MIPVU to the identification procedure.

Another element to take into account is that the criteria used to establish the dictionary meaning of a word as more basic are somewhat different in MIP in relation to MIPVU. Thus, in MIP (Pragglejaz Group, 2007), we find the following list of elements to determine the basic meaning of a word:

- "more concrete; what they evoke is easier to imagine, see, hear, feel, smell, and taste.
- related to bodily action.
- more precise (as opposed to vague).
- historically older.
- Basic meanings are not necessarily the most frequent meanings of the lexical unit."

(Pragglejaz Group, 2007, p. 3)

A final aspect that needs to be highlighted relates to the consideration of a part of speech as a boundary that may be crossed in the determination of a word as metaphorically used. Thus, a verb like 'squirrel', which has only one meaning in the dictionary (i.e., "to hoard items or save money", Pragglejaz Group, 2007, p. 28), is considered as metaphorical even if no contrast is made to a basic meaning (as we have said it only has one) because the meaning of the verb provides a metaphorical link to the noun ('squirrel', an animal), which is considered as the basic meaning in this case. In other words, word class is not considered in the analysis.

Metaphor Identification Procedure Vrije University (MIPVU)

The researchers from the VUAMC group, who as we saw were among the most active in the elaboration of MIP, continued to work in refining this procedure in order to apply it to the project they were involved in, whose aim was to analyse the use of metaphor in four different registers (fiction, academic discourse, conversations and news). This further refinement work resulted in the publication of a book (Steen et al., 2010) entitled *A method for linguistic metaphor identification: From MIP to MIPVU*. This new volume collects a detailed account of the decisions made.

MIPVU, as already explained, incorporated new features to MIP. However, the basic identification procedure described for MIP was not altered in its main guidelines. There were indeed some changes, some of which we have already discussed, but MIPVU was mainly intended to give a more exhaustive account of the presence of metaphor in texts by introducing some conceptual distinctions that could help in the exploitation of the VUAMC corpus more fully. These fine-grained categorisations were then incorporated into the corpus as new tags (Krennmayr & Steen, 2017). Let us examine each of them individually.

1 Metaphor Related Words (MRWs). In MIPVU, the basic contrast is between metaphorical related words vs words not related to metaphors, which overrides MIP's basic distinction between metaphorical language vs non-metaphorical language. The expression 'metaphorical related word' comes from the need to find a word encompassing the different types of metaphorical language that MIPVU covers in its analysis and that extend beyond indirect metaphorical uses. Some of these types have already been explained but the scope of the MRWs can be best perceived if we list them again and explain their main features:

   a Indirect metaphor. This is the only type of metaphor considered in MIP and is basically the result of the contrast between the contextual meaning of a word and its basic meaning. This is the case, explained above, of the word 'condense' when used in a sentence like "it just needs to be condensed".

   b Direct metaphor. This type of metaphor does not actually involve the use of a metaphorical word or expression like in the example, also explained, "writing is like hiking" or another sentence that we find in MetCLIL, "scientific theories are like fiction". Here the language refers to or evokes a conceptual metaphor, but the linguistic expression used is not metaphorical because there is no contrast between the contextual meaning and the basic meaning of the words *hiking* or *fiction*. These words are used with their own basic meanings to create a comparison.

c   Implicit metaphor. To explain this metaphor, we can use an example taken from Krennmayr (2011): "The All Black would treat such an outmoded <u>approach</u> with the scorn *it* deserves (...)" (p. 31). In this sentence, the pronoun *it* implicitly recovers an indirect metaphor previously used, i.e., *approach*. *It* is therefore an implicit metaphor as the contrast between the contextual and the basic meaning only happens by its implicit reference to the word *approach*. Some cohesion markers like personal (e.g., it, they) or demonstrative pronouns (e.g., this, that) are typically used in implicit metaphor.

2   When in Doubt Leave It In (WIDLII). This tag did not introduce a conceptual distinction as such. It is more related to a methodological decision to be "maximally inclusive" (Krennmayr & Steen, 2017, p. 1060) in order to identify all words with a metaphorical potential in the discourse even if there may be some doubts about their status. Thus, when the context does not make completely clear whether a word can be interpreted metaphorically or not, this tag is applied. This can be seen in the following example from the Dutch seminar in MetCLIL: "what needs to happen then is that people <u>come together</u> and merge their own merge their disciplines eh create new knowledge based on two different worlds". Here the expression "come together" can have a literal meaning in the sense that people actually meet, or it can have a metaphorical interpretation, the most likely, if we assume that this 'coming together' only entails the idea of 'working as a team' without necessarily meeting in person. WIDLII are therefore "borderline cases" (Krennmayr & Steen, 2017, p. 1060).

3   Metaphor flags (MFlags). This addition is the result of the need to tag the words that are used to signal direct metaphors. Typically, these are words such as *like* or *as*, which introduce similes. This would be something that we can find in the following utterance: "yeah (.) the theory building as MFlag an art of simplicity". Metaphor flags are therefore used to signal metaphor use.

To summarise, we can conclude with a comparison between MIP and MIPVU. Krennmayr and Steen (2017, p. 1061) provide a table (see Table 5.1) that clearly outlines the similarities and differences between the two procedures. They include points that have been elaborated in greater detail above, especially those concerning the types of metaphor coded and the crossing of word class boundaries when identifying metaphor. Other aspects such as the definition of basic meaning and the use of dictionaries will be touched upon below when specific aspects of the MetCLIL methodology will be developed.

Table 5.1 Main differences between MIP and MIPVU (Krennmayr & Steen, 2017, p. 1061)

	MIP	*MIPVU*
Definition of basic meaning	More concrete, related to bodily action, more precise (as opposed to vague), historically older	More concrete, related to bodily action, more precise (as opposed to vague)
Lexical units	Crosses word class	Does not cross word class
Dictionaries	Macmillan English Dictionary for Advanced Learners	Macmillan English Dictionary for Advanced Leaners; Longman Dictionary of Contemporary English Online; Oxford English Dictionary
Type of metaphor coded	Metaphor and non-metaphor	Metaphor-related words (indirect metaphor, direct metaphor, implicit metaphor), metaphor signals, ambiguous metaphor, possible personification[2]

Table 5.2 Summary of words analysed in MetCLIL

Adjectives	Analysed
Adverbs	Analysed
Auxiliary verbs (do, have)	Not Analysed
Light verbs (have, get, do ...)	Analysed
Modals	Not Analysed
Nouns	Analysed. For proper nouns check "proper nouns" in the following table.
Phrasal verbs	Analysed. We analyse each of the items that made up the phrasal verb as different units. To determine the basic meaning of the verb, we choose the basic meaning of the verb per se, not the meaning of the phrasal verb.
Prepositions	Analysed except for "of" and "for"
Lexical verbs	Analysed
Prepositional verbs	Analysed. We analyse the items as different units (similar procedure as that of phrasal verbs). * Example: 'deal with'. We would analyse *deal* and *with* as separate forms. In the case of *deal*, we would determine whether it is an MRW in relation to the basic meaning of deal (1. to give cards to the people playing a game of cards).

Particular cases of metaphor analysis

Once we have seen the two most important identification procedures and their similarities and differences, we now turn to the presentation of the specific decisions taken when our corpus, i.e., MetCLIL, was tagged for

Table 5.3 Mipping decisions regarding certain word categories

Terminology	**Analyse.** Stick to MIPVU. If a more basic meaning in the dictionary is found, the term is metaphorical. Examples: *course, credit, and degree* are metaphors when used in university contexts. * When in MM, there is a separate entry for the specialised term, establish the basic meaning by only considering this entry.
General meanings	**Analyse.** There are some cases in which the basic meaning is quite broad so it can include more specific senses. In these cases, the word is analysed and is tagged as "Not metaphor". * Example: The word *development* in "so as you can see the theme is aid and development". According to MM, development is "the process of creating a new product or method". As this definition is inclusive enough, it comprises the contextual meaning ("the process of improving the economy of a country or region by increasing the amount of business activity"), so we conclude that this *development* is not a metaphor.
Vague forms (things, stuff …)	**Analyse.** Vague forms are identified as metaphors when the context does not point to a concrete thing.
Discourse markers	**Analyse.** Analyse them and mark them as non-metaphorical (e.g., okay, so, well, you know …).
Unconventional uses	**Analyse.** Unconventional uses, resulting from L1 interference, are marked as "unconventional" and are analysed as any other word.
Acronyms	**Don't Analyse.** Acronyms per se are are discarded (DFMA). Not metaphorical when used in full.
Quantifiers (many, much, more …)	**Don't Analyse.** Discard them, as they are not very interesting for our analysis.
Conflation	**Analyse.** Very likely to be WIDLII. * Example: the verb 'see' as in "we are going to see the content", implies that they are "seeing" them both physically **AND** conceptually at the same time.
Metonymy	**Don't Analyse.** Some Metonymical words could correspond to the WIDLII category. In this case, analyse.
Compounds	**Analyse.** We first need to check whether it is a compound. According to the MIPVU procedure, to be regarded as a compound, a term needs to (1) appear in the dictionary in a separate entry and (2) be pronounced as a compound, that is, with the stress placed in the first item. For example, footprint /ˈfʊtˌprɪnt/ is a compound, whereas carbon footprint / ˈkɑːbən ˈfʊtprɪnt/ is not a compound although it has a separate entry in the dictionary. 'Carbon footprint' would be analysed as a modifier + head.

(*Continued*)

Table 5.3 Continued

Modifier + head	**Analyse.** We analyse the items as different units. * Example: 'a rural context': in this case, both, *rural* and *context* are marked as non-metaphorical.
Self-correction	**Don't Analyse.** We discard (DFMA) the first word or chunk and analyse the second. Example: in a phrase like 'the context...the contest', 'contest' is discarded and only the word 'context' is analysed.
Proper nouns	**Analyse.** Mark them as "not metaphor" and tag as "proper noun".
L1 words	**Don't Analyse.** Tag them as DFMAs.
Grammaticalised expressions	**Don't Analyse.**
MRW polywords (*out of* and *in front of*)	**Analyse.** Example: The word 'out' only works as a preposition in two cases: *out the door* and *out the window*. In the rest of the cases, the preposition is *out of*.
Truncated words	**Don't Analyse.** Tag them as DFMAs. Example: ca- capabilities.

metaphor. These decisions were taken within the framework of MIPVU, which constitutes the main reference for the methodology used in MetCLIL and for the present book. However, the peculiarities of the identification process in a corpus of non-native speakers make it necessary to introduce modifications that we will explain below in detail. Some of these features were already identified by MacArthur (2019) in an article explaining why the analysis of metaphor in English for lingua franca contexts (ELF), where L2 users are a majority, may differ from the majority of the discursive contexts, in which L1 speakers are predominant, to which MIP and MIPVU have been applied. MacArthur, who uses examples from the other corpus of ELF tagged for metaphor, i.e., the European Corpus of Academic Talk (EuroCoAT, see MacArthur et al., 2014), pinpoints four major problematic areas in the process of metaphor identification: determining the appropriate lexical units to be mipped; identifying the target or contextual meaning intended by the speakers; establishing the basic meaning; and deciding on the metaphorical meaning, especially when an unconventional meaning is used. We will touch on each of these elements separately.

Determining lexical units

As explained above, the first step in the procedure, i.e., understanding the text to be analysed, is followed by a second stage, which involves determining lexical units to be subjected to metaphor analysis. This seems fairly straightforward, but it means providing an answer to the question: what exactly do we understand by a lexical unit?

The term 'lexical unit' was carefully chosen by MIPVU to encompass units with different sizes. Thus, a first answer to the question would be that a lexical unit is an individual non-decomposable meaningful unit, which corresponds to a word, understood as a string of orthographical symbols with linguistic meaning and separated from other words by spaces or punctuation marks. However, it is important to note that a lexical unit may also consist of multiple words, which can create difficulties in determining its boundaries. These multiword units present the most significant challenges in defining lexical units.

When it comes to identifying multiword units in corpora primarily consisting of L2 speakers, it is important to recognise that L2 speakers process these units differently from L1 speakers. MacArthur (2019) argues that this well-established psycholinguistic finding should be reflected in how multiword units are delimited in such corpora. As MacArthur explains, the approach used to determine the (potential) decomposability of multiword units should consider the fact that L2 speakers do not use or process chunks in the same way as L1 speakers. Previous research conducted by Wray and her colleagues has highlighted this processing difference (Wray, 1999, 2005; Wray & Fitzpatrick, 2008 cit. in MacArthur, 2019). Therefore, a rigorous methodology for identifying metaphors in EFL corpora should take into account that multiword units, as defined by other metaphor projects, may not be entirely applicable.

In the following, the main multiword lexical units are considered and the methodological decisions adopted are explained.

POLYWORDS

According to MIPVU, polywords are "fixed multiword expressions that are analyzed as one lexical unit in the BNC, on the grounds that they are grammatical units which designate one specific referent in the discourse" (Steen et al., 2010, p. 27). As already explained in the tokenisation section, these multiword units are important in corpus linguistics because they can have an important impact on the word count of a large collection of texts. As can be seen from the citation, these multiword units are defined with reference to the BNC, which is the corpus (more specifically the BNC-Baby) that the VUAMC group tagged for metaphor. As already indicated, in this project, we have considered as polywords those included in the BNC list (www.natcorp .ox.ac.uk/docs/multiwd.htm). This list includes expressions such as *according to* or *as regards* that are considered as a single unit where the whole expression is analysed for metaphor use and not the individual words.

The present project differs from the criteria adopted by MacArthur (2019) and the EuroCoAT project (MacArthur et al., 2014) with regard to some of these multiword expressions. For them, the reference should not be the BNC list but the MM dictionary. Besides, in that project it was necessary to carry out a test of *internal modification* (cf. MacArthur, 2019) in order to determine whether these multiword expressions should be analysed. Thus, for this author, an expression like *a bit* should not be considered as a lexical unit because in English it is possible to find expressions like *a little bit of* or *a tiny bit of* which show that the expression is not completely fixed. This would mean that each of the words of the expression, including the word *bit*, would be analysed for metaphor use. However, even though it was considered as methodologically sound, this option was discarded by MetCLIL as it involved a lot of manual analysis of each of the candidates.

COMPOUNDS

A special case of multiword units are compounds, which are not typically included in the BNC list cited above. In order to identify compounds, we followed the procedure established by MIPVU. According to this procedure, a compound needs to meet both these criteria: (1) having a separate entry in the reference dictionary used (cf. section 2 below); and (2), showing the typical phonological contour of this word class, which entails that the accent falls on the first of its constituent words. For example, *business card* /ˈbiznəs kɑ:d/ is a compound, whereas carbon footprint /ˈkɑ:bən ˈfʊtprɪnt/ is not a compound although it has a separate entry in the dictionary.

MULTIWORD VERBS

Another particular case of multiword units is the broad category of multi-word verbs, which sometimes some dictionaries mistakenly equate to phrasal verbs, but which in fact is much wider as it not only includes phrasal verbs proper, but other groups of multiword verbs such as prepositional verbs or phrasal prepositional verbs (see Alejo-González, 2010 for a review on the terminological confusion). In the metaphorical analysis of these words, we separate from the procedure established by MIPVU and follow MacArthur (2019), who suggests that the way L2 users process these verbs makes it advisable to analyse their constituent words separately. These are the specific cases:

1   Adverb particles following verbs, i.e., phrasal verbs. Phrasal verbs are treated as fully decomposable regardless of whether or not the unit has a more basic meaning in the *Macmillan English Dictionary* (MM). For example, *narrow down* has only one meaning in MM, but is still treated as metaphor related. That is, each phrasal verb will be analysed as consisting of two (e.g., 'narrow down') or three lexical units (e.g., "put up with"). Pinning down the basic meaning of each LU may be difficult (e.g., what's the basic meaning of "with"?) but nevertheless each will be counted as an LU.
2   Prepositional verbs with a unitary meaning. In MM these are called "phrasal verbs" but strictly speaking they are not. For example, 'look after' is a prepositional verb ('Can you look after him/my son?') while "look up" is a phrasal verb ('Why don't you look the word up /look it up'?). Nevertheless, prepositional verbs like "look after" have this unitary meaning which makes them very similar to PVs. In these cases, the two elements are treated as 2 LUs, exactly the same as we do with PVs.
3   Prepositional verbs proper. The difference between bound prepositions and 'free' ones is that they depend on the lexical element before them, rather than the prepositional object. For example, 'depend on someone/something' versus 'put something in/on/under something'. Basically, we say that certain verbs, adjectives or nouns 'take' a certain preposition. Some examples are 'keen on', 'angry at', 'rely on', 'key to' or 'confide in'. Again, these combinations will be treated as two LUs (given that L2 users frequently decompose them and sometimes get them wrong) and will be submitted to metaphor analysis. MM usually records the combination as a fixed one.

WORDS NOT INCLUDED IN THE ANALYSIS

To conclude this section, it is important to clarify a specific methodological decision made in the current research project in connection with their lexical status. MetCLIL, following MIPVU, made the decision that only certain words will be considered suitable for a metaphor analysis. This is because not all words can be used to create metaphors or carry metaphorical meanings. The words to be analysed were open-class words (nouns, adjectives, adverbs, verbs and prepositions except for 'of' and 'for', whose polysemy and ambiguity makes it difficult to reach an agreement on their contextual meaning). This means that nearly all 'function' words (i.e., the closed system items that form the bedrock of the grammar of English) were not submitted to metaphor analysis (see Table 5.2). These include the following:

1   Pronouns. These tend to be co-referential with lexical units (sometimes proper nouns) but have no lexical content on their own. This means that we have excluded the *implicit metaphor* category included in MIPVU (cf. Steen et al., 2010) from our analysis.
2   Other referential words and expressions that have a stand-in relation with a preceding/following expression. Typical examples are demonstratives (this/that/these/those) and determiners (own, several, many, etc.).
3   Other types of elements contributing to textual cohesion are 'here', 'there', 'the above', 'the following', etc. i.e., spatial expressions referring to the discourse, not space.
4   Auxiliaries and modals. All elements that make up the verb group will be discarded for metaphor analysis except the lexical verb (or head of the verbal group), e.g. in 'they wouldn't have wanted' only 'wanted' is analysed as potentially metaphorical.
5   Other closed system items like conjunctions (and, so, but) or existential 'there'.

Establishing the basic meaning

When lexical units were identified, the next step is deciding whether the contextual meaning of the LU identified corresponds to the basic sense of the word. In this project, we had the opportunity to consult the database of basic meanings agreed on by the MIPVU team in their analysis of the BNC.[3] If the basic meaning was not available in that database, it was retrieved in the first place the from MM; if further clarification was needed, the *Longman Dictionary of Contemporary English* (LDCE) was consulted. As established by MIP, the basic meaning is understood as the more physical, concrete, human-oriented sense.

A database with basic meanings was created for this project for internal use. The contextual meaning was identified using MM preferably, and LDCE as second option. Given the difficulty sometimes involved in deciding whether a particular meaning was more concrete than the contextual meaning of the lexical unit (easier to imagine, see, hear, etc.) or related to bodily action, the historical development of a lexical unit was sometimes considered of significance when deciding on its basic sense. In this case, we consulted etymological dictionaries (i.e., the *Oxford English Dictionary*, OED).

MacArthur (2019) explains how such a procedure was effective in determining the basic meaning of *reflect* as used in an office hour conversation (part of the EuroCoAT corpus, cf. MacArthur et al., 2014). The contextual meaning of this verb as it was used in the conversation could be interpreted as 'deflect', in the sense of 'to turn away or aside' (cf. OED, cit. in MacArthur, 2019) and was not attested by MM. This could have led to the conclusion that *reflect* was metaphorically used. However, as MacArthur argues, this sense is in fact more basic as it is equally concrete as one of meanings attested in MM ("to shine back" – light, rays or images –) but it is also historically older.

Deciding metaphor analysis

The final step in the methodology is to determine whether a lexical unit is metaphorical. In this respect, MetCLIL followed the basic principles already explained in the section on MIPVU. The process involves the following decisions:

1   The first decision concerned whether the lexical units selected for analysis were unusual or unexpected in relation to the overall context of a text.
2   After that, attention should be paid to whether this unusual lexis signals some sort of cross-domain mapping where a lexical unit from a specific domain or conceptual area (source) is used to talk about a different domain (target).
3   Next, it is essential to verify whether this cross-domain mapping is reflected explicitly and directly in the text. As a result, a cross-domain comparison between the source and target domains gives rise to a linguistic expression that incorporates vocabulary from both domains. This would be a direct metaphor.
4   If the incongruous lexical unit used is not part of a direct metaphor, the next step is to determine whether its contextual meaning differs from its basic sense, thus indicating an indirectly performed cross-domain comparison.
5   Finally, a tag was used in the database (see transcription sample in Appendix K):
    • _i (Indirect metaphor): used when the LU is considered metaphorical but there is not a direct reference to the metaphor.
    • _d: Direct: used when the LU is considered metaphorical and there is a direct reference to the metaphor.
    • _f (Metaphor flag): this is usually, although not always, an indicator of a direct metaphor e.g., 'like' which is used to connect the two concepts compared.
    • DFMA (discarded from metaphor analysis): used when the LU are not analysed because they are not target words or they are incomplete utterances.

- _w (WIDLII): The problem faced in this step is to identify if there is a real contrast in both meanings in order to consider a lexical unit metaphorical. When the meanings are not exactly the same, but they are not sufficiently different, the tag used is: WIDLII (when in doubt leave it in). We include in this tag metonymy, personification and conflation.
- There is an extra mark-up: unconventional. This is used when the metaphors speakers used are not typical of conventional English. They are analysed as any other LU.

For this last step, metaphor analysis, the research team was organised in pairs, where one expert researcher and one novice worked together on the same fragment of the corpus (usually one seminar) in order to discuss possible disagreements in problematic LUs. Once the pairs had finished analysing their seminar, all seminars were gathered together and revised by two other researchers.

Since the application of general criteria is always problematic, the MetCLIL team thought it important to build a table where the decisions regarding some frequent categories of words were recorded. Table 5.3 reflects some of the decisions made by the MetCLIL team with regard to important word categories or tokens found in the corpus. These are the instructions given to the team and they were necessary because there were both experts and non-expert mippers collaborating in the metaphorical tagging of the corpus.

Conclusion

The first part of the book concludes here. It has focused on introducing the conceptual and methodological framework. This chapter completes the section on methodological aspects, as I have reviewed major metaphor identification procedures in the literature and then introduced the decisions made in the development of the MetCLIL corpus. In the second part of the book, I will present some examples of the quantitative and qualitative analyses that can be carried out using MetCLIL.

Notes

1 Here I use the term 'word' to be clear about the typical unit that is considered in this second step. However, as we shall see later on there are exceptions where multi-word expressions, like compounds for example, are the unit of analysis.
2 Personification has not been dealt with in the present account.
3 MetCLIL is grateful to Gerard Steen and his team for allowing us to access their database.

References

Alejo-González, R. (2010). Making sense of phrasal verbs: A cognitive linguistic account of L2 learning. *AILA Review*, 23(1), 50–71.

Cameron, L. (1999). Identifying and describing metaphor in spoken discourse data. In L. Cameron, & G. Low (Eds.), *Researching and applying metaphor* (pp. 105–132). Cambridge University Press.

Cameron, L. (2006). *MetNet: The metaphor analysis project.* Retrieved 2/3/2007, from http://creet.open.ac.uk/projects/metaphor-analysis/index.cfm

Krennmayr, T. (2011). *Metaphor in newspapers* (Dissertation). LOT Dissertation Series, Utrecht.

Krennmayr, T., & Steen, G. (2017). VU Amsterdam metaphor corpus. In N. Ide & J. Pustejovsky (Eds.), *Handbook of linguistic annotation* (pp. 1053–1071). Springer.

LDCE. Pearson Education Limited. (2018). *Longman English dictionary of advanced English.* Retrieved March 31, 2023, from https://www.ldoceonline.com/dictionary/

MacArthur, F. (2019). Linguistic metaphor identification in English as a Lingua Franca. In S. Nacey, A. G. Dorst, T. Krennmayr, & W. G. Reijnierse (Eds.), *Metaphor identification in multiple languages: MIPVU around the world* (pp. 289–312). John Benjamins.

MacArthur, F., Alejo, R., Piquer-Piriz, A., Amador-Moreno, C., Littlemore, J., Ädel, A., Krennmayr, T., & Vaughn, E. (2014). *EuroCoAT. The European corpus of academic talk.* Retrieved December 20, 2022, from http://www.eurocoat.es

MM. Macmillan English Dictionary. (n.d.). Retrieved March 31, 2023, from https://www.macmillandictionary.com/

Nacey, S. (2013). *Metaphors in learner English [metaphor in language, cognition, and communication 2].* John Benjamins.

Nacey, S., Dorst, A. G., Krennmayr, T., & Reijnierse, W. G. (2019). *Metaphor Identification in multiple languages. MIPVU around the world.* John Benjamins.

OED. Oxford English Dictionary Online. (n.d.). Oxford University Press. Retrieved March 31, 2023, from https://www.oed.com/

Pragglejaz Group. (2007). MIP: A method for identifying metaphorically used words in discourse. *Metaphor and Symbol*, 22(1), 1–39. https://doi.org/10.1080/10926480709336752

Steen, G. (2007). *Finding metaphor in grammar and usage.* John Benjamins.

Steen, G. (2017). Identifying metaphors in language. In E. Semino & Z. Demjén (Eds.), *The Routledge handbook of metaphor and language* (pp. 73–87). Routledge.

Steen, G. J., Dorst, A. G., Herrmann, J. B., Kaal, A. A., & Krennmayr, T. (2010). Metaphor in usage. *Cognitive Linguistics*, 21(4), 765–796.

Wray, A. (1999). Formulaic language in learners and native speakers. *Language Teaching*, 32(4), 213–231.

Wray, A. (2005). *Formulaic language and the lexicon.* Cambridge University Press.

Wray, A. & Fitzpatrick, T. (2008). Why can't you just leave it alone? Deviations from memorized language as a gauge of nativelike competence. In F. Meunier & S. Granger (Eds.), *Phraseology in foreign language learning and teaching* (pp. 123–148). John Benjamins.

6 Quantifying metaphor use
The role of external variables

Quantitative methods in the study of metaphor

As we have already seen in previous chapters, the use of corpora in the study of metaphor has transformed the field of cognitive linguistics, as it provides a systematic and data-driven approach to understanding the complex relationship between language and meaning. By analysing large collections of texts, researchers can gain insights into the ways in which metaphorical expressions are used in natural language, and how their meaning is shaped by the context in which they are used.

As Geeraerts (2010) highlights, this approach is based on the affinity between cognitive semantics and the distributional analysis of corpus data. Cognitive semantics emphasises the role of conceptual structures and mental representations in shaping meaning, while the distributional analysis of corpus data involves analysing the patterns of co-occurrence of words and expressions in large collections of texts. By combining these two approaches, researchers can gain a better understanding of how words combine to provide meaning in real texts.

In addition to highlighting the contextual and variational nature of language, the use of corpora in the study of metaphor also allows for an important addition that has not played a major role in cognitive-linguistic research: quantification. By quantifying linguistic data, researchers can test hypotheses about the relationship between language and cognition and identify patterns that may not be apparent through qualitative analysis alone.

Furthermore, the use of corpora is particularly apt for many of the phenomena that have attracted the attention of cognitive linguistics. For example, the study of metaphor often involves analysing the distribution of metaphorical expressions in different genres or registers, as we will see below. By using corpora to study metaphor, researchers can gain a better understanding of how these expressions are used in different contexts, and how their meaning might vary accordingly.

While the use of quantification in the study of metaphor has been generally seen as a positive development, there are some who have expressed reservations about its utility. One prominent figure in the field who has been vocal in expressing such reticence is Ray Gibbs (cf. 2015, 2017a). Gibbs

DOI: 10.4324/9781003400905-6

has argued that quantification can sometimes obscure the rich and complex nature of metaphorical meaning in discourse. More specifically he points out that frequency is sometimes not the best way to establish the importance of metaphor in a text. Thus, there are moments when a single metaphor can be used to structure the whole text and many of the inferences provided by it are expressed through literal language. He believes that the study of metaphor should focus more on the experiential and embodied aspects of meaning, rather than trying to quantify it in abstract terms.

Despite these concerns, however, many researchers in the field continue to use quantitative methods to study metaphor, arguing that they provide valuable insights into the ways in which metaphorical expressions are used in natural language. They point out that by quantifying linguistic data, they can identify patterns and relationships that might not be apparent through qualitative analysis alone.

Quantitative studies in register and genre variation

The quantitative study of metaphor has provided some interesting examples in the metaphor literature. For example, as recently shown by Semino et al. (2018), metaphor can be of great help to understand and explain the experience of cancer patients. In this book, Semino and colleagues explore how metaphors are used in talking about cancer by three different groups of people: patients, carers and health professionals. Using the concept of framing, i.e., language used to shape the interpretation of events and situations, they found that the frequency of metaphor varied depending on the perspective adopted by the participants analysed in the study. Thus, they found that JOURNEY and VIOLENT metaphors are the ones more frequently used and that patients are more prone to use ANIMAL metaphors to express how they feel.

A different approach can be found in the work of the Vrije Universiteit Amsterdam Corpus (VUAMC) team (Dorst, 2011; Herrmann, 2013; Kaal, 2012; Krennmayr, 2011, 2015; Steen et al., 2010) who study metaphor in different contexts, written academic language being one of them. By using texts from the BNC-Baby corpus and coding them using the Metaphor Identification Procedure designed at the Vrije Universiteit, Amsterdam (MIPVU) (Steen et al., 2010). As already explained in chapter 2, these researchers calculated the metaphor density of the four registers identified in their corpus (i.e., fiction, academic discourse, conversation and news) and, as we saw, academic discourse and news had a higher metaphor density than fiction and conversation. Despite having a high metaphor density, academic discourse had the fewest direct metaphors, which can be attributed to the need for abstractness and complexity in the expression used in specialised subjects.

It is crucial to bear in mind that this examination of metaphor is significantly influenced by the concept of register and is intricately linked to the dimensions proposed by Biber (2006) and Biber & Conrad (2009). This means that they incorporate metaphor as one of the linguistic elements that help categorize a text based on language's functional dimensions. Berber Sardinha (2015) also used Multidimensional Analysis to determine if metaphors could be integrated into these dimensions established by Biber. The conclusion was that a high 'information' score predicts more metaphors, while a high 'involvement' score predicts fewer. This explains the higher metaphor densities in academic texts due to their low 'involvement' scores.

A different framework is used by another group of researchers who study metaphor in academic discourse. They rely more on the study of genre and typically focus on academic lectures, as they hold a prominent position in the network of oral academic genres. The main references in this field are Corts and Pollio (1999); Littlemore et al. (2011); Low et al. (2008) and Low (2010) and their findings can hardly be considered as conclusive as Low himself (2011) acknowledges: these studies covered only a small number of lectures. The preliminary conclusions from the study of lectures are diverse and sometimes far from homogenous. Thus, a preliminary assessment appears to provide a density for university lectures that falls between values comprised between 11% and 13% (Low, 2011), which is certainly low compared to the high density of academic written discourse (18.6%). This observation suggests that metaphor density appears to be significantly influenced in the academic context by the mode of communication, specifically by whether it is oral or written. Also, the genre can be characterised by the use of clusters at key moments of the discourse of the lecturer (Corts & Pollio, 1999), although Low et al. (2008) did not find such conclusive evidence and were only able to identify the presence of a final cluster with the clear rhetorical objective of ending lectures on a high note. Moreover, the use of personification seems to be widespread, as in all academic discourse, and it is normally used "to make the argument more interesting, or to allow access to everyday terminology and thus condense the argument or make it conceptually more accessible" (Low, 2011, p. 13). Finally, university lecturers do not make use of many similes (Low, 2010, 2011; Low et al., 2008) and this finding would be related to the fact the teachers may want to preserve this figure of speech for special cases where they really want to signal the mapping usually with a didactic purpose in the way laid out by Beger (2011) for example.

The other spoken academic genre studied from a quantitative perspective is office hour consultations (e.g. Alejo-González, 2022; MacArthur, 2016a). The novelty of this research is that it addressed, for the first time, the use of metaphor in face-to-face conversations involving L2 speakers of English in an academic context. While previous studies had confirmed that metaphor fulfils important functions in academic discourse and that these language uses often prove problematic for international students, the types of communication addressed were mainly monologic (but see MacArthur, 2011 or MacArthur & Littlemore, 2011, for some insights into metaphor in intercultural conversations). The growing internationalisation of European higher education, encouraged above all by the Erasmus programme, made it imperative to understand more fully what roles metaphor plays in academic mentoring and how its use affects the quality of the interaction. Accordingly, 27 conversations (or just over five hours of face-to-face interaction) were recorded at five different universities (one in Ireland, one in England, one in The Netherlands and two in Sweden) between Spanish undergraduate students and their lecturers. These semi-guided conversations turned on three topics that were of special concern to the students spending between five and nine months as Erasmus students at universities where teaching is carried out in English: the systems of assessments used for the course being taken; an assignment the students had recently completed or were in the process of completing; and problems being experienced in understanding the course contents. The lecturers had different first languages (14 native speakers of English and 6 non-native speakers).

Among the most interesting results of this research was the finding that lecturers appear to use metaphor even more frequently when advising their students on academic topics than they do when delivering a lecture. The figures reported in Low et al. (2008, p. 435) for metaphor use in three university lectures (which varied between 10% and 13%) are lower than the density of metaphors produced only by the lecturers in these conversations: 13.61%. These more frequent uses of metaphor in the academic mentoring sessions can be related to the important role played by metaphor when giving advice and feedback on students' work (especially with realisations of the metaphoric theme THINKING AND UNDERSTANDING IS LOOKING AND SEEING [MacArthur et al., 2015]) and in explaining complex topics. The study of the dispersion of metaphor across the different conversations revealed that bursts of metaphor activity on the part of the lecturer participants responded to great efforts being made to explain concepts the student was having difficulty understanding. The metaphors used tended to cluster at these points in the conversations, with lecturers using overt or direct metaphors (e.g. "think of it as a pyramid") or systematically repeating and developing indirect metaphors (Alejo-González, 2022; MacArthur, 2016a). In contrast, the students used words and phrases metaphorically far less frequently than their interlocutors, a somewhat unsurprising finding, given the overall asymmetry of these interactions, and the fact that the students tended to adopt relatively passive roles in them (MacArthur, 2016b).

Metaphor density in MetCLIL

Overall metaphor density

From a Dynamic System Theory perspective (cf. Gibbs, 2017b), metaphor use can be seen as a dynamic and complex process that involves a delicate balance between stability and instability, and patterns of regularities and variability that shape and are shaped by the specific interaction taking place. In the case of MetCLIL one of the regularities is marked by the specific genre chosen in its compilation – i.e., the discussion seminar. The first part of the present section will deal with a general characterisation of MetCLIL as a way to establish how metaphors are used in a genre whose main purpose is to provide a context for more interactive academic discussions.

In this general characterisation of MetCLIL, I will begin by providing an overview of the presence of metaphor in the corpus and comparing it with the density of metaphor found in different registers analysed in the literature (cf. Steen et al., 2010). This will enable us to understand how the discussion seminar genre fits within the spectrum of registers identified (academic prose, news, fiction, and conversation). By comparing the density of metaphor in the discussion seminar genre to that of registers, we can gain insights into how metaphor is used in this specific context and how it differs from other types of discourse to which it is related. This comparison will also provide a better understanding of the role that metaphor plays in CLIL instruction and the ways in which it is used to facilitate learning.

The description presented here is based on the various types of metaphors identified using MIPVU and the specific adaptations discussed in the previous chapter. Therefore, we must bear in mind that the fundamental distinction established in MIPVU is between Metaphor Related Words (MRWs) and non-Metaphor Related Words (non-MRWs). The category of Metaphor Related Words (MRWs) includes not only direct or indirect metaphors, but also two additional groups, one of which is strictly metaphorical while the other is not. The metaphorical group is the WIDLII category (cf. Chapter 5), which comprises borderline metaphorical cases that are nonetheless considered as metaphor both in MIPVU and in this analysis. The other group corresponds to Metaphor Flags, which are used to signal metaphorical language in the immediate context but are not themselves metaphors. Table 6.1 presents a breakdown of MRWs for each of these categories.

Table 6.1 Number of metaphor related words and density in MetCLIL

		Tokens	%
Metaphor related words (MRWs)	Indirect + direct metaphors	15,209	13.76
	WIDLIIs or borderline metaphors	511	0.46
	Total metaphors	**15,720**	**14.22**
	Metaphor flags	52	0.05
Non-MRWs		94,721	85.73
Total		**110,493**	**100**

Table 6.2 Number of metaphors by main types

	Tokens	%
Indirect metaphors (comprising WIDLII)	15,646	14.20
Direct metaphors	74	0.06
Total metaphors	**15,720**	**14.22**

As can be seen from Table 6.1, the total number of metaphors is quite high with a percentage of metaphor density of 14.2%. We only have to compare this figure with the ones provided by the VUAMC team for the different registers to understand their exact nature. Thus, for example, the register of conversation (Kaal, 2012) only has a metaphor density of 7.7%, whereas Herrmann (2013) demonstrates that the metaphor density of academic written discourse is certainly much higher (18.5%). So, it can be concluded that the density of this type of oral academic discourse, discussion seminars, which is more interactive than the lecture, is closer, in terms of metaphor use, to written academic language than to conversation. In fact, if we compare the figure to the one obtained for another interactive oral genre like office hour consultations (11.9%), where L2 speakers were also involved (cf. Alejo-Gonzalez, 2022), this figure is even higher.

The scarcity of flagged metaphors may be linked to the frequency of different types of metaphors in the corpus, with a tendency to flag direct metaphors more often than other types, although this is not always the case. For the purposes of this discussion, I will focus on indirect metaphors, as the third type proposed by MIPVU (implicit metaphors) was not tagged in MetCLIL, as it was not deemed worthy of study. The final count of these two main types of metaphors is introduced in Table 6.2

The percentage of direct metaphors is really low, but this should be no surprise since except for fiction (Dorst, 2011) where we can find 165 direct metaphors representing 0.4% of all the metaphors found in that specific BNC-Baby subcorpus. The rest of the registers studied by the VUAMC group (Herrmann, 2013; Kaal, 2012; Krennmayr, 2011) show similar numbers to the ones given here for MetCLIL corpus.

Variation in MetCLIL

Comparing seminars

One of the most evident sources of variation is the specific seminar, as it determines the immediate context of the interaction, where factors such as the topic or the particular teaching strategies may play an important role.

Table 6.3 shows that the densities of direct and indirect metaphors together, expressed in percentages. Overall, the data suggests that the levels

Table 6.3 Metaphor density in MetCLIL seminars

Seminars	Country	Seminar total tokens	Indirect metaphor tokens	Direct metaphor tokens	Density	Residuals
Sem 1	Spain	12,039	1,752	4	14.6%	1.3
Sem 2		12,085	1,852	10	15.4%*	3.9
Sem 3		10,200	1,548	3	15.2%*	3.1
Sem 4	Italy	8,674	1,202	0	13.9%	-.8
Sem 5	Portugal	8,681	1,232	0	14.2%	0.1
Sem 6	Norway	14,854	2,191	22	14.9%*	2.2
Sem 7	Sweden	10,708	1,203	2	11.3%*	-9.1
Sem 8		12,135	1,350	5	11.2%*	-10.2
Sem 9	The Netherlands	21,117	3,316	28	15.8%*	15.7
	Total	110,493	15,646	74	14.2%	

*Significantly different densities: p<.000; Chi-Square: 237.327; Cramer's V: 0.046

of metaphorical density in the seminars are relatively similar, with the highest density of 15.8% in Sem 9 at the Dutch university and the lowest density of 11.2% in Sem 8 at the Swedish university. However, after performing a Chi-Square analysis, we can notice that some differences in density are statistically significant (marked with *), although the effect size (Cramer's V) is certainly very small. In other words, even such small differences should not be dismissed, especially when we know that the difference in metaphorical density between academic prose and news registers is also small (18.5% and 16.4%, respectively, see Steen et al., 2010). Such small differences may be indicative of other disparities.

Interestingly, by only looking at the metaphor densities, we can already notice certain trends. Thus, for example, the Dutch seminar appears to have a metaphorical density that is closer to academic prose (18.5%), while the Swedish seminars have a density that is closer to conversational language (7.7%). In interpreting these numbers, we face the specific nature of the discussion seminar as an academic genre characterised by oral interaction, which can lead to a fluctuation in the use of metaphors between academic and conversational features. Since the topic of discussion is usually specialised, the use of metaphors may also reflect the language of the academic register and, at the same time, the face-to-face conversational nature of the discourse may lead participants to adopt a more oral style in their use of metaphors. In this sense, metaphor use may be reflecting a dual characterisation that had already been observed in the case of L1 academic lectures:

> [U]niversity classroom communication features aspects of both academic writing and face-to-face conversation, thus supporting Biber et al.'(2004) contention that university classroom communication mixes characteristics of oral and literate discourses.
>
> (Lee, 2020, p. 84)

In the case of metaphor analysis, it may be valuable to employ a second type of analysis similar to the one conducted by the VUAMC group to examine the use of metaphors in various registers. In this approach, the frequency of metaphors is analysed by part of speech. As demonstrated by Steen et al. (2010) in their research on numerical data, metaphor densities not only vary across registers, but this disparity extends to the different parts of speech (nouns, verbs, etc.) used in the different registers. Therefore, focusing on the two registers of interest, academic prose and conversation, as they are the ones referred to by Lee in the citation above, it is noticeable that in academic prose, metaphorical prepositions and verbs are the most commonly used, with nouns also being overused (cf. Herrmann, 2013). In contrast, in conversation all parts of speech tend to show a certain degree of underuse of metaphorical words in comparison to the rest of registers, although with metaphorical prepositions (and also with determiners and adjectives) this trend is less pronounced (Kaal, 2012).

Table 6.4 contains information from the Chi-Square analysis that aimed to identify the parts of speech that were metaphorically used more frequently in each seminar. It includes the metaphor count, the expected count, the percentage of the total count of that part of speech in the seminar, and the adjusted residuals. Adjusted residuals greater than 2 or less than -2 indicate statistical significance when the chi-square and the Cramer's V are also significant. In this case, the only PoS that shows non-significant results is the category of Adjectives, which has a p value greater than 0.05 and a Cramer's V of 0.051. The rest of p values are highly significant (p <.000) although with moderate Cramer's V value (Adv.=0.079, Other=0.025, Verb=0.054). However, both nouns and prepositions show a greater Cramer's V (with 0.118 and 0.137 respectively) indicating that the strength of the results found is greater.

Given these results, there is one seminar that fits the description given above for the metaphorical use of the different parts of speech. This seminar is the Dutch seminar, which shows overuse of metaphorical nouns, prepositions and verbs. This would indicate that the patterns of metaphor used in this seminar approach it to the more academic end of the spectrum defined above. The seminar is clearly the one adopting a more theoretical stance as can be seen from the following example:

> in books of logic (.) they describe it as basically that there is no er (.) there's no real (.) credible <u>link between</u> one (.) eh? (.) one er <u>target</u> literature and the <u>ground</u> literature so this correspondence it doesn't actually <u>work</u> (2) erm (1) and this is erm (.) weirdly enough if you (.) er (.) if if I review a paper that <u>comes in</u> and people use analogies that's usually the <u>thing</u> that is <u>going</u> wrong (.) is that that assumptions are just <u>bringing in</u> and you forget to actually <u>make</u> it a credible analogy eh that it actually <u>works</u> so-that they call it here the <u>structural soundness</u> is er is er <u>off</u> the <u>mark</u> so you need to do some actual intellectual <u>handwork</u> craft to <u>make sure</u> that the analogy is is believable

The distribution of different parts of speech among the remaining seminars is not as clear-cut, but we can still perceive some trends. On the one hand, Sem 6 (Norway) also shows a tendency, typical of the Dutch seminar and academic prose, to overuse metaphorical nouns, prepositions and adverbs, although the use of metaphorical verbs is not as frequent. On the other, while the majority of the other seminars do not exhibit a distinct pattern, the two Swedish seminars can be categorised as approaching the pattern of metaphor use in the conversational register due to their underuse of metaphorical prepositions and verbs. As for metaphorical nouns, both do not show underuse, but one of them is close to significance with a residual of -1.8. Here we have an example from the Swedish Sem 7 where the difference with the example above can be noticed:

Table 6.4 Statistical analysis of metaphorical PoS by seminar

		Spain Sem1	Spain Sem2	Spain Sem3	Italy	Portugal	Norway	Sweden Sem 1	Sweden Sem 2	The Netherlands	Total
Adj. (p=059, Cramer's V=051)	Count	90	82	96	80	93	99	119	114	229	1002
	Expected count	106	89.2	93	100.2	88.4	105.8	103.9	106	209.6	1002
	% within seminar	14.50%	15.70%	17.60%	13.70%	18.00%	16.00%	19.60%	18.40%	18.70%	17.10%
	Adjusted residual	-1.8	-0.9	0.4	-2.3	0.6	-0.8	1.7	0.9	1.7	
Adv. (p<.000, Cramer's V=0.079)	Count	110	91	94	24	52	152	69	46	239	877
	Expected count	99.1	94.5	95.1	50.5	53.8	107.8	83.2	81.7	211.2	877
	% within seminar	10.1%	8.8%	9.0%	4.3%	8.8%	12.9%	7.6%	5.1%	10.3%	9.10%
	Adjusted residual	1.2	-0.4	-0.1	-4	-0.3	4.8	-1.7	-4.3	2.3	
Noun(p<.000, Cramer's V=0.118)	Count	384	407	331	370	266	578	303	365	993	3997
	Expected count	442.2	441.8	372.4	430.2	360.1	520.6	332.9	394.9	702	3997
	% within seminar	20.6%	21.8%	21.0%	20.4%	17.%	26.3%	21.6%	21.9%	33.5%	23.7%
	Adjusted residual	-3.4	-2	-2.6	-3.5	-5.9	3.1	-2	-1.8	13.8	

(Continued)

		Spain Sem1	Spain Sem2	Spain Sem3	Italy	Portugal	Norway	Sweden Sem 1	Sweden Sem 2	The Netherlands	Total
Other(p<.000, Cramer's V=0.025)	Count	25	15	8	6	14	34	9	8	22	141
	Expected count	14.5	15.2	12	9.6	10.4	19.9	15.1	17	27.3	141
	% within seminar	0.5%	0.3%	0.2%	0.2%	0.%	0.5%	0.2%	0.1%	0.2%	0.3%
	Adjusted residual	2.9	0	-1.2	-1.2	1.2	3.4	-1.7	-2.3	-1.1	
Prep. (p<.000, Cramer's V=0.137)	Count	496	632	502	348	321	620	306	362	848	4435
	Expected count	543.4	570.4	433.1	400.1	342.1	524.6	378.2	447.9	795.1	4435
	% within seminar	46.4%	56.3%	58.9%	44.2%	47.7%	60.1%	41.1%	41.1%	54.2%	50.%
	Adjusted residual	-3.1	3.9	5	-3.9	-1.7	6.3	-5.5	-6.1	3	
Verb (p<.000, Cramer's V=0.054)	Count	647	625	517	374	486	708	397	455	985	5194
	Expected count	595.9	576.2	512.5	400.7	446.1	742.8	459.2	550.3	910.4	5194
	% within seminar	26.8%	26.8%	24.9%	23.0%	26.9%	23.5%	21.3%	20.4%	26.7%	24.7%
	Adjusted residual	2.6	2.5	0.2	-1.6	2.3	-1.6	-3.5	-4.9	3.1	

Table 6.5 Metaphorical type/token ratio

Seminars	Country	Metaphor tokens	Metaphor types (C)	Metaphorical type/token ratio
Sem 1	Spain	1,756	414	0.236
Sem 2		1,862	399	0.214
Sem 3		1,551	348	0.224
Sem 4	Italy	1,202	368	0.306
Sem 5	Portugal	1,232	379	0.308
Sem 6	Norway	2,213	462	0.209
Sem 7	Sweden	1,205	305	0.253
Sem 8		1,355	352	0.260
Sem 9	The Netherlands	3,344	760	0.227
	Total	15,720	1,859	0.118

SQD, SWEDEN Sem 7: yes yes in the case of my country erm it's quite m-- it has a-lot of influences from different other countries so you have (.) especially in terms-of religion you have the Muslim religion it's very strong in the north side of my country and em so when like certain kind of products and and companies that want to go up north or either they will not succeed so much if it's like in the food sector and you you of course you just meat that is (swin) em it will not succeed probably because most of the population is Muslim and also the approaches for marketing for the marketing campaigns needs to be different needs to be readjusted and erm it needs to be inclusive erm like we have done have done some campaigns and they had to include all diversities of erm different people

The type/token ratio in the metaphors used is another indicator of the specific academic nature of certain seminars. Thus, a high type/token ratio would be indicative of a large variability in the use of metaphors which counter expectations is not typical of the academic register:

> The results thus suggest that journalists draw on a variety of metaphorical lexical items to transfer a message to the audience, while writers of academic texts tend to reuse metaphorical nouns that are perceived as conventional by the expert audience. Thus academic writers seem to value consistency, whereas journalists tend to aim for stylistic variation.
>
> (Krennmayr, 2017, p. 175)

In MetCLIL, the low type/token ratio of metaphors precisely occurs in those seminars (see Table 6.5) that we had already identified as sharing some of the characteristics of metaphor use in the academic register. Sem 6 (Norway) and Sem 9 (The Netherlands), together with Sem 2 and 3 (Spain) are the ones showing a lower type/token ratio.

Comparing groupings

The interactional nature of the discussion seminar as a genre is most evident when we analyse the different types of activities devised with the aim of facilitating the participation of students. One of these activities is small group discussions in which students are asked to share their thoughts and ideas, and to actively listen to the contributions of their peers, while at the same time allowing them to build on and respond to each other's ideas, sometimes using a prompt provided by the lecturer.

This type of grouping is adopted in several of the seminars of MetCLIL, for example in the case of Sem 6 in Norway. However, the logistics of the recording did not allow us to record more than one of the small group inter-actions in that seminar. Fortunately, the case of the three Spanish seminars is different since it was possible to record the small groups working in parallel.

These seminars aimed to enhance students' skills in presenting and pro-moting themselves or their ideas by incorporating a series of interactive activities based on the concept of an 'elevator pitch' – a concise, compelling speech used in Marketing to pitch an idea, product, service or oneself. The seminars were divided into three main stages, each with different dynamics.

During the first stage, which lasted 50 minutes, each student presented a 30-second 'short pitch' to the entire class, aiming to sell their idea or them-selves to a hypothetical employer or investor. The presentations were fol-lowed by a whole-class discussion, facilitated by the lecturer, where students provided feedback to the presenter and suggested areas for improvement.

In the second stage, the class was divided into two subgroups, and each student presented their pitch in an extended format of 90 seconds. The sub-groups provided feedback and comments on each presentation, and the lec-turer observed without interfering. At the end of this stage, the subgroups selected the best pitch from their respective groups.

In the final stage, the most successful 90-second pitches were presented to the whole class, followed by comments on different strategies and tech-niques used by the presenters to sell themselves or their ideas. The session concluded with a reflection on what made some pitches more successful than others.

The dynamics of the seminars could, as a result, be divided into two dis-tinct forms of interaction: whole-group discussions and split group discus-sions. In each of these two forms of interaction, the context for students to use language was different. As a result, I thought that this could have an impact the way they engaged in the use of metaphor.

According to Table 6.6, where only the students' data are considered, the metaphor densities of activities conducted in split groups (6 groups total across 3 Spanish seminars) were consistently lower than those of activities conducted in whole groups. These findings suggest that the nature of group interactions may impact the use of metaphors in communication. It would seem that while whole class activities tended to use densities more typical of

Table 6.6 Use of metaphor by type of interaction

Students		Whole group	Split groups
Sem 1	Tokens	2,973	5,511
	Metaphors	432	705
	Density	14.5%	12.8%
Sem 2	Tokens	6,093	4,070
	Metaphors	1,006	532
	Density	16.5%	13.1%
Sem 3	Tokens	2,410	4,034
	Metaphors	383	535
	Density	15.9%	13.3%

academic language, small group interactions allowed for a style where the demands for metaphor use was not as high, even when the central focus of students' speech was delivering a marketing pitch.

Comparing subcorpora: The Northern vs Southern EMI divide

In Chapter 3, it was already emphasised that one of the main design features of MetCLIL was aimed at investigating the North-South divide in the implementation of English-Medium Instruction (EMI) programmes in the European Higher Education Area (EHEA). This divide was identified by Wächter and Maiworm (2014), who not only reported a significant rise in the number of EMI programmes implemented in European universities over the previous 20 years, growing by 239% within a 7-year period (2007–2014), but also emphasised that the increase was also not uniform across countries, with Northern European countries (Nordic and West Central European countries) having a far higher number of EMI programmes (60.6% and 44.5% of universities, respectively) compared to South Western European countries (17%). This data suggest that the longer teaching tradition of Northern institutions in English-Medium Instruction (EMI) or English-Taught Programmes (ETP) may result in a more sophisticated use of academic registers, which could in turn contribute to a greater comfort level with using metaphors in teaching and communication. This could be due to a greater familiarity with the nuances of academic language, which allows for more creative use of metaphors to convey complex ideas.

However, the results in Table 6.7 show that this is not the case of the seminars from the Southern European institutions recorded in MetCLIL. Obviously, there may be other factors at play (e.g., the proficiency level of the students, the topics of the seminar, etc.) that could have greater impact than the institutional context and tradition of the universities where the seminars take place. We will see some of them in the following chapter.

Table 6.7 Metaphor density: the North/South divide

Country	# Seminars	Tokens	# Indirect metaphors	# Direct metaphors	Density
Southern EMI	Sems (1-5)	51,679	7,586	17	14.7%
Northern and Central EMI	Sems (6-9)	58,814	8,060	57	13.8%
Total		110,493	15,646	74	14.2%

Metaphor frequency

To end this more global characterisation of MetCLIL, I will deal with the most frequent metaphorical lemmas used in all the seminars that make up the corpus. Table 6.7 lists the metaphors most frequently used in MetCLIL with information that corroborates that their frequency is not the result of the entrenchment of a particular metaphor by a concrete speaker nor the consequence of its use in a particular seminar. This is why two measures included in Sketch Engine are provided. On the one hand, the acronym DOCF indicates the number (F) of documents (DOC) where the lemma was found in such a way that the maximum in MetCLIL would be 9, which corresponds to the total of seminars. On the other, the Average Reduced Frequency (ARF) is a measure intended to counterbalance frequencies derived from a high concentration of tokens in a portion of the corpus. In this way, the ARF of lemmas that are spread out through the corpus would be higher than the one of those only appearing in one seminar. Besides, I also include the frequency, the metaphoricity and the normalised frequency of the metaphorical lemmas. Metaphoricity measures the ratio of metaphorical uses of the lemma in relation to the total number of hits of that lemma. Finally the two last columns give the rank order in MetCLIL and also in EuroCoAT, the corpus of office-hours consultations.

The lemmas appearing in the list are mostly prepositions (*in, about, on, with, from, at, by*) and light verbs like *get* and *give* (see Table 6.8). In fact, if we compare the most frequent metaphorical lemmas of MetCLIL and EuroCoAT, we can see that there is a high degree of overlap between the two lists, which indicates that there seems to be a core of metaphorical lemmas for academic oral interaction.

Conclusion

In summary, this chapter has offered an in-depth exploration of metaphors within the MetCLIL corpus. Our analysis of corpus density reveals that the discussion seminars under scrutiny exhibit a notably high degree of metaphorical usage, especially when compared to other genres and registers. This

Table 6.8 Frequent metaphorical lemmas in MetCLIL

Item	Frequency	DOCF	ARF	Met frq	Metaphoricity	Metaphor norm. Frq. per 10k	Rank in MetCLIL	Rank in EuroCoAT
in	1724	9	986.53516	1256	0.728838	113.6724	1	1
have	1621	9	948.56	648	0.39975	62.809	2	2
about	696	9	377.62482	694	0.97126	62.80941	3	3
on	559	9	300.45679	520	0.930233	47.0618	4	5
with	524	9	296.5553	396	0.755725	35.83937	5	-
thing	346	9	195.52211	346	1	31.3142	6	6
from	407	9	223.48636	333	0.818182	30.13766	7	-
get	287	9	145.05849	274	0.954704	24.79795	8	8
give	268	9	122.96332	253	0.94403	22.89738	9	15
at	322	9	178.45439	240	0.745342	21.72083	10	7
way	224	9	125.12481	217	0.96875	19.63925	11	16
make	266	9	142.56065	213	0.800752	19.27724	12	12
look	238	9	112.81658	199	0.836134	18.01019	13	14
go	271	9	149.33289	175	0.645756	15.83811	14	9
see	213	9	118.95137	153	0.71831	13.84703	15	13
up	146	9	78.56924	143	0.979452	12.942	16	21
take	128	9	67.92859	126	0.984375	11.40344	17	18
culture	115	7	33.83518	115	1	10.4079	18	
point	140	9	67.32046	112	0.8	10.13639	19	
pitch	112	4	32.28881	110	0.982143	9.955382	20	
by	160	9	85.38183	109	0.68125	9.864878	21	
come	189	9	96.53522	106	0.560847	9.593368	22	
article	103	8	33.7999	103	1	9.321857	23	
feel	106	9	49.24885	96	0.90566	8.688333	24	
part	99	9	45.26969	89	0.89899	8.054809	25	

heightened metaphorical presence underscores the academic nature inherent in the speech events that constitute this corpus. Nonetheless, we cannot unequivocally assert uniformity in metaphor frequency across all the diverse speech events, as our analysis has unveiled certain variations. These variations are discernible in factors such as the nature of the speech event itself (ranging from academically inclined to less academically oriented), the grouping dynamics within the classroom (encompassing whole seminar discussions versus smaller group interactions), and the specific choice of metaphorical expressions. It is noteworthy that more academically focused subjects, whole seminar discussions, exhibit a greater density of metaphorical language with a preference for prepositions and light verbs. However, it is important to highlight that our hypothesis regarding Southern-based universities displaying a lower degree of metaphor density than their Northern counterparts does not find support in the data. In the next chapter, the analysis of individual variables, instead of the contextual ones analysed here, will be undertaken.

References

Alejo-González, R. (2022). Metaphor in the academic mentoring of international undergraduate students: The Erasmus experience. *Metaphor and Symbol, 37*(1), 1–20. https://doi.org/10.1080/10926488.2021.1941969

Beger, A. (2011). Deliberate metaphors? An exploration of the choice and functions of metaphors in US-American college lectures. *Metaphorik. de, 20*, 39–60.

Berber-Sardinha, T. (2015). Register variation and metaphor use: A multi-dimensional perspective. In J. B. Herrmann & T. Berber Sardinha (Eds.), *Metaphor in specialist discourse* (pp. 17–52). John Benjamins.

Biber, D. (2006). *University language: A corpus-based study of spoken and written registers.* John Benjamins.

Biber, D., & Conrad, S. (2009). *Register, genre, and style.* Cambridge University Press.

Biber, D., Conrad, S., & Cortes, V. (2004). *If you look at...*: Lexical bundles in university teaching and textbooks. *Applied Linguistics, 25*(2), 371–405.

Corts, D. P., & Pollio, H. R. (1999). Spontaneous production of figurative language and gesture in college lectures. *Metaphor and Symbol, 14*(2), 81–100.

Dorst, A. G. (2011). *Metaphor in fiction: Language, thought and communication.* Box Press Uitgeverij.

Geeraerts, D. (2010). *Theories of lexical semantics.* Oxford University Press.

Gibbs, R. W. (2015). Counting metaphors: What does it reveal about language and thought? *Cognitive Semantics, 1*(2), 155–177.

Gibbs, R. W. (2017a). *Metaphor wars.* Cambridge University Press.

Gibbs, R. W. (2017b). Metaphor, language, and dynamical systems. In E. Semino & Z. Demjén (Eds.), *The Routledge handbook of metaphor and language* (pp. 56–69). Routledge.

Herrmann, J. B. (2013). *Metaphor in academic discourse: Linguistic forms, conceptual structures, communicative functions and cognitive representations* (Dissertation). LOT Dissertation Series, Utrecht.

Herrmann, J. B. (2015). High on metaphor, low on simile? An examination of metaphor type in sub-registers of academic prose. In J. B. Herrmann & T. Berber Sardinha (Eds.), *Metaphor in specialist discourse* (pp. 163–190). John Benjamins.

Kaal, A. A. (2012). *Metaphor in conversation.* Uitgeverij Box Press.

Krennmayr, T. (2011). *Metaphor in newspapers* (Dissertation). LOT Dissertation Series, Utrecht.

Krennmayr, T. (2015). What corpus linguistics can tell us about metaphor use in newspaper texts. *Journalism Studies, 16*(4), 530–545.

Krennmayr, T. (2017). Metaphor and parts of speech. In E. Semino & Z. Demjén (Eds.), *The Routledge handbook of metaphor and language* (pp. 165–177). Routledge.

Lee, J. L. (2020). Spoken classroom discourse. In E. Friginal & J. A. Hardy (Eds.), *The Routledge handbook of corpus approaches to discourse analysis* (pp. 82–97). Routledge.

Littlemore, J., Chen, P. T., Koester, A., & Barnden, J. (2011). Difficulties in metaphor comprehension faced by international students whose first language is not English. *Applied linguistics, 32*(4), 408–429.

Low, G. (2010). Wot no similes? The curious absence of simile in university lectures. In G. D. Low, Z. Todd, A. Deignan, & L. Cameron (Eds.), *Researching and applying metaphor in the real world* (pp. 291–308). John Benjamins.

Low, G. (2011). "Pin me down a bit more." Researching metaphor in university lectures. *International Journal of Innovation and Leadership in the Teaching of Humanities, 1*(1), 6–22.

Low, G. D., Littlemore, J., & Koester, A. (2008). Metaphor use in three UK university lectures. *Applied Linguistics, 29*(3), 428–455.

MacArthur, F. (2011). On the use of metaphor in office hours' consultations carried out in English between lecturers and students with different first languages. *International Journal of Innovation and Leadership in the Teaching of Humanities, 1*(1), 23–44.

MacArthur, F. (2016a). Beyond engaged listenership: Assessing Spanish undergraduates' active participation in academic mentoring sessions in English as academic lingua franca. In J. Romero-Trillo (ed.) *Yearbook of corpus linguistics and pragmatics 2016: Global implications for culture and society in the networked age* (pp. 153–178) Springer.

MacArthur, F. (2016b). Overt and covert uses of metaphor in the academic mentoring in English of Spanish undergraduate students at five European universities. *Review of Cognitive Linguistics, 14*(1), 23–50.

MacArthur, F., & Littlemore, J. (2011). On the repetition of words with the potential for metaphoric extension in conversations between native and non-native speakers of English. *Metaphor and the Social World, 1*(2), 201–238.

MacArthur, F., Krennmayr, T., & Littlemore, J. (2015). How basic is "understanding is seeing" when reasoning about knowledge? Asymmetric uses of sight hours in office hours consultations in English as Academic Lingua Franca. *Metaphor and Symbol, 30*(3), 184–217.

Semino, E., Demjén, Z., Hardie, A., Payne, S., & Rayson, P. (2018). *Metaphor, cancer and the end of life: A corpus-based study.* Routledge.

Steen, G. J., Dorst, A. G., Herrmann, J. B., Kaal, A. A., & Krennmayr, T. (2010). Metaphor in usage. *Cognitive Linguistics, 21*(4), 765–796.

Wächter, B., & Maiworm, F. (Eds.). (2014). *English-taught Programmes in European higher education: The state of play in 2014.* Lemmens.

7 Individual variables

In the previous chapter, some ways in which the use of metaphors is influenced by the immediate context were considered. Specifically, the quantitative analysis focused on the results metaphor density obtained in the genre of discussion seminars, which was one of the key parameters in the compilation the MetCLIL corpus. While the analysis started at the generic level, the results were also contrasted with those obtained for a broader context of use defined by different registers, as well as with the lower level of specific activities within the seminars involving smaller groupings. It was considered important to take into account different levels of context as a single level does not cover all possible influencing factors. In fact, in addition to examining those contextual levels, the chapter ended with the exploration of the 'cultural' context defined by the specific academic institutions where the seminars took place. This allowed us to consider how the importance and tradition of EMI programmes might influence metaphor use.

In this chapter, however, the focus is shifted to the individuals who use those metaphors. Specifically, the individual differences that may be found in metaphor use will be explored. It is posited that metaphor use reflects not only the constraints imposed by the context, but also the individual characteristics of the users. The analysis of individual differences in the analysis of a corpus is only possible because of the questionnaire passed to the different participants during the recording which allowed us to gather important information from the participants.

Individual variables in metaphor use

The field of Psychology has long been associated with the concept of individual differences, giving rise to a specialised area of research known as Differential Psychology or Individual Difference Research, but while this perspective has been widely applied to Second Language Acquisition (e.g., Dörnyei & Ryan, 2015), the same cannot be said for metaphor studies. Some researchers have even described the situation in the following way: "[I]ndividual differences in metaphoric thinking have received almost no attention" (Fetterman et al., 2016, p. 258). It would seem that the main schools concerned with the study of metaphor, described in Chapter 1, have imposed a programme focused

DOI: 10.4324/9781003400905-7

on describing general rather than specific metaphor use associated with individuals. Winter et al. (2020), citing Dabrowska (2016), label the ignorance of individual differences as one of the 'deadly sins' of cognitive linguistics.

In her recent book on the sources of variation in embodied metaphor, Littlemore (2019) not only makes reference to individual differences as one of the sources of variation, but also gives an overview of the most important ones. Chapter 8 of the book specifically deals with some of these differences, which she categorises into two main groups: internally driven individual differences and externally driven (social) sources of variation. Among the former, Littlemore mentions individual differences such as analogical reasoning ability, conscientiousness, body consciousness, need for power, need for cognition, creativity and psychopathy, while in the latter we can find ideology and political persuasion and religious and spiritual beliefs. Thus, to give some examples she mentions, it has been found that positive metaphors (e.g., "thinking outside the box") result in improved creativity, whereas negative ones (e.g., "burnt out") reduce it and this transfer effect is stronger in people scoring high on analogical reasoning (cf. Marin et al., 2014). Similarly, a study she carried out together with Frank Boers (Boers & Littlemore, 2000) shows how holistic thinkers are more likely to use creative metaphors that are more easily explained as the result of a blending process (e.g., "this surgeon is a butcher" described by Fauconnier & Turner, 2008), while imagers were more prone to use conventionalised metaphors of the kind described by CMT (cf. Chapter 1). Finally, within the group of externally driven (social) individual differences, we find that people with different political beliefs may use different metaphors to describe the same concept, reflecting their different worldviews.

The majority of studies on individual differences cited by Littlemore (2019) have a psychological bent. This means that there is a preference for the use of tests in controlled situations and for more experimental approaches of the kind cited by Gibbs (2017, Chapter 5). This involves a preference for techniques such as, for example, describing thoughts after speaking metaphorically, reflecting on metaphorical meaning, generating metaphorical mappings, measuring the time employed in understanding metaphor meanings and studying the mental images formed by individuals. Corpus-based methodologies would thus be left to studies concentrating on the study of metaphor use in discourse since the data obtained are not considered to be helpful to understand elements related to metaphor processing in both language production and comprehension.

However, some corpus analyses have already been used to study how the individual features of the language have been shown to correlate with personality traits. Thus, Gill (2004 cit. in Barlow, 2013) has studied how certain combinations of words (e.g., *forward to, I'll* or *as well*) were associated with high extraverts, whereas low extraverts would have a preference for other combinations (*I don't, all the, one of,* or *I can*). But it is the recently growing field of Learner Corpus Research (LCR) where the attention to individual variables has been given relevance mostly because learner corpora have incorporated richer information from the speakers and, most importantly, because the new analyses in the field have helped to dispel "[the] common-place misconception among non-corpus linguists that corpora only contain massive pools of data collapsed over anonymized speakers, with no option to tie data points to the individual speaker who produced them" (Wulff & Gries, 2021, p. 193).

At the end of this chapter, certain individual variables, for which data was gathered via a questionnaire in the compilation of MetCLIL, will be explored. However, before delving into that analysis, a review of the literature pertaining to those variables that are linked to the presented data will be conducted.

L2 metaphor use

Metaphorical competence

The literature has connected the use of metaphor by second language (L2) speakers to the concept of "metaphorical competence" (Danesi, 1992, 2008, 2016; Littlemore, 2001; Littlemore & Low, 2006a). Danesi's notion of "Conceptual Fluency" (1992) equates metaphorical competence in L2 acquisition to communicative competence, with the former being defined as the learners' mental capacity to use figurative discourse systematically. This implies that, like other aspects of the L2, figurative language can be taught systematically. Low's (1988) definition emphasises the importance of learners developing metaphorical competence to be seen as competent users of the target language. Littlemore (2001) goes further to identify four main components of metaphorical competence: originality of metaphor production, fluency of metaphor interpretation, ability to find meaning in metaphor, and speed in finding meaning in metaphor. Littlemore and Low (2006b) highlight the importance of figurative language in L2 learning and demonstrate that learners encounter aspects of metaphor at all stages of proficiency and in all dimensions of communicative competence. All of these accounts of metaphorical competence illustrate the intrinsic complexity of the construct and the applied linguists' concerns regarding its applicability in the foreign language learning process.

Recently, there have been proposals to empirically measure L2 learners' metaphorical competence based on these theoretical notions. Thus, O'Reilly (2017) and O'Reilly and Marsden (2021, 2023) have recently developed a battery of tests (available on www.iris-database.org), based on Low and Littlemore's construct to measure what they called productive illocutionary metaphoric competence (MC), metaphor language play, topic/vehicle acceptability and grammatical MC. The tests were administered to 112 L1 Mandarin speakers of L2 English and 31 L1 English speakers in order to measure the validity of both the theoretical constructs and the tests designed obtaining good results. Furthermore, Castellano-Risco and Piquer-Píriz

(2020) propose the analysis of a specific dimension of metaphorical competence, specifically, the understanding/recognition of metaphor (which corresponds to Littlemore's [2001] third dimension: "ability to find meaning in metaphor"), as they consider that L2 learners' understanding of metaphorical meanings is part of their general lexical competence which is defined as the ability to recognise and use the words of an L2 in a native-like way (cf. López-Mezquita, 2005).

In summary, it could be said that metaphorical competence is strongly linked to a more global capacity in the sense of Danesi's "conceptual fluency" or Littlemore and Low's "figurative thinking" that consists in the ability to use our knowledge of concrete things to understand abstract concepts. As is well known, this is the basis of the Cognitive Linguistic paradigm (Lakoff & Johnson, 1980, 1999). This natural ability is conceptual and, therefore, not restricted to the way we reason in our native language but also applicable to other languages we may happen to speak. Any understanding of metaphorical competence as a strategy employed by L2 learners cannot be seen in isolation.

Metaphor in L2 production

Although there has been an attempt to relate learners' metaphorical competence and their overall language proficiency (Teymouri & Dowlatabadi, 2014), the bulk of research studies in this area, and the most interesting one for the present book, consists of corpus work that has focused on measuring learners' production of metaphor (Littlemore's [2001] first component, i.e., "originality of metaphor production") in their written outputs. For example, Nacey (2013) reports a comparison between Norwegian, advanced learners' texts extracted from the Norwegian subset of the International Corpus of Learner English (NICLE) and those produced by British L1 novice writers from the Louvain Corpus of Native English Essays (LOCNESS); and Turner (2014) analyses the presence of metaphor in exam-based written production of French and Japanese learners of English. One of the most comprehensive and ambitious studies into learners' production of metaphor so far is Littlemore et al. (2014). Using the Cambridge Learner Corpus of exam scripts, they analysed two hundred essays produced by successful Greek and German learners of English across five of the levels (A2 to C2) established by the Common European Framework of Reference for Languages (CEFRL) in order to determine the amount of metaphor employed at the different stages and the different functions for which learners used those metaphors. The authors found that metaphor usage increased as students progressed through the levels, and so did the sophistication of the function for which learners used metaphors. However, error rates involving metaphor remained significantly higher than general error rates, even at the higher levels, and L1 transfer was seen to have an effect on metaphor-related errors. Along this line of research, Hoang and Boers (2018) have also explored the association of advanced, EFL learners' writing proficiency and their use of metaphorical language in a more homogenous corpus consisting of 252 essays produced by language majors from three year levels in an undergraduate programme at a university in Vietnam. Correct metaphor use was also found to be strongly correlated with the students' year levels and the grades awarded to the essays.

L1 induced variation: the role of transfer

The influence of a speaker's L1 cannot be ignored when exploring a corpus of L2 speakers, as demonstrated by the extensive literature on language transfer (e.g., Odlin, 1989). It is highly likely that the L2 linguistic production of the speaker will incorporate certain features of their L1, including phonological, morphological and syntactic aspects, as well as lexical and pragmatic factors.

However, as suggested by Jarvis and Pavlenko (2008) there are other features of a more conceptual nature that may not be as easily noticeable as they do not rely on formal similarities or differences between languages. Metaphor obviously falls under this last category as is recognised in the following quotation:

> L2 acquisition involves learning another way of thinking-for-speaking (Cadierno, 2004) or learning to re-think for speaking (Robinson & Ellis, 2008), that is, learning to re-categorize and construe "the world" like the L2 native speakers of the foreign language. This also involves acquiring the linguistic metaphors and metonymies that are characteristic of the L2 as well as their underlying conceptual metaphors and metonymies.
>
> (Cadierno & Hijazo-Gascón, 2014, p. 102)

The above quotation also establishes a connection, obviously related to cognition, between the predictions made by the 'thinking for speaking' hypothesis (Slobin, 1996, 1997, 2000, 2003) and the acquisition and use of metaphors in an L2. In fact, this is not strange since this hypothesis mostly refers to the linguistic patterns associated with motion events, and as we know the domain of MOTION is one which is typically used as a source domain in language (e.g., *he needs to get over his fear of public speaking*), and more specifically academic language (e.g., *this research is moving in the right direction*).

To put it simply, according to this hypothesis, learners who have the same lexicalisation patterns for motion events in their L1 and L2 are likely to experience positive transfer and find it easier to learn the form-meaning pairings in the L2. Conversely, if the learner's L1 belongs to a different typological group from the L2 they are learning, they may struggle with negative transfer or avoidance. However, although the experiments conducted by Slobin and colleagues only involving the L1 of the speakers, confirm the hypothesis, the experiments conducted by Cadierno (2004) and Cadierno and Ruiz (2006) to test this prediction for L2 speakers have produced mixed results. At the same time, though, studies examining the simultaneous use of language and gesture (Kellerman & Van Hoof, 2003; Stam, 2006) have shown that the analysis of gesture can reveal thinking-for-speaking patterns that are not otherwise observable.

As can be seen, the predictions made by the 'thinking for speaking' hypothesis are related to the typology of the L1 of the L2 speaker. As with transfer above, we move here again between the traditional language typologies connected to genetic aspects, i.e., to the linguistic origin of the L1, and a proposal inspired by Cognitive Linguistics. If we take into account the former, we could find how, for example, the languages of an Indo-European origin, the most frequent L1s in MetCLIL, are divided into different linguistic families such as Germanic languages (e.g., English, Dutch, German, Norwegian, Swedish), Romance Languages (e.g., Spanish, Portuguese, Italian, French) or Slavic Languages (e.g., Russian, Serbian, Czech). For its part, a cognitive-linguistic typology establishes a basic distinction, based on how the languages encode motion events, between satellite-framed and verb-framed languages (Talmy, 1985, 1991, 2000), which has more recently being completed with other categories (e.g., equipollently framed). Thus, in satellite-framed languages, such as English and Slavic languages, the path of motion is typically encoded by a main verb (*She crept* [motion/manner] *out* [path] *of the room*), while manner of motion and other event components are expressed through particles or adverbs that function as satellites, hence the name of this group of languages. In verb-framed languages, such as Spanish and Romance languages, the path and motion are typically encoded by a single verb, which explains the name used, while manner of motion and other event components are expressed separately (Spanish: *entró* [motion/path] *corriendo* [manner]; he entered running).

Using this basic framework, Castellano-Risco et al. (2022) analysed the use of Metaphorical Motion Events (MMEs) in the Spanish section of MetCLIL (i.e., Sems 1, 2 and 3). The study concluded that L1 typological considerations were not determining and that contextual factors may be more explanatory of the differences found between participants. In the present chapter, the whole of MetCLIL will be analysed from this perspective.

Speaker's role

Within Systemic Functional Linguistics (SFL), a theory of language that examines the relationship between language and its social and cultural context, there is key concept – tenor – that describes the social relationship between the participants in a communicative event and how it influences language use.

Specifically, tenor refers to the social roles and relationships of the speakers, such as their status, power and familiarity with one another. These factors can impact the style, register and tone of language used in a given interaction. For example, a conversation between a teacher and a student would have a different tenor than a conversation between two close friends.

The role of tenor in metaphor usage is probably taken for granted, but only a limited number of studies have been conducted to actually explore it in depth. Among these studies, the book by Deignan et al. (2013) stands out as a particularly relevant contribution since the authors employ the concept of tenor, together with other SLF concepts such as field and mode, to comprehensively analyse metaphor use in various contexts. In some of these contexts, for example, the similes used by experts were shown to be of importance to allow non-experts to gain access to subject-specific knowledge that they lack.

Deignan et al. (2013) highlight the central role of the tenor concept in Chapter 5, where they analyse how a university lecturer explains, in two different exchanges to two different people, some theoretical models related to her discipline in the field of business. In the first interaction, the interlocutor was a colleague from the same department, although not exactly the same area of specialisation, whereas a post-graduate student is the participant in the second exchange. In a way, both these meetings would represent examples of expert-expert and expert-novice interactions and were analysed quantitatively and qualitatively to see if there were differences. The quantitative analysis indicates that within a general trend of high figurative density, the expert-novice exchange shows a higher metaphor density (17.4% vs 15.4%) and approximately the same metonymic density. However, these figures are not considered conclusive, since it is the qualitative analysis that shows that in the expert-expert exchange, metaphors were mostly used to "build rapport" and in the expert-novice they were used pedagogically. This last conclusion, relating to the expert-novice, is also confirmed by a similar analysis carried out by Woodhams (2014), where a mentor uses metaphor to help the enculturation process of an intern in an accounting department of a government office in New Zealand.

The role of tenor in academic contexts usually refers to the different status in terms of knowledge and authority that lecturers and students hold. This imbalance will naturally anticipate a difference in their use of metaphor in their interactions, but here the research is also scarce. One of the few studies is the one conducted by Alejo-Gonzalez (2022) on a situation related to the focus of the present book: the use of metaphor in mentoring sessions – i.e., office hour consultations – by Erasmus students. The quantitative analysis of the conversations revealed that lecturers exhibit a significantly higher density of metaphors in their language production compared to students (13.3% vs 8.9%). The explanation seems to point to the fact that lecturers are part of research communities, are well-versed in academic registers that utilise metaphors extensively (Herrmann, 2013; Low et al., 2008), which sets them apart from students who are still in the process of becoming familiarised with disciplinary practices in a language that is not their L1. The study also reveals that lecturers made statistically significantly more frequent use of certain lemmas than their student counterparts. These include three prepositions (to, at, from), two light verbs (get and give), two SIGHT metaphors (see and look), a MOTION metaphor verb (go), and a discourse marker (*exactly*). This finding may be related to the fact that students are developing metaphorical competence and that they show a tendency towards vocabulary simplification, particularly with closed-class elements like prepositions and light verbs, which results in incomplete mastery of academic English phraseology.

Analysis of individual variables in MetCLIL

L2 proficiency in MetCLIL

Although MetCLIL is not a learner corpus as defined in Chapter 2, the information collected from the participants in the seminars included (especially, Question 9, Appendix F) gave us information about their proficiency level, which was incorporated into the tag set available through Sketch Engine. This means that it is possible to select a specific proficiency level when searching for metaphors in MetCLIL. However, it has to be taken into account that not all students participated actively and made verbal contributions in the seminars. Thus, from the initial list of people attending the seminars, the number of participants making a contribution was 91, which is a high enough figure to be able to study whether the proficiency level has some influence on the number of metaphors and metaphor densities of those participants. It was considered important to leave out both the lecturers, since in their case other factors related to their role, and the native speakers of English, which obviously could not be compared to the rest in this respect. The One-way Anova performed to the data (p=0.434) showed that there were no differences in the metaphorical performance of the different proficiency levels.

As can be seen from the results in Table 7.1, where the speakers of the B1 and B2 groups are conflated, the densities are not very different and the smaller density of the C1 group may be due to the greater number of speakers that are included in that group.

The proficiency variable was therefore not enough to explain the different metaphor densities. However, the possibility that the proficiency level could interact with other variables, especially the L1 of the participants, was considered. This analysis was also possible because the L1 of the participants was also incorporated into the tags. It was hypothesised that those speakers with an L1 genetically related to English could have a higher metaphorical performance. This would mean that both the level and the L1 of the students combined could have an influence on the metaphorical densities observed. In fact, the data appearing in Table 7.2 already seem to indicate that the

Table 7.1 Metaphor density by proficiency level

Proficiency level	# Speakers	# Metaphors	# Tokens	Metaphor density
B1-B2	25	1,708	12,042	14.18
C1	46	3,734	27,384	13.64
C2	14	2419	16,830	14.37

Table 7.2 Metaphor density: proficiency and L1

	Speakers	# Metaphors	# Word tokens	Density
B1-B2	**25**	**1,708**	**12,042**	**14.18**
Germanic	4	642	4,408	14.56
Romance	16	722	5,536	13.04
Slavic	1	200	1,248	16.03
Other (Turkic, Greek, Latvian, Indo Aryan, African, Arabic, Chinese)	4	130	765	16.99
C1	**46**	**3,734**	**27,384**	**13.64**
Germanic	11	1,164	8,191	14.21
Romance	22	1,422	10,269	13.85
Slavic	5	279	2,502	11.15
Other (Turkic, Greek, Latvian, Indo Aryan, African, Arabic)	8	869	6,422	13.53
C2	**14**	**2419**	**16,830**	**14.37**
Germanic	6	983	5,616	17.50
Romance	5	935	7,202	12.98
Slavic	2	482	3,861	12.48
Other (African)	1	19	151	12.58

density behaviour of L1 Germanic speakers of English (Dutch, Norwegian, Swedish and German) seems to show a more coherent pattern in the use of metaphor. This pattern would not distinguish between the B1-B2 and the C1 levels within Germanic speakers (14.56 and 14.21), but it would certainly separate these two levels from C2 Germanic L1 speakers (17.5) indicating that the top level – C2 – constituted for these speakers the level at which there was a change in their metaphorical production. This configuration could not be observed in the rest of the L1s where the results were less consistent in this respect.

To check that the data could really support the possibility of the interaction between proficiency level and L1 of the speakers, a two-way ANOVA test was performed. In this case, the two independent variables or fixed factors were proficiency level and the main L1 typologies of the speakers. The typologies were rearranged since there were certain groups (such as Chinese or even Slavic languages) that did not have a big enough number of speakers per proficiency level. Thus, the resulting groups of L1 typology were Germanic, Romance and Others.

The two-way ANOVA (see Table 7.3) shows that the model as such is significant ($p<0.05$) and that apart from the interaction between typology and level, which is also significant at $p<0.005$, there is no other significant result. This means that there is no significant main effect for typology or level considered separately, but that the interaction is significant.

To end this section, we provide the data for the contrast between native and non-native speakers in the corpus (Table 7.4). As mentioned above, native speakers were left out of the analysis dealing with proficiency level. Obviously, the difference in the density percentages is not statistically significant since the number of native speakers is very small and the data are not comparable.

L1-induced variation

In the previous section, it was already pointed out that, although some apparent differences were noticed, the L1 typology of the participants (not considering either lecturers or native speakers of English) was not a factor influencing their metaphor production on its own. It was only when interacting with the proficiency level that metaphor densities were affected. In this section, the data for the individual languages are provided. Besides, an analysis of the difference in metaphor production between satellite-framed and verb-framed languages will be carried out.

The data in this table, which, as already said, are not statistically significant, are interesting in so far as the L1s represented by several speakers (>5) and intervening in more than one seminar are more likely to be representative of the impact of that language in metaphor production. In the rest of the cases, idiosyncratic features of the speaker or the constraints imposed by the type of communication in that particular seminar may play a more important role.

Table 7.3 Interaction L1 typology and proficiency level: Two-way ANOVA results

Tests of between-subjects effects

Dependent variable: Density_level

Source	Type III Sum of squares	df	Mean square	F	Sig.	Partial eta squared
Corrected model	292.074[a]	12	24.340	2.090	0.028	0.258
Intercept	6621.309	1	6621.309	568.444	0.000	0.888
Typology	43.023	4	10.756	.923	0.455	0.049
Levels	53.595	2	26.798	2.301	0.108	0.060
Typology*levels	238.765	6	39.794	3.416	0.005	0.222
Error	838.665	72	11.648			
Total	17528.745	85				
Corrected total	1130.740	84				

a. R squared = .258 (Adjusted R squared = .135)

Table 7.4 Native vs non-native metaphor densities

	# Speakers	# Metaphors	# Word tokens	Density
Native	7	601	3950	15.2
Non-native	85	7,847	56,171	14.0

In this respect, it could be hypothesised that L1 Dutch exerts a stronger push in the production of metaphors than L1 German. For this hypothesis to be confirmed, a larger corpus involving more seminars and speakers would be necessary. For its part, within the group of Romance L1, it is possible to see a quite consistent behaviour of all the languages represented with more than five speakers participating in at least two seminars.

Finally, following on the work by Castellano-Risco et al. (2023), a comparison between the L1 languages that the cognitive-linguistic literature cited above has categorised into verb-framed and satellite-framed languages was conducted. Within the verb-framed category, we have all Romance languages (Spanish, Catalan, Portuguese, French and Italian) and some other languages such as Turkish and Arabic also represented in the corpus, while in the satellite-framed group, we have all Germanic and Slavic languages (see Table 7.5) together with Finnish and Greek. Other languages such as Urdu, Swahili, Twi, Sinhala and Latvian, whose categorisation was not found, were left out of the analysis.

The results of the T-test run are not statistically significant and, as can be seen from Table 7.6, the two groups of speakers did not show great differences in their metaphor densities. These results seem to confirm those already obtained for the three Spanish seminars and for a small subgroup of metaphors (motion) analysed by Castellano-Risco et al. (2022). It would seem that the categorisation, which has been shown so useful in the study of literal motion events, does not have a translation in metaphor use.

However, since Özçaliskan (2004, 2005) demonstrated a difference between English and Turkish writers not only in the amount but also in the variety of metaphorical verbs of motion, the possibility that there might be a difference not in the metaphorical density but in the number of types was considered (see Table 7.7). In this case, the results of the T-test were not significant either, but they were closer to it ($p=0.06$).

Comparing the metaphor production of lecturers and learners

A final comparison relates the role of speakers in the seminars. The only previous analysis comparing the metaphor density of lecturers and students was conducted by Alejo-Gonzalez (2022), who found that there were significant differences in the metaphor densities of these two groups. It has to

Table 7.5 Metaphor density according to L1 typology

L1 Typology	# Speakers	# Seminars	# Metaphors	Total tokens	Density
English	7	4	601	3950	**15.2**
Germanic	21	4	2789	18215	**15.3**
Dutch	6	2	981	5905	16.6
Norwegian	9	1	1027	6632	15.5
Swedish	2	2	135	927	14.6
German	4	4	646	4751	13.6
Romance	43	6	3079	23007	**13.4**
Romanian	1	1	99	550	18.0
Italian	7	4	224	1609	13.9
Spanish (including Catalan bilinguals)	10	1	815	5958	13.7
Portuguese	9	4	761	5747	13.2
Catalan (including Catalan-Spanish bilinguals)	10	1	818	6342	12.9
French	6	3	362	2801	12.9
Slavic (Bulgarian, Croatian, Czech, Russian, Serbian)	8	5	961	7611	12.6
Turkic (Azeri, Turkish)	4	3	342	2252	15.2
African languages (Swahili/Kikuyu, Twi)	2	1	46	394	11.7
Arabic	2	1	364	2790	13.0
Chinese	2	1	53	417	12.7
Indo-Aryan (Bengali, Sinhala, Urdu)	3	2	127	985	12.9
Other languages (Finnish, Latvian, Greek)	3	2	104	651	16.0

Table 7.6 Metaphorical densities of satellite vs verb-framed L1s

		Speakers	Density
Density level	Satellite-framed	34	14.0
	Verb-framed	46	13.7

Table 7.7 Number of metaphorical types: satellite vs verb framed L1s

		Speakers	Metaphorical types	Standard deviation
Density level	Satellite-framed	34	58.12	45.114
	Verb-framed	46	42.07	31.793

F=11.165, T=1.868, df=78, p=0.06

be remembered that the data in that study corresponds to a very specific academic situation, i.e., office hour consultations by Erasmus students in different European universities, including some Irish and English institutions, where the majority of lecturers were L1 speakers of English. While both that study and MetCLIL examine oral academic interactions, it is important to bear in mind several notable differences between them. First, they differ in terms of the genres of academic interactions that they focus on, with the former concentrating on office hour and the latter on discussion seminars. Second, there are differences in the number of lecturers involved, with the former having 27 and the latter only 9. Additionally, the L1 status of both the lecturers and students also varies significantly between the two studies: in the former, more than half of the lecturers are L1 English speakers, while all students are L1 Spanish speakers; in contrast, MetCLIL features a more diverse mix of L1 backgrounds among both the lecturers and students.

As Table 7.8 shows, the results of Alejo-Gonzalez (2022) are not replicated and the difference in metaphor density is not statistically significant. In fact, the data in the table show a big disparity in the metaphorical behaviour of the lecturers from the different seminars.

One possible explanation for this result may lie in the different role that the lecturers adopt in the different seminars. Thus, while in some cases they may limit themselves to making specific points to be understood by the students or to encourage discussion, in other cases they may adopt a more teacher-centred stance with a more formal approach.

Conclusion

After thoroughly examining key contextual variables associated with metaphor usage, this chapter has adopted an approach that centres on individual variables. The findings reveal that a majority of these individual variables do not exhibit significant effects. However, it is worth noting that the students' L1 typology comes close to achieving significance, especially when considering the number of metaphor types, and eventually attains full significance when considering the interaction with the proficiency level of students. In the final chapter, the mostly quantitative method adopted in Chapters 6 and 7 will be replaced by a more qualitative approach, allowing for a more individualised exploration of metaphor use.

Table 7.8 Metaphorical density: lecturers vs students

Country	Seminars	Lecturers		Students		Density	
		Word tokens	Metaphor tokens	Word tokens	Metaphor tokens	Lecturer	Students
Spain	Sem 1	3,515	619	8,524	1,137	17.6	13.3
	Sem 2	5,638	966	6,438	895	17.1	13.9
	Sem 3	3,705	633	6,495	918	17.1	14.1
Italy	Sem 4	7,598	1,036	1,059	162	13.6	15.3
Portugal	Sem 5	4,191	507	4,487	725	12.1	16.2
Norway	Sem 6	7,016	1,017	7,733	1,186	14.5	15.3
Sweden	Sem 7	2,130	245	8,541	960	11.5	11.2
	Sem 8	3,984	388	8,095	967	9.7	11.9
The Netherlands	Sem 9	11,545	1,748	9,559	1,596	15.1	16.7
		49,322	7,159	60,931	8,546	14.5	14.0

$F=0.60$; $t=-0.50$, $df=95$, $p=0.961$

References

Alejo-González, R. (2022). Metaphor in the academic mentoring of international undergraduate students: The Erasmus experience. *Metaphor and Symbol, 37*(1), 1–20.

Barlow, M. (2013). Individual differences and usage-based grammar. *International Journal of Corpus Linguistics, 18*(4), 443–478.

Boers, F., & Littlemore, J. (2000). Cognitive style variables in participants' explanations of conceptual metaphors. *Metaphor and Symbol, 15*(3), 177–187.

Cadierno, T. (2004). Expressing Motion Events in a Second Language: A Cognitive Typological Perspective. In *Cognitive Linguistics, Second Language Acquisition, and Foreign Language Teaching* edited by Michel Achard and Susanne Niemeier, 13–49. Berlin/New York: Mouton de Gruyter.

Cadierno, T., & Ruiz, L. (2006). Motion events in Spanish L2 acquisition. *Annual Review of Cognitive Linguistics, 4*, 183–216.

Cadierno, T., & Hijazo-Gascón, A. (2014). Cognitive linguistic approaches to second language Spanish. A focus on thinking-for-speaking. In K. L. Geeslin (Ed.), *The handbook of Spanish second language acquisition* (pp. 96–110). John Wiley.

Castellano-Risco, I., Martín-Gilete, M., Hijazo-Gascón, A., & Ibarretxe-Antuñano, I. (2023). Metaphors set in motion in the context of L2 academic spoken discourse. *Vigo International Journal of Applied Linguistics, 20*, 77–105.

Castellano-Risco, I., & Piquer-Píriz, A. M. (2020). Measuring secondary-school L2 learners vocabulary knowledge: Metaphorical competence as part of general lexical competence. In A. M. Piquer Píriz & R. Alejo González (Eds.), *Metaphor in foreign language instruction* (pp. 199–218). Mouton de Gruyter and De Gruyter Mouton.

Danesi, M. (1992). Metaphorical competence in second language acquisition and second language teaching: The neglected dimension. In J. E. Alatis (Ed.), *Language communication and social meaning* (pp. 489–500). Georgetown University Press.

Danesi, M. (2008). Conceptual errors in second language learning. In S. De Knop & T. De Rycker (Eds.), *Cognitive approaches to pedagogical grammar* (pp. 231–256). Mouton de Gruyter.

Danesi, M. (2016). Conceptual fluency in second language teaching: An overview of problems, issues, research findings, and pedagogy. *International Journal of Applied Linguistics and English Literature, 5*(1), 145–153.

Deignan, A., Littlemore, J., & Semino, E. (2013). *Figurative language, genre and register*. Cambridge University Press.

Dörnyei, Z., & Ryan, S. (2015). *The psychology of the language learner revisited.* Routledge.

Fauconnier, G., & Turner, M. (2008). *The way we think: Conceptual blending and the mind's hidden complexities*. Basic Books.

Fetterman, A. K., Bair, J. L., Werth, M., Landkammer, F., & Robinson, M. D. (2016). The scope and consequences of metaphoric thinking: Using individual differences in metaphor usage to understand how metaphor functions. *Journal of Personality and Social Psychology, 110*(3), 458.

Gibbs, R. W. (2017). *Metaphor wars, conceptual metaphors in human life*. Cambridge University Press.

Herrmann, J. B. (2013). *Metaphor in academic discourse: Linguistic forms, conceptual structures, communicative functions and cognitive representations* (Dissertation). LOT Dissertation Series, Utrecht.

Hoang, H., & Boers, F. (2018). Gauging the association of EFL learners' writing proficiency and their use of metaphorical language. *System, 74*, 1–8.

Jarvis, S., & Pavlenko, A. (2008). *Crosslinguistic influence in language and cognition*. Routledge.

Kellerman, E., & Van Hoof, A. (2003). Manual accents. *International Review of Applied Linguistics, 41*, 251–269.

Lakoff, G., & Johnson, M. (1980). *Metaphors we live by*. University of Chicago Press.

Lakoff, G., & Johnson, M. (1999). *Philosophy in the flesh: The embodied mind and its challenge to western thought*. Basic Books.

Littlemore, J. (2001). The use of metaphor in university lectures and the problems that it causes for overseas students. *Teaching in Higher Education, 6*(3), 333–349.

Littlemore, J. (2019). *Metaphors in the mind*. Cambridge University Press.

Littlemore, J., Krennmayr, T., Turner, J., & Turner, S. (2014). An Investigation into metaphor use at different levels of second language writing. *Applied Linguistics, 35*(2), 117–144.

Littlemore, J., & Low, G. D. (2006a). Metaphoric competence, second language learning, and communicative language ability. *Applied Linguistics, 27*(2), 268–294.

Littlemore, J., & Low, G. D. (2006b). *Figurative* thinking and foreign language learning. Palgrave Macmillan.

López-Mezquita, M. T. (2005). La evaluación de la dimensión léxica a nivel receptivo: Un marco para el diseño de instrumentos de medida. In M. L. Carrió Pasto (Ed.), *Perspectivas interdisciplinares de la lingüística aplicada* (Universitat de València pp. 381–390).

Low, G. D. (1988). On teaching metaphor. *Applied Linguistics, 9*(2), 125–147.

Low, G. D., Littlemore, J., & Koester, A. (2008). Metaphor use in three UK university lectures. *Applied Linguistics, 29*(3), 428–455.

Marin, A., Reimann, M., & Castano, R. (2014). Metaphors and creativity: Direct, moderating and mediating effects. *Journal of Consumer Psychology, 24*(2), 290–297.

Nacey, S. (2013). *Metaphors in learner English*. John Benjamins.

O'Reilly, D. (2017). *An investigation into metaphoric competence in the L2: Alinguistic approach* (Unpublished PhD dissertation). University of York.

O'Reilly, D., & Marsden, E. (2023). Elicited metaphoric competence in a second language: A construct associated with vocabulary knowledge and general proficiency? *International Review of Applied Linguistics. 61*(2), 287–327.

O'Reilly, D., & Marsden, E. (2021). Eliciting and measuring L2 metaphoric competence: Three decades on from Low (1988). *Applied Linguistics, 42*(1), 24–59.

Odlin, T. (1989). *Language transfer: Cross-linguistic influence in language learning*. Cambrige University Press.

Özçalışkan, Ş. (2004). Typological variation in encoding the manner, path, and ground components of a metaphorical motion event. *Annual Review of Cognitive Linguistics, 2*(1), 73–102.

Özçalişkan, Ş. (2005). Metaphor meets typology: Ways of moving metaphorically in English and Turkish. *Cognitive Linguistics, 16*(1), 207–246.

Slobin, D. I. (1996). Two ways to travel: Verbs of motion in English and Spanish. In M. Shibatani & S. A. Thompson (Eds.), *Grammatical constructions: Their form and meaning* (pp. 195–220). Clarendon Press.

Slobin, D. I. (1997). Mind, code, and text. In J. Bybee, J. Haiman, & S. A. Thompson (Eds.), *Essays on language function and language type: Dedicated to T. Givón* (pp. 437–467). John Benjamins.

Slobin, D. I. (2000). Verbalized events: A dynamic approach to linguistic relativity and determinism. In S. Niemeier & R. Dirven (Eds.), *Evi- dence for linguistic relativity* (pp. 107–138). John Benjamins.

Slobin, D. I. (2003). Language and thought online: Cognitive consequences of linguistic relativity. In D. Gentner & S. Goldin-Meadow (Eds.), *Language in mind: Advances in the study of language and thought* (pp. 157–192). The MIT Press.

Stam, G. (2006). Thinking for speaking about motion: L1 and L2 speech and gesture. *International Review of Applied Linguistics*, *44*, 143–169.

Talmy, L. (1985). Lexicalization patterns: Semantic structure in lexical forms. In T. Shopen (Ed.), *Language typology and syntactic description* (pp. 36–149). Cambridge University Press.

Talmy, L. (1991). Path to realization: A typology of event conflation. *Berkeley Linguistic Society*, *7*, 480–519.

Talmy, L. (2000). *Toward a cognitive semantics, Vol. 1: Concepts structuring systems*. The MIT Press.

Teymouri Aleshtar, M., & Dowlatabadi, H. (2014). Metaphoric competence and language proficiency in the same boat. *Procedia - Social and Behavioral Sciences*, *98*, 1895–1904. https://doi.org/10.1016/j.sbspro.2014.03.620

Turner, S. L. (2014). *The development of metaphoric competence in French and Japanese learners of English* (Doctoral dissertation). Birmingham, UK University of Birmingham.

Winter, B., Duffy, S. E., & Littlemore, J. (2020). Power, gender, and individual differences in spatial metaphor: The role of perceptual stereotypes and language statistics. *Metaphor and Symbol*, *35*(3), 188–205.

Woodhams, J. M. (2014). 'We're the nurses': Metaphor in the discourse of workplace socialisation. *Language & Communication*, *34*, 56–68.

Wulff, S., & Gries, S. T. (2021). Exploring individual variation in learner corpus research: Methodological suggestions. In B. Le Bruyn & M. Paquot (Eds.), *Learner corpus research meets second language acquisition* (pp. 191–213). Cambridge University Press.

8 Exemplary study of speech metaphors[1]
Corpus exploration of a target domain

Corpus studies of speech metaphors

Introduction

In the same way as the analysis of the SPEECH domain, and more particularly that of speech verbs, is closely connected to the origins of Pragmatics as a linguistic discipline (Austin, 1962), the interest in speech events from a metaphor perspective has been present in the research ever since the inception of the Conceptual Metaphor Theory (CMT) movement (Grady, 1998; Johnson, 1987; Lakoff & Johnson, 1980; Reddy, 1979). This initial interest was continued by Semino (2005, 2006) with the analysis of SPEECH metaphors in a large corpus of written genres. Based on the previous work by CMT scholars, but more concerned with a bottom-up description of conceptual metaphors, Semino was able to establish the body of conventionalised metaphorical models that native speakers of English use when referring to SPEECH. Thus, to give but one example she uses, English L1 speakers would have a preference for referring to SPEECH as TRANSFER as shown in expressions such as "deliver a message", "issue a warning", "leave a message" or "throw a question" (cf. Semino, 2006, p. 48ff.).

However scarce the research on the topic, its interest in theoretical debates (e.g., the CONDUIT metaphor [Reddy, 1979] vs primary metaphors [Grady, 1998]) or the concern with the description of metaphorical models used at a high level of generality, i.e., disregarding specific users or settings, makes it necessary to explore more definite contexts where this general characterisation is put to the test. In other words, it makes sense to assume a methodology where the analysis is made within "a particular socio-cultural or discourse community" (p. 324). And this approach is all the more required in the case of situations that do not readily conform to the monolingual users that the existing research had in mind. I refer to English as a Lingua Franca (ELF) contexts, and more concretely to the emerging subfield of English as a Medium of Instruction (EMI), areas introduced in Chapter 2 (cf. Mauranen, 2012 for ELF and Macaro, 2018 for EMI), but which have so far received very little attention from the perspective of metaphor (Pitzl, 2018 for an exception).

DOI: 10.4324/9781003400905-8

In this chapter, I intend to analyse the speech metaphors produced in seminars 1–3 of the Spanish section of MetCLIL, which deal with the subject of digital marketing, since they suited my purposes in several ways. First, the students in the seminars had to provide feedback on the presentations made by their colleagues, which meant they needed to refer to what they had said (i.e., to their SPEECH). Second, the short presentations, which all students had to make individually, did not consist in discussing a topic, but instead in the delivery of a marketing genre, an 'elevator pitch', already a metaphor (and a metonym) that could be exploited in so far as it alludes to the communication process, as made clear in the following quotation:

> Pitch has been usually defined using the baseball pitcher metaphor (Belinsky & Gogan, 2016) and the elevator pitch cliché (Denning & Dew, 2012). The baseball metaphor supposes a person (the entrepreneur) throwing an idea (pitching) to a specific audience (stakeholder) (Belinsky & Gogan, 2016). The elevator pitch cliché, on the other hand, represents the idea of an oral presentation occurring in the time lapse of an elevator ride (e.g., from the first until the tenth floor), in which an innovator has to be able to sell his or her idea to an investor on such a short time.
>
> (Sabaj et al., 2020, p. 55)

This specific situation provided me with a perfect context for the situated analysis of speech metaphors in an EMI context. As a result, the aim of the present paper was to explore the extent to which the conventionalised ways of metaphorically referring to SPEECH already described were used by L2 speakers or they had to resort to new metaphorical models. To put it more vividly, or figuratively if you want, it would be interesting to know whether participants represent themselves, and others, more as 'senders' or 'deliverers' or, on the contrary, as 'pitchers', 'catchers' or even 'sellers' of their pitch content.

Background

As a preliminary terminological clarification, it is important to define here the actual scope of the present analysis. Like many authors in the field (cf. Grady, 1998; or Semino, 2005, 2006), I do not only include metaphors referring to a speaker's verbal activity or production, but also metaphors used for the whole communication process, including the communication response or reception (Grady [1998], for example, refers to how meaning is *acquired* by addressees). In fact, Kövecses, in his list of common target domains (2010, pp. 23–28), refers to COMMUNICATION, not SPEECH, as a common target domain, a decision supported by the connection established between speech acts and mental states (Sweetser, 1987).

This explanation is in place because, given the role of speech acts in Pragmatics, the research on SPEECH in its narrower sense has been extensive and has often dealt solely with verbs (see Caballero's [2018] introduction for an overview). However, these analyses and, among them, the ones more closely connected to Cognitive Semantics are of interest here. This is particularly the case of Caballero and Paradis' (2018) analysis of Speech Framing Expressions (SFEs), as they call them to include 'verbs of saying' and their co-text. By identifying the different verbal frames used to introduce direct speech in a large corpus of fictional texts, they are able to classify the main domains these verbs draw on, to wit, Speech (e.g., *say, reply*), Activity (*add, continue*), Perception (*hear, see*), Cognition (*reason, muse*), Emotion (*explode, burst out*) and Auxiliary (*be, appear*) SFEs. This classification and the accompanying list of verbs give us an approximation to the range of different general source domains used to refer to speech in English and Spanish.

However, as already pointed out, the research on SFEs only focuses on verbs, usually with a speech act value, and less so on other word categories, including nouns, which refer to speech activity more generally (cf. Semino, 2005). Besides, this research does not strictly deal with metaphor, a goal initially undertaken by researchers mostly concerned with conceptual metaphors. In this respect, it is important to highlight the ground-breaking article by Reddy (1979), who proposed the CONDUIT metaphor as the main metaphorical model explaining human communication. According to this view, when we communicate, we send or transfer our ideas (or any other mental content, which Reddy refers to as Repertoire Members) by means of linguistic signals (e.g., words) with the aim of being understood by our interlocutors. Lakoff and Johnson (1980) expanded on this model and disaggregated the metaphors making up the CONDUIT metaphor into three main mappings, i.e., IDEAS AND MEANINGS ARE OBJECTS; LINGUISTICS EXPRESSIONS ARE CONTAINERS; and COMMUNICATION IS SENDING. Grady (1998), in contrast, rebuts both these accounts and suggests that many of the mappings involved are not exclusive to the SPEECH domain but are the result of basic mappings (i.e., primary metaphors) used in many other contexts and not just communication. According to Grady, it is not possible to posit a "unified scenario involving the transfer of containers from one person to another" (1998, p. 14).

Using a discursive approach, Semino (2005, 2006) concurs with Grady (1998) that many Speech metaphors are not specific to communication and that they are usually basic mappings (i.e., primary metaphors). However, Semino moves away from Grady in three fundamental aspects. First, her conclusions are based on a corpus-based analysis. Second, although she admits that the different metaphors do not always provide a consistent pattern, she thinks they can be "interpreted in terms of a physical scenario" (Semino, 2005, p. 4), a conclusion corroborated for their analysis of verbs by Caballero and Paradis (2018), when they say "In contrast to the mental focus in Spanish, there is a tendency in English to focus on the physical and dynamic aspects of speech events" (p. 25). And third, this physical scenario is not structured on a set of conceptual metaphors, but on the basis of the different source domains, to which speakers resort when conventionally referring to SPEECH. Ordered by their relative frequency and accompanied by their percentage share of the total number of identified metaphors, the list includes the following source domains (cf. Semino, 2006, p. 57): TRANS-FER (OF OBJECTS) (45/21%), VISIBILITY/VISUAL REPRESENTATION (28/13%), PHYSICAL CONSTRUCTION (OF OBJECTS) (27/12.6%), PHYSICAL AGGRESSION (27/12.6 %), MOVEMENT (14/6.5%), PHYSICAL PROXIMITY (9/4.2%), PHYSI-CAL PRESSURE (7/3.1%), or PHYSICAL SUPPORT (4/1.8%).

In summary, as already expressed, except for the valuable work of Semino, to the best of my knowledge, no other research has been carried out on speech metaphors using a corpus-based methodology, let alone analysed their import in specific contexts of use such as the one described here.

The importance of SPEECH in the seminars: a keyword analysis

As a first step in my analysis, I wanted to show, by using the USAS tool in Wmatrix (Rayson, 2008), the thematic make-up of the seminars. This is elaborated by automatically assigning a semantic tag to the words in the cor-pus and by comparing it to the list obtained from the reference corpus, in our case the BASE files cited above. The statistical comparison of the two lists, which takes into account the significance (LL, Log Likelihood) and the effect size (%Difference), gives as a result the topics that are overused (+) or under-used (-) in the corpus. If you look at Table 8.1, you can see that topics such as 'Money generally', 'Geographical terms' and 'Cause&Effect/Connection' are underused in the three seminars, whereas 'Evaluation:Good', 'Pronouns', 'Work and Employment', 'Education in general', and 'Degree:boosters' are overused. This would point, in the first place, to a difference in the specific subject matter, more connected to the area of labour in my corpus and more related to financial issues in BASE, but perhaps most importantly towards a difference in discursive features, which seem to be more characteristic of conversation (e.g., pronouns or boosters) versus the more academic discourse features of BASE (e.g., Cause&Effect). However, what is of special interest to us is the overuse in our seminars of the 'Q2.1 Speech: Communicative' tag. The 76.61% difference clearly indicates that in the three seminars the refer-ence to speech activity is quite salient as can be expected from the activity that takes place in the seminars studied.

Literal vs metaphorical SPEECH

Speech or pitch

The basic choice that seminar participants faced was whether to frame SPEECH metaphorically or, on the contrary, use a literal expression. This basic choice is initially illustrated by the way students refer to the actual presentation they make during the seminar, i.e., to the marketing genre that is the focus of the seminar activity. On the one hand, they can resort to the literal use of the word 'speech', while on the other hand they can make use of the expression 'elevator pitch', most often truncated as 'pitch'. In the first case, the speech

Table 8.1 Comparison of SPEECH words in the MetCLIL corpus and BASE

Semantic tag	MetCLIL Corpus	Standard frq.	BASE Soc Sc.	Standard frq.	Overuse	LL	% Difference
I1 Money generally	67	0.20	1273	3.56	-	1261.51	-94.45
A5.1+ Evaluation: Good	752	2.22	343	0.96	+	257.45	171.26
Z8 Pronouns	5978	17.63	4939	13.80	+	163.05	27.75
I3.1 Work and employment: Generally	259	0.76	78	0.22	+	112.54	250.46
PI Education in general	229	0.68	62	0.17	+	111.15	289.83
W3 Geographical terms	15	0.04	125	0.35	-	92.91	-87.33
A13.3 Degree: Boosters	576	1.7	321	0.90	+	87.91	89.39
A2.2 Cause & Effect/Connection	139	0.41	337	0.94	-	74.59	-56.47
Q2.1 Speech: Communicative	589	1.74	352	0.98	+	73.81	76.61

event is referred to by a noun, 'speech', which can be considered as a general and neutral way of referring to the words addressed to an audience, while in the second, the use of the more specific term 'pitch' would mean drawing on a metaphor, and a metonym if accompanied by 'elevator' (cf. Sabaj et al.'s [2020] citation above).

An analysis of the collocations of both these words ('pitch' and 'speech'), using the Word Sketch Difference tool from Sketch Engine, shows that, in this context, they are almost considered as close synonyms given that both show a preference to combine with the same verb ('to be') and with the same adjective ('good'). Besides, their frequency is also quite similar: 'speech' appears 125 and 'pitch' 112 times. This probably shows that speakers are not aware of the metaphorical meaning of 'pitch' and that they use it in a terminological way, a hypothesis that seems to be confirmed by the lack of exploitation of BASEBALL, and more generally of SPORTS, as a source domain. This is an exception as other words to refer to SPEECH more clearly convey the metaphorical meaning on the part of the participants, even if this framing is in most cases conventional.

Literal SPEECH

The words used to refer to the domain of SPEECH in a literal way are the ones to be expected (see Table 8.2). I only deal with nouns and verbs as it is difficult to find other word classes expressed literally. Thus, the most frequent verb is 'say', which is used 257 times, followed by other general SPEECH verbs like 'talk', 'tell', 'speak', typically used by participants to refer to the presentation their colleagues have made (e.g., *cut the part where you say you are Dutch*). Similarly, they use nouns like 'speech', used to talk about the actual presentation, 'name', whose frequency is due to the self-introduction students make at the beginning of the speech (*My name is Raul and ...*), and other vocabulary items like 'word' and 'question', used to refer to elements in their pitches. In general terms, the literal vocabulary referring to SPEECH that we find in these seminars follows the lexical simplification strategies characteristic of ELF contexts: "the most frequent items tend to be even more frequent" (Mauranen, 2012, pp. 116–117).

Metaphorical SPEECH

The situation of verbs and nouns used to refer to SPEECH metaphorically is different. Not only are there a number of tokens that is very similar to those used literally but, what is more significant, the number of types for both parts of speech is greater, which indicates that in the case of metaphorical framing of SPEECH there is greater variation, and therefore less lexical simplification, than in its literal counterpart.

However, we still find repetition in the most frequently used metaphorical lemmas and they correspond to semi-fixed conventionalised combinations belonging to two main groups: *light verb constructions* and *particle/prepositional verbs*. Thus, light verbs such as 'give', 'make', or 'put' are collocated

Table 8.2 Frequency of literal and metaphorical types in the corpus

	Verbs	Nouns
TOTAL LITERAL TOKENS 915 (52.2%)	*say (257) talk (55) tell (39) speak (32) read (31) ask (24) mention (22) hear (17) explain (12) understand (12) prove (12) differentiate (11) listen (11) agree (8) develop (4) pronounce (3) state (3) improvise (3) specify (3) convince (3) discuss (2) summarise (1) list (1)* Total number of literal verb tokens: 566; Total types: 23	*speech (125) name (47) word (29) question (18) voice (17) example (16) speaking (15) tone (11) language (10) anecdote (9) comment (8) statement (8) speaker (4) introduction (4) answer (4) sentence (4) argument (3) advice (3) listener (3) detail (3) talk (2) phrase (2) critique (1) adjective (1) conversation (1) silence (1)* Total number of literal noun tokens: 349; Total types: 26
TOTAL METAPHORICAL TOKENS 838 (47.8%)	give (51) add (31) make (29) catch (16) get (15) break (14) put (13) go (13) run (12) keep (12) have (10) miss (9) do (9) express (9) pull (9) hit (9) apply (8) set (7) feel (7) take (7) build (6) allow (6) settle (5) move (5) connect (5) transmit (5) sound (4) prepare (4) bring (4) share (4) stop (4) let (4) aim (4) acquire (4) structure (3) flow (3) change (3) attract (3) sell (3) polish (3) come (3) leave (3) split (2) project (2) cut (2) separate (2) fill (2) mix (2) stand (2) follow (2) stress (2) link (2) emphasise (2) shorten (2) lose (2) introduce (2) switch (1) end (1) wrap (1) play (1) exchange (1) combine (1) treat (1) form (1) skip (1) present (1) start (1) generate (1) stretch (1) base (1) throw (1) condense (1) understand (1) reinforce (1) develop (1) relax (1) align (1) rise (1) engage (1) bear (1) stick (1) rush (1) area (1) say (1) carry (1) appeal (1) act (1) send (1) fix (1) deliver (1) twist (1) hurry (1) work (1) inject (1) avoid (1) internalise (1) Total number of metaporical verb tokens: 446; Total types: 96	pitch (96) thing (69) part (31) structure (14) end (14) mark (12) sense (12) message (10) stuff (9) area (8) pace (7) story (6) script (6) feedback (6) middle (6) asset (5) content (5) message (5) account (5) touch (4) aim (4) storyteller (3) stage (3) turn (3) ice (3) contact (3) strength (2) emphasis (2) answer (2) job (2) name (2) engagement (2) bit (2) speed (2) piece (2) magic (2) voice (2) capture (1) baggage (1) feeling (1) set (1) summary (1) side (1) trick (1) feature (1) back (1) package (1) subject (1) start (1) break (1) stop (1) treat (1) approach (1) section (1) intrigue (1) vehicle (1) actor (1) sandwich (1) Total number of metaphorical noun tokens: 392; Total types: 58

Table 8.3 Frequent light verb constructions with a metaphorical meaning

Light verb	Repertoire members (RM) found in the corpus
Give	Fact/number/sense/speech/example/pitch/information/something/idea
Make	Point/sense/contact/explicit/clear
Put	Emphasis/information
Get	Attention/feedback/sense/comment/advice/message

with nouns such as 'facts' or 'point', which generally correspond to what Reddy (1979) calls Repertoire Members, i.e. the material that is communicated (see Table 8.3). For their part, particle/prepositional verbs are also frequently used metaphorically with frequent use of verbs such as 'give away', 'point out', 'put out', or 'get through'.

An analysis of source domains for SPEECH metaphors

The metaphors found in the corpus can be classified according to the metaphorical models they use. In this section, I follow Semino (2005, 2006) and the different uses of systematic metaphor she proposes for SPEECH, separating or deviating from her proposal when our data did not fit her categories. Besides, given that I deal with a more restricted context, I have placed great emphasis on identifying the main functions that the different models fulfil in the seminars, thus connecting them with the rhetorical function they may play. Finally, I will also make reference to the number of metaphorical verbs and nouns referring to SPEECH that I have identified in each model. I just keep a tally of these two word categories for the purposes of establishing a comparison with the figures given by Semino (2006), as she did not consider other parts of speech in her tally.

MOTION

Source and path of *MOTION*: thematic initiation and progression

An important preliminary remark should be made so that the scope of this systematic metaphor is properly understood. In the seminars, there is no rich description of speech activity as motion. To be more specific, JOURNEY metaphors, which is the way other researchers (e.g., Cameron, 2011 or Semino et al., 2018) have referred to this use of metaphor, are not fleshed out in the most typical manifestations they find in their corpora (e.g., *journey, route, path, pathway*). Instead, the metaphors found in my corpus are less fully elaborated and refer only to the source-path-goal schema.

The reference to this schema is reflected, in the first place, in the use of two very general, or neutral, motion verbs like *go* and *move*. The use of *go* in the seminars, as is also the case with *continue*, is mostly connected to interaction management, i.e., to indicate when to start (or proceed with) a pitch, usually in student-student exchanges ('Do you wanna go first?').

Move is used to refer to the progress made by the speaker in his/her delivery of the pitch. The implication is that the different elements in the speech are like stages in the progression of the discourse:

(1) I think it was very good [the pitch] ... because you <u>move</u> forward from questions,
(2) when you have to pause two seconds breathe in breathe out and <u>move forward</u>

The last example also shows how the idea of motion is sometimes implicitly combined with its opposite, i.e., the lack of progress in the speech. The lecturer conveys the idea that it is sometimes necessary to 'stop for air' before 'moving forward'. This idea is taken up by two students when they say:

(3) when you're going to say something important <u>stop</u> and then
(4) you could make some <u>stops</u> like before you said before you say this random fact ... it will catch even more the audience's attention

As a result, the idea being emphasised, both by the teacher and the students, is that this shift between motion and stasis is important in making a good speech.

A second set of metaphors in this group focuses on the manner of movement. This is the case of a verb like *skip*, which is used to convey an idea that is usually associated with the JOURNEY scenario, i.e., the obstacles typically found 'en route'.

(5) yes so like <u>skip</u> the never that then like

In contrast, participants use another manner verb, *flow*, to map smooth steady motion onto pitches and to indicate that the pitch does not meet significant obstacles in its thematic progression:

(6) going to well it's going to <u>flow</u> more naturally okay
(7) have to read it anymore it will <u>flow</u> more naturally i think okay but

Finally, attending to the structure of the MOTION domain (cf. Sullivan, 2013), a relevant element, also related to manner, is the 'speed of motion', which is profiled in many of the expressions referring to SPEECH. This dimension is expressed by means of different linguistic resources like the use of verbs like *hurry up* and *slow down*, nouns like *pace* and *speed*, or adjectives like *fast* and *slow*. The emphasis on this element is connected with an important characteristic of 'elevator pitches': their compact nature. Since students only have 30 seconds, for the pitch delivered for the whole group, and 90 seconds, for the one given to the split group, it is important that they strike a balance between the need to provide information in such a short time and the need not to give the impression of being rushed.

Overall, the importance of MOTION in our corpus is highlighted not only by a great number of tokens (117, making up 13.2% of speech metaphors) but also by the highest number of different types of all metaphorical models (36).

Goal of MOTION: successful pitch

This group of metaphors is also related to MOTION, but I deal separately with them because they are used to focus on the destination of that movement, following the conceptual metaphor ACHIEVING A GOAL IS REACHING A DESTINATION. Most of the metaphors in this group are used to frame the criteria describing a successful pitch and they are fundamentally related to two aspects: time constraints and main point(s) addressed in the pitch.

As already indicated, time is of the essence in the production of 'elevator pitches' given the scarce time available in business communication. Thus, many of the expressions produced refer to the need to stick to the time limit trying not to go over or under it. This idea is mostly emphasised by the lecturer, who repeatedly uses the expression *hit the (ninety/thirty-second) mark* (7 times) to remind students of this requirement. In other cases, we see how the *hit the mark* metaphor is mixed with a reference to the time constraint as an explicit destination:

(8) you have long words that can give you like more the sense of desperation about about not <u>hitting the time</u> and also when you have so much information well you are you get anxious about well i'm not getting there i'm not <u>getting there</u> i'm not <u>getting there</u>

The second ingredient for a successful pitch refers to the clear identification by students of what they want to communicate or as the lecturer puts it in the slides introducing the theoretical part of the lesson, "knowing your goal will allow you to communicate more efficiently and confidently" (personal communication).

(9)   what <u>straight</u> to the <u>point straight</u> to the <u>point</u> yeah
(10) she can offer and it was very <u>straight</u> to the <u>point</u> but but clear

Some of these metaphors are reminiscent of the CONDUIT metaphor described by Reddy (1979):

(11) to well to have your message well *straight through through* people ok
(12) that helps you to get your message straightforward eh through people yeah

In general, it can be said that, although participants are using quite a lot of conventionalised MOTION metaphors as seen in our previous section, GOAL metaphors are less frequent (only 31 tokens) and mostly the result of repeating the same types (4).

Combining MOTION and CONTAINMENT: amount of information in the pitch

Even if the CONDUIT metaphor as a unitary whole has been subjected to criticism (cf. Grady, 1998), the idea of metaphoric containment is undoubtedly present in the language used to refer to everyday communication: "You are *putting* too many ideas *into* a single sentence" (cf. Kověcses, 2010, p. 26). The question that arises is whether this same metaphor is present in the language non-native speakers use to refer to specialised forms of communication like the 'elevator pitch'.

As can be seen from the following examples, the metaphor is mirrored by the participants in the seminar, with the pitch acting as a CONTAINER:

(13) things that you can pull out to give or well *put in* the pitch to give a more sense about
(14) what can you take from the ninety second to *put into* the thirty second one what can

This mapping is reinforced with the use of other verbs, in combination with prepositions, which can be considered as variations on the basic notion of CONTAINER:

(15) can use on your ninety-second pitch is to *inject* a-little bit of emotion to it so think
(16) to be condensed a little bit yeah so maybe *take out* some erm some things some facts

Sometimes, this metaphorical model is so entrenched, as shown by the 116 instances (13.1%) found in the corpus, that participants produce metaphors that are not wholly acceptable:

(17) to see you are going to notice if you need to *pull out* some things from the speech so
(18) what you can do is when you check on it again *pull out* some things that you might

The metaphorical construal of the pitch as a CONTAINER also brings with it the associated metaphor of CONSTITUENTS ARE CONTENTS (cf. Grady, 1998). In our case, this means that the pitch is not just a recipient, but it also has the function of holding a whole array of communication contents, which go beyond the "ideas", "emotions", "thoughts" or "meanings" originally pointed by Reddy (1979) as Repertoire Members and are also built metaphorically. In a way, the CONTAINER metaphor is also profiling the reification of the discourse.

Visual metaphors

Visual metaphors have usually been listed under the conceptual metaphor UNDERSTANDING IS SEEING, which have been shown to be so productive in general discourse (Danesi, 1990 or Sweetser, 1991) and in the academic language used with L2 speakers (MacArthur et al., 2015).

According to Semino (2005), a first group of visual metaphors is closely associated with the CONTAINER schema, as "understanding corresponds to the emergence of the meanings/contents from the words/container" (p. 21). However, in my corpus there is only one use of *reveal*, and even so, the sentence used is not completely conventional (see ex.19).

(19) interesting story can use Cosme to *reveal* the the speech what about the being a

It is interesting to note here the case of *give away*, used 17 times by the lecturer. Its most conventional and frequent meaning in standard English would lead us to assimilate it to *reveal*. However, its contextual meaning, obviously related to an unconventional L2 use, is certainly one of TRANSFER:

(20) yeah this is very hard to to accomplish to <u>give away</u> a lot of information without

Most frequently used are other visual metaphors already present in the lectures introducing the seminars. There, the lecturer, as shown in his slides, defines 'elevator pitch' as "a short speech that communicate[sic] a clear message" or advises students "to have certain things cleared before writing your speech". He obviously does not refer to a message that is 'easy to see' but to one that is 'easy to understand' (cf. Macmillan Dictionary, senses 5 and 2 respectively). It is then no surprise that we see examples like the following:

(21) but erm it's not that it's not very <u>clear</u> okay but it was a great great exam
(22) but otherwise the information was <u>clear</u> for me i would xxxx content-wise it is

Another group of metaphors refers to examples where the visibility of the ideas to be communicated is achieved not as a result of the emergence from a CONTAINER but as a product of a non-specified movement resulting in physical isolation. Thus, speakers convey the idea of distinctiveness or salience, which are so important in the business world to achieve 'market visibility', or as in the present case, to achieve 'personal visibility' in the labour market. Physical distance or separation are, in consequence, a good means to express this:

(23) a human being e can help you to well to <u>separate</u> and differentiate you from the rest
(24) along life that help you to <u>set</u> you <u>apart</u> from the rest okay yeah (give it up)
(25) that can help can help you to <u>set</u> you <u>apart</u> because if you have been studying in

Another group comprises conventionally used expressions from the visual domain. They include metaphors already mentioned by Semino (2005): *point out, show, focus* or *look for*. This last expression is particularly useful to highlight the main objective, or message, of the pitch:

(26) I just missed what you are <u>looking for</u>

In our corpus, visual metaphors are the least frequent of the conventionalised metaphors identified by Semino (2006). I have identified only 91 instances amounting to 10.3% of the total speech metaphorical tokens.

CONSTRUCTION

So far, the metaphorical language used by both the lecturer and the students has mostly made reference to the delivery of the pitch. But there are other metaphorical expressions that are intended to refer to the conscious work students need to do to prepare their pitches. One could say that the focus here is more on the pitch as a 'product' than as a 'process'.

Some of the metaphors used in this group – *make* and *add* – were already pointed out by Semino (2005). As in her corpus of native written English, the main metaphorical uses of these two verbs are also conventionalised in the spoken language of non-natives. However, here we find a certain degree of variation in the use of these verbs with the introduction of metaphorical *do* (*did a speech*) and the use of verbs like *connect* or *break*.

However, it is also possible to find other expressions mapping, onto the pitch, the specific domain of BUILDING. This would parallel the conventional metaphor ARGUMENTS ARE BUILDINGS (e.g., "we need to construct a strong argument for that" Lakoff & Johnson, 1980, p. 125), which emphasises the idea that the pitch is also a rhetorical artefact that needs to be designed as a house or a building:

(27) pieces of context that helps you to <u>build</u> the story so that would be one thing
(28) the sides because it helps you like <u>reinforce</u> your message okay great great
(29) when you e when you give away <u>strong</u> statements with a-lot of
(30) i really liked that the way you <u>structured</u> it it shows very motivation and

This metaphorical model accounts for the highest number of tokens (223) and a high number of types (34). Indeed, this tally is related to the inclusion in this group of one of the metaphors most frequently used in academic spoken discourse (see Swales, 2001), i.e., the word *thing*, when used as a synonym for 'word'. This does not mean that we cannot conclude that it is a truly productive model as indicated by the diversity of types used.

TRANSFER

We have already explained that the seminars had as their goal to practise the 'elevator pitch' as part of their training in digital marketing and that the use of the word pitch already implied that the idea of transfer was present. The pitch would thus be a type of speech that is 'thrown' like a baseball at an audience. This can clearly be seen in the following example from the lecturer:

(31) if you use the ninety seconds pitch just to <u>give</u> and <u>throw away</u> a lot of information it's going to the the the other person is going to feel overwhelmed about the how much information you are <u>giving</u> them

However, the word 'pitch', as it is used in the seminars, is a clear example of a terminological metaphor. The participants, not even the lecturer, seem to be aware of its metaphorical motivation. We cannot see examples where the word is used in a context suggesting its origin or where its meaning is 'opened' (Knudsen, 2003). Not even does the use of *catch*, which could be considered as the reverse side, seem to explicitly refer to this conceptual metaphor as this verb is mostly found under the form of the very conventional collocation 'catch someone's attention'.

This does not mean that the transfer meaning is not frequent. On the contrary, metaphorical transfer expressions are very frequent in the seminars as they are instantiated by the regular use of light verbs mentioned above (*give* and *get*). These verbs, although delexicalised, express the idea that the production of a pitch by a student can be construed "in terms of the transfer of physical objects from one person (the speaker) to others (the addressees)"

(Semino, 2006, p. 48). Other verbs used similarly, but clearly not as frequently, are *deliver, transmit,* or *share.*

This is yet another metaphorical model which, by presenting the pitch as the transfer of objects, is objectivising or reifying communication. But in this new metaphorical model, where ditransitive verbs are frequent, a new element is being incorporated. The thing being transferred is profiled together with the audience or the listeners, i.e. the recipients, to use the term from Frame Semantics. As highlighted by verbs such as *get* or *catch*, which already perspectivised the transfer from the point of view of the recipients, when delivering the pitch, the audience is of paramount importance:

(32) giving away the important information that you want to <u>share</u> with the with the public okay oh yeah

Together with PHYSICAL CONSTRUCTION, this metaphorical model ranks among the most frequently used (195 tokens and 22.1% of the total speech metaphors). The smaller number of types (14) makes it, however, a bit less productive. Again, the explanation lies in the inclusion of the word *pitch* here.

STORYTELLING

Apart from a few metaphors drawing on BUSINESS (like *sell*, 3 times, or *asset*, 5 times), this metaphorical model is the only one not included in the list compiled by Semino (2005, 2006). Besides, it is also the only model where we encounter the very few direct metaphors found in our corpus to refer to SPEECH. This indicates a conceptualisation of the pitch being made explicit, although surprisingly this conceptualisation is not present in the lecturer's notes (i.e., slides) in the introductory class to the seminars studied here. Here is the example where the lecturer makes this comparison explicit:

(33) she is looking for a new experience and all that stuff and that helps you to give more sort of a <u>storytelling</u> figure to the to the pitch great great

And this comparison is echoed by a student, who relates it to the streamlining process that is necessary to produce the pitch:

(34) in thirty or ninety seconds you're not going to explain your whole life or your whole cv it's like a <u>story</u> yeah

Naturally, the model is also used, this time indirectly, in many other cases:

(35) brand and telling compelling brand <u>stories</u> are two of my main skills an
(36) but as annelie told er told us she is a <u>storyteller</u> all right so you can say

And extended to include elements of fiction:

(37) forward from e questions i mean from some kind of <u>intrigue</u> to you
       were talking about

However, the story being told is not written on paper, it is more a story represented as a theatre piece:

(38) remember e i told you you can practise like the <u>actors</u> do e in front the
       mirror so you can t-- you can see yourself and see what kind-of gestures
       you are

The importance of this model is not numerical (only 24 tokens and 2.7% of
the total) but the fact that it is the model that more clearly moves away from
the conventionalised patterns described by Semino (2005, 2006) and the one
where direct metaphor is used.

Conclusion

The present chapter has studied the metaphors used to refer to SPEECH in the
context of three EMI seminars. In this specific setting, where L2 users are a
majority, I have been able to examine the extent to which conventionalised
metaphorical models described for L1 contexts of use are still in place.

   A first conclusion, not directly connected to metaphor use but drawn from
a semantic keyness analysis, relates to the frequency in the seminars of a
general target domain such as SPEECH, which would not seem to be expected
from an academic communicative event such as the university seminar or
from the specialised topic dealt with – marketing. However, this finding ties
in with other linguistic features identified (i.e., frequency of pronouns and
evaluation), and confirms the particular conversational nature of the seminars and their adequacy to be contrasted with the written discourse studied
so far in the speech metaphor literature.

   As regards metaphor use, the corpus analysed shows a balance between
the literal (52.8%) and the metaphorical expressions (47.2%) referring to
SPEECH. This is in sharp contrast with the data obtained by Semino (2006),
who, in her analysis of an L1 written corpus, found that only 22% of the
expressions referring to SPEECH were metaphorical. No apparent reason can
be found for this striking fact, except perhaps for the saliency of SPEECH,
which makes it necessary for participants to draw on different expressive
resources. However, in both literal and metaphorical expressions, a similar
process of lexical simplification or overrepresentation of the most frequent
expressions is in place as expected from an ELF context (cf. Mauranen, 2012).

   Moreover, participants in the seminars use most of the conventionalised
models described by Semino (2005, 2006), albeit with some variations, addi-
tions and omissions that are worth commenting on. First, the most frequent

models in my corpus are also the ones with great frequency in her corpus, although their rank order and the percentages are somewhat different. Thus, in my corpus, PHYSICAL CONSTRUCTION (25.2%) has a greater share in comparison with the one found for the written corpus (12.6%) and takes precedence over TRANSFER (22%), which was the predominant domain in that corpus (21%). MOTION and VISIBILITY, for their part, are also present in my corpus but again with certain disparities, more significant in the first case (16.8% vs 6.5%) than in the second (10.3% vs 13%). The importance of these models is so great that they give rise to unconventional uses such as *give away* or *pull out* respectively interpreted as TRANSFER and CONTAINER expressions when they are not. Second, I have identified a source domain, STORY-TELLING/DRAMA, which was not present in Semino's corpus. This model is not very frequent, but its importance lies in that it is the only one where direct metaphors are used, thereby involving a greater prominence in the discourse. And third, some source domains identified by Semino in her corpus are not found in mine. These are PHYSICAL CONFLICT, PHYSICAL PROXIMITY, PHYSICAL PRESSURE and PHYSICAL SUPPORT and their absence may be due to the partial use in the seminars of the physical scenario posited by Semino to conceptualise the communicative process in English. As expressed by Semino (2005, p. 29), these models are typically used to refer to interactants participating in the communication, whereas, as we have seen, the focus of the seminars is set on the product of communication, i.e., on the pitch.

Finally, the situated analysis carried out has allowed us to specify, within the general physical scenario, the different uses or functions that each of the models has in the overall discourse used in the seminars. These roles are the thematic progression towards a successful pitch that MOTION metaphors express, the reference to the main ideas of the pitch through VISUAL metaphors, the careful planning of the pitch incorporated into the discourse via PHYSICAL CONSTRUCTION, the incorporation of the audience by the use of ditransitive TRANSFER expressions and the comparison of the pitch delivery with STORYTELLING or DRAMA.

Overall, the approach adopted here has afforded a more detailed description of the metaphors used to refer to SPEECH and points to the need for further research in metaphor production in contexts where English is not the L1.

Final recapitulations and suggestions for further research

As we reach the end of this chapter, it seems appropriate make some final reflections on the most important concepts and findings developed in the book. Throughout the book, the emphasis has been on providing readers with a detailed model for constructing a compact oral corpus in the context of English as a Medium of Instruction (EMI) seminars – the MetCLIL corpus. This corpus stands out for its unique feature: the incorporation of metaphor tagging, a feature that is not very frequent in the corpora available. Additionally, another goal has been to focus on how to utilise corpus-linguistic methodology to explore the use of this figure of speech in multilingual contexts.

The first part has introduced the conceptual and methodological framework used with two initial chapters introducing the theoretical and conceptual background underpinning the work as a necessary first step to its overall practical approach. Thus, the book has not only dealt with the basics of metaphor theory, drawing on the key developments of this discipline, but what is perhaps more interesting, it has focused on the latest contributions of corpus linguistics to the field, emphasising how corpus linguistic methodology has been employed by different authors to explore the role of metaphor and how this has contributed to guiding metaphor research away from a predominant cognitive approach towards one where linguistic factors have a more substantial impact. This innovative approach has proven its significance in emerging fields like English as a Medium of Instruction, which forms the primary context for the research presented in this book. This area not only demands further investigation but also calls for an agreement of the researchers as to the precise scope of the phenomenon, a dispute in which this book has opted for a more restrictive approach that will only include non-English speaking higher education institutions.

The practical aspects of the book, included in Chapters 3–5, have introduced the MetCLIL corpus used as the base of the present research and have delineated its structure, detailing key components of corpus research such as design, compilation, transcription, tokenisation, and metaphor identification and tagging. These elements, well established in corpus linguistics, have been presented systematically and practically, providing a comprehensive guide for researchers approaching metaphor analysis through a corpus-based approach. In the existing literature, there is a scarcity of works that have developed in an organised and consistent way the tasks that the corpus linguist faces when delving into metaphor research, a gap that this book has sought to fill.

The second part has emphasised the importance of quantification and statistical analysis when using corpora to analyse metaphor, an approach that has been called into question but that can provide a broader and complementary view of the role of metaphor in discourse. Besides, this need to undertake quantitative studies has been shown to be interesting with respect to the types of variables that discourse analysis has mostly readily already incorporated into their work, i.e., contextual variables, which have been analysed in Chapter 6. Other less explored variables such as individual variables of the speakers participating in the speech events recorded, have also been explored, an analysis which has highlighted the role of the L1 of the speakers. Finally, the present chapter has emphasised the need to complement quantitative studies with a more nuanced case study focusing on the use of metaphor to refer to a particular area of experience. In this case, the focus has fallen on the use of metaphor to refer to the target domain of SPEECH. Given its frequency in the three seminars recorded in Spain, this domain seemed a perfect test ground to study conventionalised metaphors in EMI contexts at both at the conceptual and the linguistic level.

Indeed, this introductory book has provided an overview of key topics within this area, yet there is still much ground to cover in dealing with the significance of metaphor within the emerging field of EMI and, more broadly, in the domain of English as a Lingua Franca. It must be acknowledged that the field of metaphor, which has been shown to exert significant influence across various domains, especially within academic discourse, requires a deeper exploration within the ever-evolving landscape of contemporary English as a Lingua Franca (ELF). In this pursuit, corpus linguistics emerges as an invaluable instrument, shedding light on the intricate mechanisms of this figure of speech.

Note

1 Based on the Online first article "Conventional metaphors in English as a lingua franca. An analysis of speech metaphors in three academic seminars" in *Review of Cognitive Linguistics*, published in November 2023. Reprinted with kind permission from John Benjamins Publishing Company, Amsterdam/Philadelphia.

References

Austin, John L. (1962). *How to Do Things with Words*. Oxford University Press.

Belinsky, S., & Gogan, B. (2016). Throwing a Change-Up, Pitching a Strike: An Autoethnography of Frame Acquisition, Application, and Fit in a Pitch Development and Delivery Experience. *IEEE Transactions on Professional Communication, 59*(4), 323–341. https://doi.org/10.1109/TPC.2016.2607804

Caballero, R. (2018). Showing versus telling: Interpreting speech events in English and Spanish. In A. M. Piquer-Píriz & R. Alejo-González (Eds.), *Applying cognitive linguistics: Figurative language in use, constructions and typology* (pp. 205–228). John Benjamins.

Caballero, R., & Paradis, C. (2018). Verbs in speech framing expressions: Comparing English and Spanish. *Journal of Linguistics, 54*(1), 45–84.

Cameron, L. (2011). *Metaphor and reconciliation: The discourse dynamics of empathy in post-conflict conversations*. Routledge.

Danesi, M. (1990). Thinking is seeing: Visual metaphors and the nature of abstract thought. *Semiotica, 80*(3–4), 221–238.

Denning, P.J., & Dew, N. (2012). The Myth of the Elevator Pitch. *Communications of the ACM, 55*(6), 38–40. https://doi.org/10.1145/2184319.2184333

Grady, J. (1998). The "conduit" metaphor revisited: A reassessment of metaphors for communication. In J.-P. Koenig (Ed.), *Discourse and cognition: Bridging the gap* (pp. 205–218). CSLI Publications.

Johnson, M. (1987). *The body in the mind: The bodily basis of meaning, imagination and reason*. Chicago University Press.

Knudsen, S. (2003). Scientific metaphors going public. *Journal of Pragmatics, 35*, 1247–1263. https://doi.org/10.1016/S0378-2166(02)00187-X

Kövecses, Z. (2010). *Metaphor: A practical introduction*. Oxford University Press.

Lakoff, G., & Johnson, M. (1980). *Metaphors we live by*. Chicago University Press.

Macaro, E. (2018). *English medium instruction: Content and language in policy and practice*. Oxford University Press.

MacArthur, F., Krennmayr, T., & Littlemore, J. (2015). How basic is "understanding is seeing" when reasoning about knowledge? Asymmetric uses of sight hours in office hours consultations in English as Academic Lingua Franca. *Metaphor and Symbol*, *30*(3), 184–217.

Mauranen, A. (2012). *Exploring ELF: Academic English shaped by non-native speakers*. Cambridge University Press.

Pitzl, M.-L. (2018). *Creativity in English as a lingua franca: Idiom and metaphor*. Mouton de Gruyter.

Rayson, P. (2008). *Wmatrix: A web-based corpus processing environment*. Lancaster University. http://ucrel.lancs.ac.uk/Wmatrix/

Reddy, M. J. (1979). The conduit metaphor: A case of frame conflict in our language about language. In A. Ortony (Ed.), *Metaphor and thought* (2nd ed., pp. 164–201). Cambridge University Press.

Sabaj, O., Cabezas, P., Varas, G., González-Vergara, C., & Pina-Stranger, A. (2020). Empirical literature on the business pitch: Classes, critiques and future trends. *Journal of Technology Management & Innovation*, *15*(1), 55–63.

Semino, E. (2005). The metaphorical construction of complex domains: The case of speech activity in English. *Metaphor and Symbol*, *20*, 35–70.

Semino, E. (2006). A corpus-based study of metaphors for speech activity in contemporary British English. In A. Stefanowitsch & S.T. Gries (Eds.), *Corpus-based approaches to metaphor and metonymy*. (pp. 36–62). Mouton De Gruyter.

Semino, E., Demjén, Z., Hardie, A., Payne, S., & Rayson, P. (2018). *Metaphor, cancer and the end of life: A corpus-based study*. Routledge.

Sullivan, K. (2013). *Frames and constructions in metaphoric language*. John Benjamins Publishing.

Swales, J. M. (2001). Metatalk in American academic talk: The cases of point and thing. *Journal of English linguistics*, *29*(1), 34–54.

Sweetser, E. (1987). Metaphorical models of thought and speech: A comparison of historical directions and metaphorical mappings in the two domains. In J. Aske, N. Beery, L. Michaelis, & H. Filip (Eds.), *Proceedings of the thirteenth annual meeting of the Berkeley linguistics society* (pp. 446–459). Berkeley Linguistics Society.

Sweetser, E. (1991). *From etymology to pragmatics: Metaphorical and cultural aspects of semantic structure*. Cambridge University Press.

Appendices

APPENDIX A - PRESENTATION LETTER

Approved by the Spanish National R+D
programme (FFI2017-86320-R)

Are you interested in taking part in the research project?

"La metáfora en el lenguaje académico oral: la producción metafórica en los seminarios de los programas AICLE en la Educación Superior"

[Metaphor in oral academic language: metaphor production in HE (Higher Education) EMI (English as Means of Instruction) seminars]?

This is an inquiry about participation in a research project where the main purpose is **study how language is actually used in seminars at university level in Europe.** In this letter we will give you information about the purpose of the project and what your participation will involve.

Purpose of the project

This project studies language in settings involving Content and Language Integrated Learning (CLIL) - that is, a course where a second or foreign language is the medium of instruction. Our focus is on language in seminars at university programmes taught in English in European countries where English is not an official language. More specifically, we want to understand how seminars work when English is used to talk about academic topics. We are not interested in language 'correctness', but rather in the natural use of language in university seminars.

This research project on CLIL has been approved by the Spanish national R+D programme and funded by the Spanish Ministry of Economy, Industry and

Competitiveness. The project is international and includes 13 researchers from six European countries: Italy, the Netherlands, Norway, Portugal, Spain and Sweden.

Who is responsible for the research project?

Professor Rafael Alejo at the University of Extremadura in Spain is the institution responsible for leading the project.

Some collaborators are: Annelie Ädele (Dalarna Univ., Sweden); Tina Krennmayr (Vrije Univ. Amsterdam, The Netherlands); Jeannette Littlemore (Univ. of Birmingham, UK); Gill Philip (Univ. of Macceratta, Italy); Margarida Coelho (Instituto Superior Politécnico de Portalegre, Portugal); Susan Nacey (Inland Norway University of Applied Sciences).

Why are you being asked to participate?

Our project specifically focuses on language used to discuss topics related to business. You have been selected for participation because you are enrolled in a relevant course at your university Business Programme.

What does participation involve for you?

Your participation involves agreeing to have a seminar video recorded by one of the project members. The video and audio data recorded for the project will only be accessible to the project members. The audio will be transcribed, where any personal data that may reveal the identity of the participants will be anonymised, and this written transcription will be made available to other researchers and teachers. Your name will not be used at any stage.

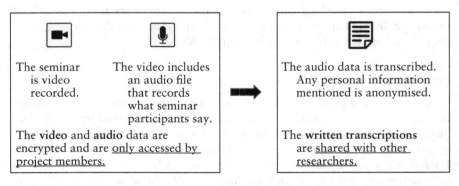

The seminar is video recorded.　　The video includes an audio file that records what seminar participants say.	The audio data is transcribed. Any personal information mentioned is anonymised.
The **video** and **audio** data are encrypted and are <u>only accessed by project members.</u>	The **written transcriptions** are <u>shared with other researchers.</u>

The written transcription will be included in a database which will be used by researchers in language and linguistics to study how language is used in university settings. The database will comprise the anonymised transcriptions from seminars in all six participating countries.

In addition, you will be asked to complete a brief questionnaire that will collect basic information about your gender, age, native language and background studying English. This information will be linked to the transcribed data and may be used in research to gain a deeper understanding of factors that may influence language use. <u>Personal data in the form of names are not referred to at all.</u> Instead, each participant is given a number which serves to connect the video, audio and metadata. The information from this questionnaire may be used in research to gain a deeper understanding of factors that may influence language use.

Participation is voluntary

Participation in the project is voluntary. If you chose to participate, you can withdraw your consent **within a period of three months after the recording date** without giving a reason, and demand the deletion of all recorded data and metadata. After the three-month period, all usage rights are transferred to the University of Extremadura, including the right to publish parts of the transcribed data for research and teaching purposes. There will be no negative consequences for you if you chose not to participate or later decide to withdraw.

Your personal privacy – how we will store and use your personal data

We will only use your personal data for the purpose(s) specified in this information letter. We will process your personal data confidentially and in accordance with data protection legislation (the General Data Protection Regulation and Personal Data Act).

The **audio data** from the recordings will be transcribed to make it easier to study the use of language. If personal data such as participants' names are mentioned in the audio recording, they will be anonymised in the written transcription.

The **audio** and **video data** will not be modified (pixellated or other), and the participants will appear as in the original recording, which means that personal identification may be possible. However, the audio and video recordings will only be accessed by the research team and will not be shared with others. The data will be stored securely with file encryption. No personal information will be published, and participants will not be recognisable in publications based on the data.

What will happen to your personal data at the end of the research project?

The project is scheduled to end *31/12/2020*. At that point, the digital recordings will be destroyed.

The anonymised written transcriptions of what is said in the seminar will be made available through open-access online channels to researchers and teachers outside of the research team.

Your rights

So long as you can be identified in the collected data, you have the right to:

- access the personal data that is being processed about you
- request that incorrect personal data about you is corrected/rectified
- receive a copy of your personal data (data portability)

What gives us the right to process your personal data?

We will process your personal data based on your consent.

Where can I find out more?

If you have questions about the project, or want to exercise your rights, contact:

The University of Extremadura (Spain) via Professor Rafael Alejo (ralejo@unex.es)

Yours sincerely, Rafael Alejo González

Consent form

I have received and understood information about the project 'Project CLIL' and have been given the opportunity to ask questions. I give consent:

- to participate in digital recording of a CLIL seminar at INN
- to participate in a written survey collecting basic information about my gender, age, native language and background studying English

I give consent for my personal data to be processed until the end date of the project, approx. [31/12/2021]

(Signed by participant, date)

APPENDIX B – CHECKLIST FOR RECORDINGS

CHECKLIST FOR RECORDINGS

TO PREPARE BEFORE RECORDING IF POSSIBLE

PROGRAMME Should be 3rd/ 4th Year B.A. or 1st Year M.A. programme in Business Studies or similar	
COURSE Should be Business, Economics, Marketing or similar (but not Auditing/Accountancy, etc.)	
COURSE DATES 1st semester or 2nd semester (2018–2019)	
COURSE TUTOR Name and contact details	
DATE FOR RECORDING	

SIZE/LAYOUT OF THE SEMINAR ROOM
(This information will allow the researcher to consider
   how feasible recording a session will be and what
   equipment will be needed.)	

Ask the course tutor about the predicted format of the seminar by referring to the following features:

	DESCRIPTION
Communicative purpose	The seminar is designed to be supplemental or additional to lectures. It gives students an opportunity to discuss the assigned reading.
Group size	Approximately 8–20 students
Degree of naturalness	What happens in the seminar is naturally occurring and largely non-scripted (so it is not the case that students give presentations *reading from a script*, for example).
Format of seminar	The seminar has a high degree of student participation (and is not a teacher-fronted session where students only answer the teacher's questions). The seminar mostly involves the whole group (and is not exclusively devoted to students working in small groups). The seminar involves a great deal of discussion. There may be presentations by the students as well, which are followed by discussion.

Permissions and consent

PERMISSION SOUGHT/GRANTED FROM LOCAL UNIVERSITY'S ETHICS BOARD	
CHECK STUDENTS' WILLINGNESS TO PARTICIPATE	• Check whether it might be possible to arrange a meeting with the students before the seminar you plan to record? to explain aims of recordings and to determine whether they consent to take part • Consider whether it would work to have the teacher send the information sheet and the consent form to the students by email and then let the teacher know if they are not willing to participate?

SEMINAR OCCASION: HANDOUTS

Distribute before recording

- **Information sheet** (make copies for all participants – students and teacher – to keep)
- **Consent form** (one copy for each participant – students and teacher – to keep and one for the researcher)
- **Questionnaire for students**

Distribute after recording

- **Follow-up questionnaire on naturalness** (for students and the teacher)

OBSERVATIONS DURING/AFTER RECORDING

SEMINAR DESCRIPTORS	*DESCRIPTION*	*COMMENTS, IF ANY*
NUMBER OF STUDENTS IN SEMINAR		
SIZE/LAYOUT OF SEMINAR ROOM		
Approximate proportion of **instructor talk** (state percentage)		
Approximate proportion of **discussion** (state percentage)		
Approximate proportion of **student presentations** (state percentage)		
Approximate proportion of **group work** (state percentage)		
Degree of perceived disruptions caused by recording the seminar		

APPENDIX C – RECORD OF VIDEO TEMPLATE

Video #	
Name:	
Country:	
University:	
Course:	
Type of class	
Type of study:	
Order:	
Date:	
Timing:	
Type of talk:	
Number of instructors:	
Professors' L1(s):	
Number of students:	
Type of students:	
Learner's home country:	
Learners' L1(s):	
Assignment:	
Topic:	
Lesson focus:	
Grouping:	
Skill(s):	
Type of room:	
Class layout:	
Professor's setup:	
Student's setup:	
Professor's posture:	
Student's posture:	
Type of interaction:	
Professor's role:	
Student's role:	
Resources:	

Description of the activity:	
Expected Metaphors on:	
Comments:	
Reflections:	

APPENDIX D – INFORMATION SHEET FOR PARTICIPANTS

Approved by the Spanish National R+D
programme (FFI2017-86320-R)

Information sheet for participants

This research project on CLIL has been approved by the Spanish national R+D program and funded by the Spanish Ministry of Economy, Industry and Competitiveness. The project is international and includes 13 researchers from six European countries: Italy, the Netherlands, Norway, Portugal, Spain and Sweden.

The aim is to study how language is actually used in seminars at university level in Europe and to understand how seminars work when English is used to talk about academic topics. The project specifically focuses on university programmes taught in English in countries where English is not an official language. The project members are not interested in language 'correctness', but hope that you will be able to take part in the seminar in a natural way, so that the recording does not interfere with what normally happens in a seminar.

Participation in the project is completely voluntary. Your participation involves agreeing to have a seminar video recorded by one of the project members. The video and audio data recorded for the project will only be accessible to the project members. The audio will be transcribed, where any personal data that may reveal the identity of the participants will be anonymised, and this written transcription will be made available to other researchers and teachers. Your name will not be used at any stage.

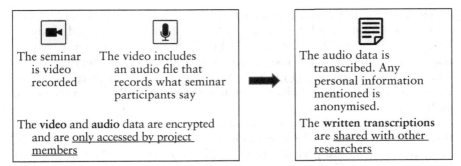

The written transcription will be included in a database which will be used by researchers in language and linguistics to study how language is used in university settings. The database will comprise the anonymised transcriptions from seminars in all six participating countries. The person in charge of the project is Rafael Alejo, from the University of Extremadura in Spain (ralejo@unex.es). Do not hesitate to contact him if you have any follow-up questions or want to know more about the research project.

If you agree to participate in the study, please fill out the consent form and the questionnaire.

APPENDIX E – CONSENT FORM

Consent form

I, ..., hereby give my consent to have audio and video data recorded of myself for the METCLIL project. I approve of the data to be used for the creation of a database which will be used to study language use in university programmes taught in English in non-English speaking countries.

The **audio data** will be transcribed to make it easier to study the use of language. If personal data such as participants' names are mentioned in the audio recording, they will be anonymised in the written transcription.

The **audio** and **video data** will not be modified (pixellated or other), and the participants will appear as in the original recording, which means that identification is made possible. However, the audio and video recordings will only be accessed by the research team and will not be shared with others. They will be stored securely with file encryption. It is only the anonymised written transcription of what is said in the seminar that may be made available to researchers and teachers outside of the research team.

The **questionnaire**, which each participant is asked to fill in, includes basic information about gender, age, native language and background studying English. This information will be linked to the transcribed data and may be used in research to gain a deeper understanding of factors that may influence language use. <u>Personal data in the form of names are not referred to at all.</u> Instead, each participant is given a number which serves to connect the video, audio and metadata.

Within a period of three months after the recording date I can revoke this consent and demand the deletion of all recorded data and metadata. After the three-month period, I transfer all usage rights to the University of Extremadura, including the right to publish parts of the transcribed data for research and teaching purposes.

I have been informed about the aim of the project and the planned use of my recorded data and metadata, and all my questions regarding this have been answered. I have received a copy of the information sheet and this consent form.

Place_____ Date_____

Signature _____

Thank you for agreeing to take part in this study.
Your contribution is very much appreciated.

APPENDIX F– QUESTIONNAIRE FOR STUDENTS

Approved by the Spanish National R+D
programme (FFI2017-86320-R)

Questionnaire for students

This questionnaire aims to collect basic information about your gender, age, native language and background studying English. Based on your participant number (again, no names are used), this information will be linked to the written transcriptions of the spoken data from the seminar. It may be used in research to gain a deeper understanding of factors that may influence language use.

Please answer the following questions. If anything is unclear, do not hesitate to ask the project member for clarification.

PARTICIPANT NUMBER: _____

1　Age: ....
2　Sex
　a　Male
　b　Female
　c　Prefer not to say
3　Are you an international student? .... Home country:
　........................
4　Are you participating in an exchange programme (Erasmus or other):.............
5　Mother tongue/native language: ....
6　How many years have you studied at university? ....
7　Number of years of English in school (before university):
　...............................
8　Number of years attending a school where content subjects (e.g. Natural Science or Mathematics) are taught in English
　...............................
9　Assess your level of English on a scale from 0–60, 60 being native-like competence (or C2 if you are familiar with the CEFR, *Common European Framework of Reference for Languages*): ....

Basic user or beginner		Independent user or intermediate		Proficient user or advanced	
0–10 (A1)	11–20 (A2)	21–30 (B1)	31–40 (B2)	41–50 (C1)	51–60 (C2)

10　Does this university programme require a specific English-language level ?

　a　Yes ☐ What level? ....
　b　No ☐
　c　Don't know ☐

Thank you very much for participating in our study and for taking the time to answer these questions!

APPENDIX G – QUESTIONAIRE FOR LECTURERS

Approved by the Spanish National R+D
programme (FFI2017-86320-R)

Questionnaire for lecturers

This questionnaire aims to collect basic information about your gender, age, native language and background studying English. Based on your participant number (again, no names are used), this information will be linked to the written transcriptions of the spoken data from the seminar. It may be used in research to gain a deeper understanding of factors that may influence language use.

1 PARTICIPANT NUMBER: _____
2 Age: ....
3 Sex
   a   Male
   b   Female
   c   Prefer not to say
4 Years of experience as a university teacher/instructor/lecturer?
5 Years of experience teaching in English?
6 Mother tongue/native language: ....
7 Assess your level of English on a scale 0-60, 60 being a native-like competence (or C2 if you know the European Framework of Reference for Languages): ....

Basic user or beginner		Independent user or intermediate		Proficient user or advanced	
0—0 (A1)	11-20 (A2)	21–30 (B1)	31–40 (B2)	41–50 (C1)	51–60 (C2)

8 Does the university programme require an English language level to enrol as a teacher?
   a   Yes ☐ What level? ....
   b   No ☐

9 I teach my classes entirely in English.
   a Yes
   b No
10 The courses I teach are specifically designed for international students

                                                      Yes
                                                      No
                                                      N/A

11 The materials I use are adapted for students whose first language is not English

                                                      Yes
                                                      No
                                                      N/A

Thank you very much for participating in our study and for taking the time to answer our questions.

APPENDIX H – FOLLOW-UP QUESTIONAIRE ON NATURALNESS FOR STUDENTS

Follow-up questionnaire for students

This is a short questionnaire aimed at gathering your views on how the session went.

1 To what extent (if at all) did you find that the fact that the seminar was video recorded affected <u>people's</u> behaviour?

   <u>Not at all</u>; the seminar was done in a typical way ☐
   <u>To a very little extent</u>; there was only a slight disturbance ☐
   <u>To some extent</u>; the seminar was different because of the video recording ☐
   <u>Very much</u>; the video recording really made the seminar different ☐
   <u>Completely</u>; the video recording changed all aspects of the seminar ☐

2 In what way do you think it affected your <u>own</u> behaviour?

   <u>Not at all</u> ☐
   <u>To a very little extent</u> ☐
   <u>To some extent</u> ☐
   <u>Very much</u> ☐
   <u>Completely</u> ☐

Thank you very much for participating in our study and for taking the time to answer these questions!

APPENDIX I – FOLLOW-UP QUESTIONAIRE ON NATURALNESS FOR LECTURERS

Approved by the Spanish National R+D
programme (FFI2017-86320-R)

Follow-up questionnaire for teachers

This is a short questionnaire aimed at gathering your views on how the session went.

1   To what extent (if at all) did you find that the fact that the seminar was video recorded affected people's behaviour?

Not at all; the seminar was done in a typical way ☐
To a very little extent; there was only a slight disturbance ☐
To some extent; the seminar was different because of the video recording ☐
Very much; the video recording really made the seminar different ☐
Completely; the video recording changed all aspects of the seminar ☐

2   In what way do you think it affected your own behaviour?

Not at all ☐
To a very little extent ☐
To some extent ☐
Very much ☐
Completely ☐

3   Is there anything else about how the class went today that you would like to comment on? Please use the space below.

Thank you very much for participating in our study and for taking the time to answer these questions!

APPENDIX J – PROJECT TEAM

Coordination

Rafael Alejo González is a lecturer at the University of Extremadura, Spain. He has extensive experience in teaching Business English at the Faculty of Economics and is currently based at the Faculty of Education where he is involved in courses relating to Applied Linguistics and Second Language Acquisition.

Several of his articles have appeared in journals such as *Cahiers de Lexicologie, The International Journal of the European Association of Languages for Specific Purposes, Ibérica, System or the Journal of Pragmatics*. He has also published books and book chapters dealing with **economic language, CLIL** and **Cognitive Linguistics** with Mouton de Gruyter, John Benjamins, Continuum and Cambridge Scholar.

He has been a member of the editorial and scientific boards of the *European association of languages for specific purposes, Ibérica,* and has refereed research articles for the *Journal of English for Specific Purposes*, the *Journal of English for Academic Purposes* and *IRAL*.

He has been the head of research projects funded by the Spanish Ministry of Education and also led a project on Content and Language Integrated Learning (CLIL) funded by the regional educational authorities in Extremadura.

Researchers

International team

Annelie Ädel joined the English Department at Dalarna University as Professor of English Linguistics in 2012. Her main research areas include discourse analysis and pragmatics, corpus linguistics, English for Specific Purposes (ESP), and learner writing.

Her methodological approach is empiricist; she believes that generalisations about language need to be supported by authentic and, where possible, substantial samples of language data. To enable empirically supported lines of enquiry, she has been involved in different projects involving corpus development, such as the Michigan Corpus of Academic Spoken English (MICASE), the Michigan Corpus of Upper-level Student Papers (MICUSP), the English-Swedish Parallel Corpus (ESPC) and the Mid-Sweden Corpus of Computer-Assisted Language Learning (McCALL).

She has been invited to give talks and seminars in Sweden, Spain, Chile, Austria, Turkey, Italy and the US. She regularly serves as a reviewer for a range of different journals and is a current or past member of the editorial boards of the *International Journal of Learner Corpus Research, Nordic Journal of English Studies, Miscelánea: Journal of English and American Studies* and *Journal of English for Academic Purposes* (2013–2016).

Margarida Coelho, PhD in Language and Cultures (University of Extremadura) and MA in English Literature and Culture (University of Lisbon), is a senior English language lecturer at the Polytechnic of Portalegre (IPPortalegre), Portugal.

She is a member of the Technical-Scientific Board of the School of Technology and Business Studies (IPPortalegre) and coordinated the Languages and Culture Centre of the Institute from 2010 to 2015.

Researcher in C3i, CETAPS / TEALS (CLIL strand), and collaborator in the CLIL research team of ReCLes.pt, her research work is mainly developed in the areas of language teaching and methodologies, particularly CLIL at tertiary level.

Tina Krennmayr is an Assistant Professor at VU University Amsterdam.

She does corpus research on metaphor variation in discourse and develops methods for metaphor identification. She also applies metaphor research to foreign language learning. She has published on the integration of corpus research in ESP teaching and has studied the development of figurative language use by non-native speakers of English across different levels of written language competency, together with Jeannette Littlemore. Her recent research focuses on teaching phrasal and prepositional verbs using teaching techniques based on cognitive linguistics.

She is involved in BA and MA programmes (English and International Communication, Minor in English, Multimodal Communication) and the Research Master Program.

Jeannette Littlemore is a Professor of Applied Linguistics in the Department of English Language and Linguistics at the University of Birmingham. Her research focuses on metaphor and metonymy and explores the facilitative and debilitative role played by metaphor and metonymy in language education and in cross-linguistic and cross-cultural communication more generally. She is interested in the creative use of metaphor and metonymy and in the ways in which figurative meaning is negotiated by speakers with different kinds of background knowledge and different emotional experiences.

Her monographs include: *Metaphors in the Mind: Sources of Variation in Embodied Metaphor* (Cambridge University Press, 2019), *Metonymy: Hidden Shortcuts in Language, Thought and Communication* (Cambridge University Press, 2015); *Figurative Language, Genre and Register* (with Alice Deignan and Elena Semino, Cambridge University Press, 2013); *Doing Applied Linguistics* (with Nicholas Groom, Routledge 2011); *Applying Cognitive Linguistics to Second Language Learning and Teaching* (Palgrave Macmillan, 2009) and *Figurative Thinking and Foreign Language Learning* (with Graham Low, Palgrave Macmillan, 2006). She is currently working on a new monograph: *Unpacking Creativity: The Role of Figurative Communication in Advertising* (with Paula Perez-Sobrino, Cambridge University Press).

Susan Nacey is a professor of English as a second/foreign language, and currently works as the Vice Dean for Research at the Faculty of Education in Hamar/Lillehammer.

Her research interests are metaphor and learner language, with a focus on Norwegian L2 English, as well as L2 Norwegian. She published a monograph entitled *Metaphors in Learner English* in 2013, dealing with metaphors produced in the written English of Norwegian students, as well as methodological issues concerning the Metaphor Identification Procedure (MIPVU). She was also responsible for collecting the Norwegian version of the LINDSEI corpus (spoken learner English) and has also been involved in the compilation of the TraWL corpus (Tracking Written Learner Language), a longitudinal corpus of English texts written by Norwegian pupils aged 10–19.

Further, methodological issues connected to metaphor research are a concern of hers, especially (linguistic) metaphor identification and valid statistical analysis. Together with A.G. Dorst, T. Krennmayr, and W.G. Reijnierse, she edited a volume entitled *Metaphor identification in multiple languages: MIPVU around the world* (John Benjamins, 2019). She is the review editor of the scientific journal *Metaphor and the Social World*, published by John Benjamins.

Gill Philip is Associate Professor of English language in the Department of Modern Languages and Cultures, University of Macerata, Italy, where she teaches modules in English corpus linguistics, English-Italian translation, cognitive linguistics, and TEFL.

Her primary research interest lies in phraseology, idiomaticity and figurative language, using mixed methodologies that draw together corpus, cognitive, and applied linguistics, with a view to understanding the interplay between cognition and linguistic communication. She has published in many scholarly journals including *Lingua, Language and Communication, or Studies in Corpus Linguistics,* she has contributed to the *Routledge handbook of metaphor and language* and published in 2011 with John Benjamins a book entitled *Colouring meaning: Collocation and connotation in figurative language.*

For the three-year term 2016–2019 she was Head of Department, and she is currently deputy-head of the School of Humanities. In addition to her present role as Secretary of the RaAM Executive Board, she also served two consecutive terms as an ordinary member (2012–2016).

UEx team

Ana Mª Piquer-Píriz is a lecturer at the Faculty of Education at the University of Extremadura (Spain), where she teaches undergraduate courses to teacher trainees and postgraduate courses in the MA programme 'Master on Bilingual Education at Primary and Secondary Levels'.

Her research interests concern EFL learning and teaching, L2 vocabulary acquisition, figurative language and, Content and Language Integrated Learning (CLIL). She is particularly interested in the acquisition of vocabulary by young L2 learners and the presence of figuration in their language and thought. Her work has appeared in journals such as *System, Language, Culture and Curriculum, Language Teaching Research, Review of Cognitive Linguistics, Metaphor and the Social World* or *VIAL* and she has also published three co-edited volumes and several book chapters with John Benjamins and Mouton de Gruyter.

She is the principal investigator of the regionally funded research project 'ICLUEx' that explores Content and Language Integration practices at the UEx. She is currently involved in two other EU-funded projects on CLIL: 'INCOLLAB' and 'CLIL4YEC', she has also taken part in the nationally funded research project EuroCoAT and is now involved in METCLIL.

Fiona MacArthur is a former Senior Lecturer in the Department of English Philology (Faculty of Arts, Cáceres) at the University of Extremadura, where she used to teach undergraduate and graduate courses on the English language and Applied Linguistics.

Her research interests are wide and varied, and include metaphor, vocabulary learning and Pragmatics. She has co-edited the volume *Metaphor in Use: Context, Culture and Communication* (Amsterdam & Philadelphia: John Benjamins, 2012) and has book chapters published by Routledge, Bloomsbury or John Benjamins and research articles in *Metaphor* and *Symbol*, the *Review of Cognitive Linguistics* and the AILA review among others.

She was the research project leader of 'EuroCoAT', a nationally funded research project which investigated the use of metaphor in office hours' consultations involving Spanish Erasmus students studying at universities in Ireland, England, Sweden and The Netherlands and was the forerunner of METCLIL.

Laura Fielden Burns originally hails from the United States, where she graduated from Appalachian State University, North Carolina, and she completed an MA in literature at the University of North Carolina, Chapel Hill. She currently teaches at the University of

She is interested in motivation in EFL, in particular pertaining to study persistence and student mindsets. She has various publications in the areas of applied linguistics and education, and is a member of national, regional and international projects.

Irene Castellano-Risco is a lecturer at the University of Extremadura, Spain, where she teaches modules related to English for Specific Purposes. She graduated in English Primary education from the University of Extremadura and holds an MA degree in Bilingual Education and an MA degree in Humanities Research. Having completed her PhD studies in 2021, her research focuses on vocabulary acquisition, Content and Language Integrated Learning (CLIL), EFL learning and teaching and language learning strategies. She has published several articles on these issues in journals like *Onomazéin* and *System*.

Marta Martín-Gilete is a PhD candidate in English Language and Culture at Universidad de Extremadura (Spain). Her main research interests lie in the areas of cognitive linguistics, applied linguistics, English language learning and teaching, and figurative language – in the field of metaphor. Her PhD research focuses on applied metaphor in the teaching of English as a foreign language.

She is currently an associate lecturer at the Faculty of Philosophy and Humanities (Universidad de Extremadura), where she teaches undergraduate courses on EFL/ESL instruction, and English Studies.

Juan de Dios Martínez Agudo is a lecturer on Didactics of the English Language at the Faculty of Education of the University of Extremadura. His main research interests revolve around the incidence of cognitive and affective aspects in the process of teaching and learning a foreign language, the variability and sequencing of the teacher's pedagogical discourse and bilingual education programmes (CLIL).

The results of his research have appeared in international journals such as *Linguistics and Education*, the *International Journal of Bilingual Education* and *Bilingualism*, the *Language Learning Journal* or *Porta Linguarum*, among others. He has published more than twenty books as an author and editor, such as the most recent: *Professional challenges and teacher training* (De Gruyter, 2017), *Emotions in teaching a second language. Theory, research and teacher training* (Springer, 2018) and *Quality in TESOL and teacher training: From a culture of results to a culture of quality* (Routledge, 2020).

Collaborators

Raquel Martín Domínguez graduated in English Studies from the University of Extremadura. She holds an MA degree in Secondary Education Teacher Training and an MA degree in Bilingual Education.

She is currently a research assistant at the Faculty of Education (University of Extremadura), where she is involved in METCLIL, a research project on the use of metaphor in academic seminars. Her research interests concern Content and Language Integrated Learning (CLIL), figurative language and EFL learning and teaching.

Lucía Blázquez López is a Linguistic and International Relations Specialist (Sub-Saharan African and MENA region). She graduated in Translation and Interpreting from the Autonomous University of Madrid, where she earned a Master's Degree in International Relations and African Studies, and a Master's Degree in Contemporary Arabic and Islamic Studies.

She is currently a research assistant at the Faculty of Education of the University of Extremadura, where she works in ICLUEX, a project devoted to the application of Content and Language Integrated Learning (CLIL) in the University of Extremadura. Her research interests are focused on linguistics applied to translation, linguistics in international relations, discourse analysis, social constructivism, Content and Language Integrated Learning and EFL language learning.

María Teresa Mendiola Romero graduated in Early Childhood Education from the University of Extremadura. She holds an MA degree in Bilingual Education. She has collaborated in a research group at the Faculty of Education (University of Extremadura).

She is currently a researcher in the English Philology Department (Faculty of Education, University of Extremadura) where she is involved in METCLIL, a European project on metaphor analysis. She is also engaged in some projects about Content and Language Integrated Learning (CLIL), vocabulary acquisition and EFL learning and teaching.

Cecilia Calderón Poves is a graduate in English Primary Education from the University of Extremadura and holds an MA degree in Bilingual Education.

She is currently a research assistant at the Faculty of Education (University of Extremadura), where she is involved in some projects about Content and Language Integrated Learning (CLIL), figurative language and EFL learning and teaching. Her research interests concern Content and Language Integrated Learning (CLIL) and EFL learning and teaching.

APPENDIX K– TRANSCRIPTION SAMPLE

<SW_SEM1_WHOLE_u_528 who=SQD_C2_PT> go_i on_i yeah <{SQD shakes her hand and makes gestures to invite SAB to talk}> </SW_SEM1_WHOLE_u_528 who=SQD_C2_PT>

<SW_SEM1_WHOLE_u_529 who=SPF_B2_CH> @@@@ </SW_SEM1_WHOLE_u_529 who=SPF_B2_CH>

<SW_SEM1_WHOLE_u_530 who=SQD_C2_PT> no i think @@ that e any product but specifically </SW_SEM1_WHOLE_u_530 who=SQD_C2_PT>

<SW_SEM1_WHOLE_u_531 who=SAC_B2/C1_RU> are we already_i on_i the fourth question </SW_SEM1_WHOLE_u_531 who=SAC_B2/C1_RU>

<SW_SEM1_WHOLE_u_532 who=SCB_C1_GE> third </SW_SEM1_WHOLE_u_532 who=SCB_C1_GE>

<SW_SEM1_WHOLE_u_533 who=SPF_B2_CH> third </SW_SEM1_WHOLE_u_533 who=SPF_B2_CH>

<SW_SEM1_WHOLE_u_534 who=SQD_C2_PT> specifically that something that has_i do_i with_i e </SW_SEM1_WHOLE_u_534 who=SQD_C2_PT>

<SW_SEM1_WHOLE_u_535 who=SAC_B2/C1_RU> it is the fourth yeah </SW_SEM1_WHOLE_u_535 who=SAC_B2/C1_RU>

<SW_SEM1_WHOLE_u_536 who=SQD_C2_PT> e things_i that have_i are related to_i </SW_SEM1_WHOLE_u_536 who=SQD_C2_PT>

<SW_SEM1_WHOLE_u_537 who=SAC_B2/C1_RU> it is the fourth yeah </SW_SEM1_WHOLE_u_537 who=SAC_B2/C1_RU>

<SW_SEM1_WHOLE_u_538 who=SPF_B2_CH> ok yeah we we we maybe could dis-- discuss this to-- together_i cause the norms is also mentioned in_i the beauty_i article_i i-- it's possible for businesses in_i the beauty_i sector_i to STOP_i producing whitening products rather-than should focus_i on_i the production of products that e would enhance nature_i or

healthy_i look_i well it depends on_i demand </SW_SEM1_WHOLE_u_538 who=SPF_B2_CH>

<SW_SEM1_WHOLE_u_539 who=SAC_B2/C1_RU> @ </SW_SEM1_WHOLE_u_539 who=SAC_B2/C1_RU>

<SW_SEM1_WHOLE_u_540 who=SPF_B2_CH> @@@@@ </SW_SEM1_WHOLE_u_540 who=SPF_B2_CH>

<SW_SEM1_WHOLE_u_541 who=SQD_C2_PT> that's what i wrote here it depends on_i demand @@@@ </SW_SEM1_WHOLE_u_541 who=SQD_C2_PT>

<SW_SEM1_WHOLE_u_542 who=SPF_B2_CH> @@@ </SW_SEM1_WHOLE_u_542 who=SPF_B2_CH>

<SW_SEM1_WHOLE_u_543 who=SCB_C1_GE> of-course it always depends </SW_SEM1_WHOLE_u_543 who=SCB_C1_GE>

<SW_SEM1_WHOLE_u_544 who=SQD_C2_PT> it depends on_i demand definitely </SW_SEM1_WHOLE_u_544 who=SQD_C2_PT>

<SW_SEM1_WHOLE_u_545 who=SGK_C2_EN> to_i me i do n't think it depends on_i demand because erm the article_i spoke_i about_i e the eastern countries and the western countries whereby e the <pvc> instan-- <{eastern}> </pvc> the eastern countries were about_i they want like most of them are into_i plastic_i surgery and they want to like go_i into_i products they think will attract_i some europeans if erm businesses stop_i producing this product which is high_i in_i the eastern countries i feel_i the consumers would have_i no no option than just adopt-- adapt to_i the what's it called_i the product to_i the market_i that 's what i feel_i well yeah </SW_SEM1_WHOLE_u_545 who=SGK_C2_EN>

<SW_SEM1_WHOLE_u_546 who=SPF_B2_CH> mhm yeah of-course if e if there there are no this kind-of product from_i the beginning then people would not e think of that but the thing_i is that e when they start to offer this kind-of product and then if e they stop_i doing that then maybe there will be some kind-of react_i </SW_SEM1_WHOLE_u_546 who=SPF_B2_CH>

<SW_SEM1_WHOLE_u_547 who=SQD_C2_PT> because needs are cre-ated </SW_SEM1_WHOLE_u_547 who=SQD_C2_PT>

<SW_SEM1_WHOLE_u_548 who=SAC_B2/C1_RU> but it's always a choice of the person </SW_SEM1_WHOLE_u_548 who=SAC_B2/C1_RU>

<SW_SEM1_WHOLE_u_549 who=SQD_C2_PT> hm </SW_SEM1_WHOLE_u_549 who=SQD_C2_PT>

<SW_SEM1_WHOLE_u_550 who=SAC_B2/C1_RU> how can you say_w no to_i a person if he or she wants that i mean there are also white_i people who wants to be more_i darker_i for-example </SW_SEM1_WHOLE_u_550 who=SAC_B2/C1_RU>

<SW_SEM1_WHOLE_u_551 who=SQD_C2_PT> hm </SW_SEM1_WHOLE_u_551 who=SQD_C2_PT>

<SW_SEM1_WHOLE_u_552 who=SAC_B2/C1_RU> they go to solarium they put_i some special creams to make_i the skin darker_i it's always a choice of the person and not e ranging of the colour of the skin so just how you feel_i

and i do n't think that we have to say_w stop_i or say_w erm do n't do s--
plastic_i surgery because it's always your choice and if you feel_i better in_i
this way_i so just do it </SW_SEM1_WHOLE_u_552 who=SAC_B2/C1_RU>

    <SW_SEM1_WHOLE_u_553 who=SPF_B2_CH> mhm yeah but as the
paper_i says_i erm the fact is that erm well beautiful people ca-- can get_i can
have_i a good job_i to get_i job_i and to get_i good paid specially in_i the
service_i erm s-- sector_i </SW_SEM1_WHOLE_u_553 who=SPF_B2_CH>

    <SW_SEM1_WHOLE_u_554 who=SQD_C2_PT> that's true_i </SW_
SEM1_WHOLE_u_554 who=SQD_C2_PT>

    <SW_SEM1_WHOLE_u_555 who=SPF_B2_CH> yeah they get_i more
tips_i @@@ </SW_SEM1_WHOLE_u_555 who=SPF_B2_CH>

    <SW_SEM1_WHOLE_u_556 who=SCB_C1_GE> yeah </SW_SEM1_
WHOLE_u_556 who=SCB_C1_GE>

    <SW_SEM1_WHOLE_u_557 who=SAC_B2/C1_RU> probably yeah </
SW_SEM1_WHOLE_u_557 who=SAC_B2/C1_RU>

Index

Printed in the United States
by Baker & Taylor Publisher Services